Twentieth-Century Reworkings of German Literature

A "literary reworking" is a fictional work based on an earlier, usually canonical, literary work. In this book, Gundula M. Sharman considers six twentieth-century examples of this phenomenon in German literature, including Peter Schneider's *Lenz* as a reworking of Georg Büchner's novella of the same title, Ulrich Plenzdorf's *Die neuen Leiden des jungen W.* as a reworking of Goethe's *Werther*, Wolfgang Koeppen's *Der Tod in Rom*, based on Thomas Mann's *Der Tod in Venedig*, and three other pairs of reworkings/original works from the genres of drama, the novella, and the novel. The indebtedness of such reworkings to the original works is openly acknowledged — often in the title — and this invites the reader to draw comparisons and to note contrasts between reworking and original. The twentieth-century author's interpretation and the reader's reception of the older work merge to form a subtext of the reworking, giving rise to a third narrative in the reader's imagination. The better the reader knows the literary model, the more multi-faceted the reworking appears. The purpose of each reworking is unique: One may demonstrate how much the world has changed since the publication of the original, while another argues that society has not changed at all. One may be conceived as an anti-work to the original, while another serves to endorse its message. However, common to all reworkings is a gain in historical depth, and in each case themes and issues arise from the relationship of reworking to original that are not immediately apparent when the reworking is considered on its own.

Gundula M. Sharman teaches in the German Department at the University of Aberdeen, Scotland.

Studies in German Literature, Linguistics, and Culture

Edited by James Hardin
(*South Carolina*)

Gundula M. Sharman

Twentieth-Century Reworkings of German Literature

An Analysis of Six Fictional Reinterpretations from Goethe to Thomas Mann

CAMDEN HOUSE

Copyright © 2002 Gundula M. Sharman

All Rights Reserved. Except as permitted under current legislation,
no part of this work may be photocopied, stored in a retrieval system,
published, performed in public, adapted, broadcast, transmitted,
recorded, or reproduced in any form or by any means,
without the prior permission of the copyright owner.

First published 2002
by Camden House

Camden House is an imprint of Boydell & Brewer Inc.
PO Box 41026, Rochester, NY 14604–4126 USA
and of Boydell & Brewer Limited
PO Box 9, Woodbridge, Suffolk IP12 3DF, UK

ISBN: 1–57113–245–7

Library of Congress Cataloging-in-Publication Data

Sharman, Gundula.
    Twentieth-century reworkings of German literature: an analysis of six fictional reinterpretations from Goethe to Thomas Mann / Gundula M. Sharman
    p. cm. — (Studies in German literature, linguistics, and culture)
Includes bibliographical references and index.
ISBN 1–57113–245–7 (alk. paper)
    German literature—20th century—History and criticism. 2. German literature—19th century—History and criticism. I. Title. II. Studies in German literature, linguistics, and culture (Unnumbered)

PT401. S53 2002
830.9'.0091—dc21

2002019369

A catalogue record for this title is available from the British Library.

This publication is printed on acid-free paper.
Printed in the United States of America.

To my family

Contents

Preface	ix
Acknowledgments	xi
Abbreviations of Works Frequently Cited	xii
Introduction	1
1: Allusion to Classicism: Friedrich Schiller's *Die Jungfrau von Orleans* and Bertolt Brecht's *Die heilige Johanna der Schlachthöfe*	16
2: Ironic Reproduction: Friedrich Hebbel's and Franz Xaver Kroetz's *Maria Magdalena*	45
3: Fragmentation: Thomas Mann's *Der Tod in Venedig* and Wolfgang Koeppen's *Der Tod in Rom*	71
4: Integration: Georg Büchner's and Peter Schneider's *Lenz*	96
5: Quotation: Goethe's *Die Leiden des jungen Werther* and Ulrich Plenzdorf's *Die neuen Leiden des jungen W.*	123
6: Constellation of Character: Goethe's *Die Wahlverwandtschaften;* Hugo von Hofmannsthal's *The Chandos Letter;* and John Banville's *The Newton Letter*	151
Conclusion	175
Works Cited	187
Notes	195
Index	215

Preface

> Wer nicht von 3000 Jahren
> Sich weiß Rechenschaft zu geben,
> Bleibet im Dunkeln unerfahren.
> Mag von Tag zu Tage Leben.
> *Goethe*

WHILE IT IS NOT THE INTENTION OF this study to delve as far back as three thousand years, the practice of authors revisiting outstanding works of the past, and commenting on the relevance of the classics to the present culture, can be regarded as an endeavor pursued in the spirit of Goethe's dictum above. In some cases this commentary comes in an unusual form, namely as a "fictional reinterpretation," or, to introduce the term that is used throughout the study, as a "literary reworking." No work of art stands in isolation. In one way or another it will have evolved from a form that has been created before, and, likewise, it may itself have an influence on future developments and set trends in a given genre. Literary reworkings distinguish themselves from other literary works by referring openly and explicitly to a previous fictional model. The author draws parallels and creates contrasts to the chosen model, and the new work rejects or endorses the content and the sentiments expressed in the older work. Most important, the literary reworking seeks to involve the reader in participating actively in the process of reading the new while remembering the old. However, in the reworking, the predicament is usually resolved in a new way, as the specific socio-political context of each different era changes. The more effective a reworking is, the more productive and rewarding the reading process becomes, so that we can say: *a reworking is a work that openly and explicitly refers to a literary predecessor and engages with its model to such an extent that the resulting dialogue between model and reworking will significantly open up the interpretation of the later text. At the same time it will aid and clarify our reception of the model, whether we are sympathetic to the new treatment of the work, or not.* Thus, the literary reworking, understood in the light of its respective literary model, provides a unique opportunity to study the past as it is perceived from the present, and to understand how the present is shaped by the past.

The current work examines the nature of the construction of six such literary reworkings in the context of German literature ranging from Goethe and Schiller to Ulrich Plenzdorf and Peter Schneider. I will analyze two examples from each genre, the drama, the novella, and the novel respectively: Brecht's play *Die heilige Johanna der Schlachthöfe*, which is conceived as an anti-work to Schiller's romantic tragedy *Die Jungfrau von Orleans*, and Hebbel's bourgeois tragedy *Maria Magdalena*, which is reproduced in the shape of Franz Xaver Kroetz's comedy of the same title; Wolfgang Koeppen's *Der Tod in Rom*, which deconstructs Thomas Mann's novella *Der Tod in Venedig*, and Peter Schneider's *Lenz* narrative into which essential features of Büchner's novella *Lenz* have been absorbed; and lastly, the two Goethe novels *Die Leiden des jungen Werther* and *Die Wahlverwandtschaften*, which reappear in the guise of Ulrich Plenzdorf's *Die neuen Leiden des jungen W.* and John Banville's *The Newton Letter* respectively.

The focus of this study is to provide an overview of the range of different aesthetic purposes that can be achieved by applying this literary technique. The effect of the reworking, when read in conjunction with its literary model, is strikingly different in each case. But, as will be demonstrated, common to all reworkings is a gain in historical depth, and in each case new themes and issues arise that are not immediately apparent when the reworking is considered on its own. This study embraces some important works of the last three hundred years in German literature, and has been written in the hope that it may go a little way towards countering the state of spiritual poverty referred to above that is threatening our culture as we move into the new millennium.

Acknowledgments

FIRST THANKS ARE DUE TO Professor Gordon J. A. Burgess, who guided and directed me in producing the manuscript in its initial form. My appreciation also goes to my colleagues in the German Department of the University of Aberdeen, who were always willing to engage in constructive discussions on particular questions, made useful suggestions, and offered unstinting support. I am especially grateful to Mrs. Barbara Wibbelmann, who gave her time and skills to assist with the proofreading. The publication of this volume has been made possible through the assistance of the Carnegie Trust, Scotland, and the University of Aberdeen.

And finally, my gratitude goes to my husband and my children, without whose sympathy and practical help in matters concerning the real part of living I could not have completed this study.

G. M. S.
June 2002

Abbreviations of Works Frequently Cited

BFA	Bertolt Brecht. *Werke: große kommentierte Berliner und Frankfurter Ausgabe*. 30 vols. Berlin and Weimar: Aufbau, Frankfurt am Main: Suhrkamp, 1988–98.
BW	Georg Büchner. *Lenz*. Vol. 1 in *Sämtliche Werke und Briefe: Historisch-kritische Ausgabe mit Kommentar*. Hamburg: Christian Wegner, 1967.
EB	Hugo von Hofmannsthal. *Ein Brief*. Vol. 31 in *Sämtliche Werke*. Frankfurt am Main: Fischer, 1991.
GW	Johann Wolfgang Goethe. *Die Leiden des jungen Werther* in *HA*, 6.
HA	Johann Wolfgang Goethe. *Goethes Werke. Hamburger Ausgabe in 14 Bänden*. Hamburg: Christian Wegner, 1948–60.
HJ	Bertolt Brecht. *Die heilige Johanna der Schlachthöfe* in *BFA*, 3.
HMM	Friedrich Hebbel. *Maria Magdalena* in *HW*, 1.
HW	Friedrich Hebbel. *Werke*. 5 vols. Munich: Carl Hanser, 1963–67.
JO	Friedrich Schiller, *Die Jungfrau von Orleans* in *NA*, 9.
KMM	Franz Xaver Kroetz. *Maria Magdalena*. In *Stücke II*. Frankfurt am Main: Suhrkamp, 1989.
NA	Friedrich Schiller. *Schillers Werke. Nationalausgabe*. 42 vols. Weimar: Hermann Böhlhaus Nachfolger, 1943–2000.
NL	John Banville. *The Newton Letter*. London: Minerva, 1992. First published in London: Warburg & Secker 1982.
PL	Ulrich Plenzdorf. *Die neuen Leiden des jungen W*. Frankfurt am Main: Suhrkamp, 1976. First published in *Sinn und Form*, 1973.
SL	Peter Schneider. *Lenz. Eine Erzählung*. Berlin: Rotbuch, 1973.
TR	Wolfgang Koeppen. *Der Tod in Rom*. Frankfurt am Main: Suhrkamp, 1954; 4th edition, 1982.
TV	Thomas Mann. *Der Tod in Venedig*. Vol. 8 in *Gesammelte Werke*. Frankfurt am Main: Fischer, 1974.
WV	Johann Wolfgang Goethe. *Die Wahlverwandtschaften* in *HA*, 6.

Introduction

> Daß immer mal wieder neuere Leute sich große
> alte Titel und Themen unter den Nagel reißen,
> ist mir eine alt-ehrwürdige Unverschämtheit.
> Wolf Biermann

A Story is Conceived . . .

IN THE OPENING PARAGRAPH of his novella *Romeo und Julia auf dem Dorfe* (1856), Gottfried Keller claims that there is only a very limited number of basic plots in literature, and that those are reworked over and over again. According to this view almost *all* literature is constituted of reworkings of one kind or another.

> Diese Geschichte zu erzählen, würde eine müßige Nachahmung sein, wenn sie nicht auf einem wirklichen Vorfall beruhte, zum Beweise wie tief im Menschenleben jede jener Fabeln wurzelt, auf welchen die großen alten Werke gebaut sind. *Die Zahl solcher Fabeln ist mäßig;* aber stets treten sie in neuem Gewande wieder in Erscheinung und zwingen alsdann die Hand, sie festzuhalten.[1]

The title of Keller's novella immediately evokes the classic character constellation of doomed lovers, and yet the protagonists of Keller's narrative do not bear the names of their respective literary predecessor, nor indeed, those of the title. The rural setting, the social conditions of the age, and the geographical location, even the literary genre, are quite different from those of Shakespeare's tragedy. However, by means of the allusion in the title, the reader anticipates the tragic outcome of the narrative before even being introduced to the characters, and is constantly invited to draw comparisons between the dilemma of Shakespeare's archetypal lovers and Keller's nineteenth-century counterparts.

Other such classic conflicts, which form the basis of countless plots in literature from all over the world, include the relationships between parents and their children, sons and mothers, fathers and daughters. The figure of Oedipus signifies a particular type of these relationships. Within German literature the incestuous affair between Sabeth and Faber in Max Frisch's *Homo faber* (1957) may serve as an example of a reversed instance of the Oedipus story.² On a slightly different note, any reference to Goethe's *Die Leiden des jungen Werther* (1774) immediately creates an association with the eternal triangle in love-relationships and implies a protagonist of extreme sensibility possessed of an excess of feeling. Again, the pattern can be varied endlessly. In short, in the above quote Keller refers to typical character constellations that offer a potential source of conflict and thus give rise to an infinite number of reproductions in fiction, as, indeed, in real life.

As Keller implies, one source of material that has been taken up time and again in literature throughout the centuries is found in ancient myths and legends. For example in a European context, the figure of Iphigenie, first dramatized by Euripides in 412 B.C., has been used over the centuries to symbolize contrasting, even contradictory sentiments, depending on the historical events at the time of the conception of a new work. In Goethe's drama *Iphigenie auf Tauris* (1779), the figure of Iphigenie has become the very incarnation of the values and ideals of Weimar Classicism and her words and actions represent the flowering of German humanism *per se*. In contrast, in his two *Iphigenie* dramas, *Iphigenie in Aulis* and *Iphigenie in Delphi*, written in the years between 1941 and 1944, Gerhard Hauptmann uses the ancient mythology to express his utter despair over the traumatic years of the Second World War. In the post-*Wende* era, Volker Braun resurrects the classical persona in his dramatic poem *Iphigenie in Freiheit* (1990), whereas Kerstin Jentzsch introduces a prosaic and practical heroine in her novel *Iphigenie in Pankow* (1998). With every literary incarnation, the figure of Iphigenie represents a very different set of values. Antigone, Medea, Alkestis, to name but a few figures from ancient Greek mythology, have over the centuries proved to be equally irresistible to playwrights and novelists.

In the Christian era the Arthurian tradition has been a vast source of mythical and historical characters who have been taken up by authors of all major European literatures since the Middle Ages, culminating in Richard Wagner's operas *Tristan und Isolde* (1859) and *Parsifal* (1882). The interest of writers and readers alike shows no sign of abating, taking into account recent film versions featuring the knights of the Round Table and publications such as Christoph Hein's drama *Die Ritter der Tafelrunde* (1990). A further example of a story that never loses its appeal can be found in the *Faust* legend, the first written record of which is found in 1587 in Spies's *Faustbuch*. Again, the fascination with the material has transcended cultural and linguistic boundaries and has been taken up time and again in drama, novel, film, and opera. The literary preoccupation with the material spans from the early version by Christopher Marlowe, circa 1594, to the twentieth-century novel *Doktor Faustus* by Thomas Mann, not to mention Goethe's *Faust* and countless lesser known works. As regards historical figures, Mary Stuart and Joan of Arc are just two heroines whose life has been retold countless times both in English and French as well as in German literature.

All of the above examples manifest the engagement of an author with commonly known and previously published material. Each time the reader's knowledge of the original fable is played upon to emphasize the parallels and contrasts between the original and the new literary treatment of the story, which has resulted from the author's particular purpose. From this vast field of reworkings in a general sense, the present investigation focuses on a particular type of twentieth-century reworking taken from German literary models, which we describe as a "literary reworking."[3] More specific than Keller's archetypal character constellations or, alternatively, going beyond a general engagement with any particular mythical, legendary, or historical figures, a literary reworking in the sense that we want to define it is not necessarily a work constructed along the lines of a well-known fable or conflict, but is modeled on a particular *literary* work. After first establishing what constitutes a literary reworking, the main concern of the following chapters is initially to analyze the narrative devices used to establish the links between model and reworking, and then to reflect on the effect this technique has on the reader's reception of the reworking. In order to limit the field, literary adaptations, which belong to the tradition of a particular legendary or historical figure, have been excluded, because the thematic links often form a continuous evolution and it would be more appropriate to analyze the treatment of a specific figure or character constellation vertically through the ages. The aim of this study is rather to introduce and analyze the very diverse range of literary reworkings from across a number of literary genres, all of which occur in the context of German literature and have been written in the twentieth century.

What Are Literary Reworkings?

Common to all literary reworkings, in the sense defined in this study, is the phenomenon that the reworking is directly and explicitly based on a previous *literary,* that is *fictional* work, or as Hans Mayer puts it: "Kunstschaffen mit Hilfe einer bereits vorhandenen Kunst."[4] The new work deliberately and openly refers to one or more well-known texts with the result that the narrative of the literary model is present in the mind of the reader side-by-side with that of the contemporary creation. The more familiar the reader is with the literary model, the more complex becomes the dialogue between author and author, between author and reader and, indeed, between the various protagonists of the two narratives. The mingling of different narrative discourses adds depth to the understanding not only of the reworking, but occasionally even to the reception of the literary model. Hans-Robert Jauss even goes so far as to argue that the new and creative reproduction of a canonical text not only constitutes a dialectic process between the past and the present, but also overcomes the potential one-sidedness of a traditional or purely formal renewal of the classical work.[5] As we will see, the association of model and reworking operates as an implicit commentary of one text on the other. The successful reworking, when read in conjunction with the model, will constantly suggest unexpected angles and introduce additional themes and questions. Even in the case of an Irish reworking of a German literary text, the literary allusions to the model considerably widen the interpretation of the reworking, and significantly deepen the understanding of the respective cultural context.

As we are concerned with a form of literary reworkings specific to German literature, it is remarkable that, although there is a sizeable body of secondary literature on individual pairings, there is no agreed term in German to describe the phenomenon. Whereas the English term "reworking" suggests exactly what the contemporary authors have done with their respective models — taken up particular aspects of a literary work and presented them in a new, and original fashion — the German terms *Neuerzählung* and *Wiedererzählung*, both of which are found in secondary literature, are not particularly satisfactory because neither does full justice to the inherent originality of the literary descendant. The use of *Bearbeitung*, or even *Wiederbearbeitung*, is equally problematic, because either one implies a value judgment. All of these German terms suggest an expressed intention by the author to improve on the model, something which the more neutral English term "reworking" does to a much lesser degree. This lack of a descriptive term for such a distinctive feature within German contemporary literature highlights the fact that only sporadic attempts have been made so far either in German or in English to collate and analyze a range of literary reworkings as a whole. The following chapters are intended to lay the foundation for a more comprehensive understanding of the phenomenon in the context of German literature, and to demonstrate the sometimes spectacular effect a literary reworking might have. It is hoped this study will lead to further research in the field.

In order for a reworking to be effective, it ought to be modeled on its predecessor closely enough to invite the reader to take note of parallels and contrasts between model and reworking. Two essential characteristics of a literary reworking can be summarized thus: (1) the modern literary work is consciously and deliberately modeled on an earlier literary work; and (2) the literary model is a well-known text by an established canonical writer.[6] The effect of the reworking rests on the premise that the reader will not merely recognize the allusion to the model in the title of the reworking, but that he or she will be sufficiently acquainted with the literary predecessor to appreciate the finer points of the technique. Only then will the author of the reworking and the reader engage in a silent dialogue in which the reception of the literary model and that of the reworking can be compared and explored. The process of this silent but unavoidable comparison between the model and the contemporary reworking inevitably shapes the reader's reception not only of the new work but also alters the previous understanding of the literary model. Thus, a third narrative arises in the mind of the reader, which consists of the mingling of the different voices and emotions of the protagonists of both model and reworking, as they comment on each other during the reading process.

Literary reworkings occur in all genres. Therefore, this study is divided into six chapters, discussing two examples of a reworked drama, novella and novel respectively. These, in turn, are ordered chronologically, according to the date of publication of the reworking, rather than that of the model. The selection of works is meant to introduce the widest possible range of dramatic and narrative devices and to demonstrate the scope of the literary technique. The link between model and reworking can be established by means of allusion or quotation, the names of characters and character constellations, similarities and contrasts in particular incidents, and by direct reference to the respective models. Naturally, every example of literary reworking uses a number of different narrative devices, but in each of the following chapters an attempt has been made to find the underlying principle according to which any one reworking has been constructed.

A possible list of technical criteria defining a literary reworking might include: (1) evidence of an *explicit* link between the model and the reworking, most typically, but not always, found in the title; (2) parallels and marked contrasts in the plot and/or in single incidents, in names or character constellations; (3) related or equivalent devices in the narrative perspective, the narrative construction and linguistic style and register; or (4) the use of quotes, or intentional misquotes, often marked as such. But even for the purpose of defining a literary reworking it is impossible to sort these criteria into *necessary* and *optional* devices, as the range of techniques used differs widely. More fruitful is the focus on the apparent *intention* of the reworking and, as a test of the effectiveness of the reworking, we may ask the following question: does the knowledge and integration of the literary model into the reading process of the new work add a *significant* new dimension to the understanding and interpretation of the literary reworking? And *vice versa:* in what way is the model illuminated in the light of the treatment it receives in the reworking? This latter analysis of what constitutes a creative literary reworking is concerned less with the obvious parallels and contrasts that exist between model and reworking on a factual level, and more with the dynamic processes that arise from the interaction between the two works.

All reworkings can be treated on their own merit; appraising a literary reworking is not the same as source hunting, because the very characteristic of reworkings is that the link to the model has been made explicit. It should be emphasized that the focus on those aspects concerning the elements of reworking in the newer text must be *additional* to any interpretation of the work itself and act as an enrichment of the understanding of the text. Equally, no interpretation, particularly of the literary models, offered in the following chapters, claims to be comprehensive but is naturally confined to those aspects relevant to the reworking, or to those features that emerge from re-reading the model with the reworking in mind.

Existing secondary literature tends to look at any one of the reworkings discussed in this study from a particular thematic angle, and draws on aspects concerned with the characteristics of a reworking only where and when it serves the overall argument of the paper. To my knowledge no comprehensive analysis exists that looks solely at a reworking as a reworking, or at how model and reworking are mutually affected by one another when read in conjunction. There is an extensive body of critical articles and some larger studies on individual pairings of model and reworking, the most important of which form the basis to the argument of the following chapters. However, apart from a very few notable exceptions, all of these refer to a single pair of model and reworking only. An article by Götz Grossklaus (1975),[7] and the one by Hans-Robert Jauss's "Klassik — wieder modern?" (1978, cited above) compare and contrast two sets of reworkings, but, as can be seen from the respective titles, they focus on content and reception rather than on the phenomenon of reworkings itself. Gordon Burgess's article "Büchner, Schneider and Lenz: Two Authors in Search of a Character" (1990, cited above) draws attention to the fact that other reworkings exist in German literature, but, once more, the argument in the article is limited to the *Lenz* tradition. A number of full-scale studies in book form touch upon certain aspects of the chosen field, but none prove to be particularly relevant in the quest of depicting the phenomenon of literary reworkings in its breadth and complexity. Herman Meyer's *Das Zitat in der Erzählkunst* (1961)[8] is limited to an analysis of actual quotation; Herbert Haffner's *Dramenbearbeitungen* (1980)[9] is concerned exclusively with reworkings of drama, as is Ralf Sudau's *Werkbearbeitung, Dichterfiguren* (1985).[10] An interesting aside is provided by H. J. Schueler's study *The Old Retold* (1996), but Schueler belongs to the psychoanalytical school, and is looking at archetypes in German literature based on "Northrop Frye's understanding of the nature of literature."[11]

There have been repeated calls to develop a theoretical framework for the related practices of alluding to, quoting from, and reproducing literary texts in other texts, but nothing definitive has been forthcoming to date. In the context of Schneider's *Lenz* as an example of the so-called *Verständigungstext,* a term which originated in the early 1970s, Eveline Keitel gives a possible reason for this, namely that the techniques used in these works are too diverse and varied to allow for a comprehensive theory which does not generalize and oversimplify.[12] These difficulties apply equally to the field of literary reworkings, and this study makes no claim to provide a new theoretical framework for reworkings. In the meantime, however, the practice of reworking continues, the inventiveness of the authors is growing, and with it the number of different literary devices employed.

From the contemporary author's point of view there are certain dangers attached to writing a reworking, because the technique is only really effective if the model is well-known and established in the literary canon. All too often even a very ambitious reworking pales into insignificance in comparison to the illustrious model. Some harsh judgements have been made of reworkings that do not reach the literary merit of the model they attempt to emulate, to update, or to replace. With reference to Schneider's *Lenz,* Burgess acknowledges the enrichment Schneider's narrative receives by reading it as a reworking, but dismisses the new *Lenz* as inferior to the original. "[Schneider's work] has nothing of the condensed, pregnant economy and the rich intensity of its forerunner, and in particular lacks the power to express the universal in the particular which so distinguishes Büchner's text" (223–24). The reception of Kroetz's *Maria Magdalena* has also been largely negative. "Vordergründig aktualisiert," reads the headline of the *Deutsche Volkszeitung*, and the article continues: "Die prägnanten Hebbel-Dialoge sind durch hilflos geschwätzige . . . ersetzt."[13] Another review states: "Gegen Hebbel aber tritt Kroetz mit seiner *Maria Magdalena* gar nicht erst an."[14] In most cases this sort of criticism is justified if we compare the model and reworking directly. Few modern works can compete on a formal or on a linguistic level with the often intricate and complex survivors of eighteenth- and nineteenth-century works of literature. However, the reworking element is only *one* aspect of the texts under discussion. Each work can also be read without reference to its literary model, and it would, perhaps, be more generous to regard these works as part of the contemporary literary scene, and compare them to other works of their respective period. In that way the reworking aspect becomes an additional enhancement of the text, and the skill and inventiveness of the authors concerned may be appreciated more readily.

Reworkings can play an important part in the contemporary reception of the literary works of previous centuries. Concerned with ways of bridging the historical gap that lies between the initial effect of a classical work and our present reception, Jauss, who sees the whole phenomenon of reworkings in a positive light, describes them as an *Aktualisierung* and claims that they are *necessarily* shorter than their models, and highly selective.[15] For example, Plenzdorf's *Die neuen Leiden des jungen W.*, itself hugely successful in the early 1970s, also reawakened a genuine and popular interest in Goethe's *Die Leiden des jungen Werther*, and made the classic accessible once more to a young readership curious to revisit Plenzdorf's model. In turn, this process enters the realm of fiction when the central character of Volker Braun's novella *Unvollendete Geschichte* (1977), who has read both books, is moved to draw a comparison between reworking and model.[16]

The charge of plagiarism was already leveled against what must have been the first reworking of this century, Hugo von Hofmannsthal's *Erlebnis des Marschalls von Bassompierre* (1900). Karl Kraus vigorously defended the narrative in his journal *Die Fackel*:

"Was Ungebildete hier Plagiat nennen, ist in Wahrheit Citat [*sic*]."[17] The term *Zitat,* quotation, is often used in critical reviews of reworkings, and can have several meanings. In the context of Plenzdorf's *Die neuen Leiden des jungen W.,* Ilse H. Reis characterizes the effect of a word-for-word quotation as a passage which points beyond the immediate surface of the text, the presence of which will alert the reader to look out for more direct and indirect clues hidden in the work. Thus, the reader becomes more involved with the text and enters into a sort of game with the author.[18] As we will see, Plenzdorf establishes the links between his work and Goethe's *Die Leiden des jungen Werther* not merely by acknowledged quotes, but by a whole series of structural devices which may loosely be described as "quotation" in the sense described by Herman Meyer: "In weiterem Sinne kann Zitieren bedeuten, daß man nicht den Wortlaut, sondern den Inhalt von bestimmten literarischen Stellen oder gar von ganzen literarischen Werken anführt oder auf sie anspielt" (15). This is the field in which a reworking operates in its widest sense. The thin line between plagiarism and creative reworking becomes difficult to determine. After all, by its very definition the reworking acknowledges its indebtedness to its model. We need to bear in mind that, even if the reworkings refer to serious, sometimes cathartic matters, reading fiction and visiting the theatre are first and foremost forms of entertainment. Expressions like "in-joke" (Burgess) or "Spiel" (Reis) emphasize a certain intellectual playfulness that is part of every reworking, and in some ways the severe charge of plagiarism misses the point. Furthermore, Dorothea Keuler reminds us in the prefix to her novel *Die wahre Geschichte der Effi B.* (1998): "Schon immer wurde Literatur aus Literatur gemacht. Jeder Text verweist auf andere Texte, die ihm vorausgingen oder in seinem Umfeld existieren. Das Wortspiel vom *playgiarism* bringt die Interaktion zwischen Texten auf den Punkt."[19]

The question of why reworkings of German literature occur in the first place, and why they have taken this particular form, can be answered only very tentatively, and two possible ideas have been put forward. In the larger context of European history, Karl Marx reminds us of a general tendency in the continuous treatment of literary themes: "Hegel bemerkt irgendwo, daß alle großen weltgeschichtlichen Tatsachen und Personen sich sozusagen zweimal ereignen. Er hat vergessen hinzuzufügen: das eine Mal als Tragödie, das andere Mal als Farce."[20] Elsewhere, Marx elaborates and offers us some actual examples:

Die Geschichte ist gründlich und macht viele Phasen durch, wenn sie eine alte Gestalt zu Grabe trägt. Die letzte Phase einer weltgeschichtlichen Gestalt ist ihre Komödie. Die Götter Griechenlands, die schon einmal tragisch zu Tode verwundet waren im gefesselten Prometheus des Äschylus, mußten noch einmal komisch sterben, in den Gesprächen Lucians. Warum dieser Gang der Geschichte? Damit die Menschheit heiter von ihrer Vergangenheit scheide.[21]

The same theory is also advanced, albeit in a slightly different form, by Friedrich Dürrenmatt who, in his collection of essays on the theoretical aspects of the theatre, *Theater-Schriften und Reden* (1966), argues that our age cannot produce tragedy any longer. "Doch ist das Tragische noch möglich, auch wenn die reine Tragödie nicht mehr möglich ist."[22] When we look at the actual examples of reworkings, we find that the tragic models (and they all end in death or despair) have indeed been transformed into tragi-comedies set in a world in which the ultimate punishment is to go on living.

Another, more particular German reason for this individualistic and complex reception of Germany's literary heritage has been hinted at by Jauss when he describes Wolfgang Hildesheimer's play *Mary Stuart — eine historische Szene* (1970) as "nicht einfach eine neuere *Mary Stuart*, sondern auch eine Antwort auf die Frage, welche Barrieren in Deutschland dem unproblematischen Weiterspielen der klassischen *Maria Stuart* entgegenstehen" (40). The sense of sorrow that Germany's idealistic past did not prevent the horrors of two world wars and the Holocaust lives on as an underlying question in the literary output of the postwar years. Here Jauss refers specifically to "das latente, von Max Frisch 1949 namhaft gemachte Unbehagen an der Tradition des klassischen Individualismus, die als Bildungsmacht die unmenschliche Realität des Hitlerreiches nicht hatte verhindern können" (38). This sense of unease can also be found in the implicit dialogue with the past, which forms the basis of all reworkings.

Criteria for Chosen Works

The works introduced in the following chapters are by no means the only reworkings in German literature of the twentieth century.[23] In most cases the reader is alerted to a potential reworking by the title of a work which refers openly or obliquely to a distinguished predecessor. Part of the difficulty of providing a definition of what exactly constitutes a reworking is the fact that individual reworkings are written with different objectives in mind. This will become clear even from the small selection of works introduced in this study. Since the model must be generally known to the readership, it is hardly surprising that the works of the German classical period, particularly those by Goethe and Schiller, are foremost among the literary models selected by modern authors. However, other authors whose works serve as models for modern reworkings include Georg Büchner, Friedrich Hebbel, and Thomas Mann.

With one exception the reworkings discussed in this selection were published after the Second World War, particularly in the 1970s, when a number of important and widely discussed reworkings reached the public of East and West Germany. Brecht's *Die heilige Johanna der Schlachthöfe*, written 1929–31, has been included because, as we will see, in much of his work Brecht recycled literary material so frequently that he could even be regarded as a special case in the history of reworkings. However, Brecht's version of the Joan of Arc theme targets the values of Weimar Classicism and the idealism of Schiller's *Die Jungfrau von Orleans* (1801) so specifically that we may justly regard *Die heilige Johanna der Schlachthöfe* not so much as another version of the legendary material, but more particularly, as a literary reworking of Schiller's romantic tragedy. In *Die heilige Johanna der Schlachthöfe* Brecht openly attacks the classical heritage of German literature, and parodies the poetic language and the unswerving idealism of his model, thus creating an anti-work.

Hebbel's *Maria Magdalena* (1843) has often been described as the literary successor to Lessing's *Emilia Galotti* (1772), which in turn deals with a provocative, albeit productive literary theme, a father's seduction of his daughter. Here, too, our interest lies not so much in the development through the ages of this particular theme,[24] but in the *specific* reproduction of Hebbel's tragedy that Kroetz has undertaken in his version of the plot. By rewriting Hebbel's drama as a "comedy," Kroetz turns the story on its head. The resounding message of Kroetz's *Maria Magdalena: Eine Komödie frei nach Friedrich Hebbel* (1972) is that the world that allowed the first Maria Magdalena to die 150 years previously has not changed greatly. In contrast, in Wolfgang Koeppen's *Der Tod in Rom* (1954) we are moving in a world wherein everything has changed compared to that of Thomas Mann's *Der Tod in Venedig* (1912). Mann's novella is the only model which was written in this century, but in many ways Mann, with his melancholic nostalgia for the past, can be seen as one of the last in the long line of German classical writers, and in *Der Tod in Venedig* he describes a way of life that has long since disappeared forever. By the time Koeppen wrote *Der Tod in Rom* Mann's novella was firmly established as part of the German canon.

Whereas Koeppen firmly rejects the aestheticized ideals of Mann's protagonist, Peter Schneider apparently aims to import the intense atmosphere and the sense of growing mental disintegration of its literary predecessor into his narrative. Büchner's *Lenz* (1835), already to some degree indebted to Goethe's *Die Leiden des jungen Werther*, generated a complex *Lenz* tradition that was a much-favored literary theme with the soul-searching writers of the late nineteenth century.[25] In the twentieth century the *Lenz* tradition was revived, particularly in the East German literature of the 1970s and 1980s.[26] My choice of Peter Schneider's *Lenz* (1973) over any other narrative written in the *Lenz* tradition is, once more, based on the *explicit* link to the model that is found in the title.

The most notorious reworking of the postwar era was probably Ulrich Plenzdorf's *Die neuen Leiden des jungen W.* (1973). There can be no doubt that its fame in literary circles as well as in the political arena was due to a large extent to the Goethe reference in the title. But it is equally true that the enthusiastic reception of the play (later rewritten as a novel), particularly among the youth of both Germanys, had less to do with the reworking aspects of the work, and more with the fact that, just like Goethe's Werther before him, Edgar, the new Werther, very quickly became an idol for young people who felt they could identify with his sufferings. In *Die neuen Leiden des jungen W.* the central protagonist gradually learns to understand and identify with a literary figure from the past. In contrast, John Banville's *The Newton Letter* (1982) transposes the characters of Goethe's *Die Wahlverwandtschaften* (1809) into the present, or, more specifically into a framework of our contemporary scientific paradigm. My inclusion of Banville's *The Newton Letter*, an Irish reworking of *Die Wahlverwandtschaften*, can only be justified because in some ways, ironically, it is the most spectacular example of the effect a reworking can have. Read purely as a narrative of contemporary Irish fiction, *The Newton Letter* leaves the impression of a moving, well-constructed, but otherwise unremarkable, short novel. But, as soon as we place the work into the German cultural context, and recognize the links which connect the work with not just one but two models from German literature, our reception of the narrative opens up and philosophical and literary questions emerge that go far beyond the framework of the plot, thus providing a prime example of the full potential inherent in the technique of literary reworkings. (As we shall see, Hofmannsthal's short text, *Ein Brief* [1902], commonly referred to in English as *The Chan-*

dos Letter, is as important to *The Newton Letter* as is *Die Wahlverwandtschaften.*)

Definitions

To summarize, the following chapters will introduce six examples of literary reworkings taken from drama, the novella, and the novel respectively. An important aspect of the selection criteria is to exclude the continuous literary engagement with common fables and myths, and to focus on reworkings which are explicitly linked to *literary,* that is entirely fictional, predecessors. Rather than drawing up a list of criteria as to what exactly a reworking *is,* the approach taken is to explore what it *does.*

Initially, the prime difficulty of this investigation was the problem of how to merge the very diverse forms of reworkings into a cohesive field of study. As a result, the research focuses on the question of identifying the guiding principle according to which any one reworking is linked to its respective literary model and which will most effectively reveal additional dimensions, questions, and themes that are implied either in the reworking, or in the model or, indeed, in both works. The following terms are used to describe the overarching principle applied by the author of each respective reworking.

Allusion: In his investigation *Games Authors Play* (1983), Peter Hutchinson lists "quotation," "parody," "myth," "pictures," and even "name" as various examples of "allusion."[27] All of these are present not only in Brecht's *Die heilige Johanna der Schlachthöfe,* but in all reworkings. The decision to apply the term particularly to Brecht's reworking is justified not so much because the general definition of allusion above is more relevant here than in the case of any other reworking, but because it demonstrates the particular effect of "allusion" as described by Andy Hollis:

> An allusion is a device by means of which an author hints at a context beyond the immediate one. The aim is to invite, stimulate or even challenge readers to draw comparisons. . . . Allusions, however, are not a statement of fact. . . . How we interpret any implied link between contexts is up to us.[28]

This last point is of special importance. As will be demonstrated, the connection between Brecht's *Die heilige Johanna der Schlachthöfe* and Schiller's *Die Jungfrau von Orleans* is rather general and progresses on a conceptual basis. On the level of characters and plot, Brecht's *Die heilige Johanna der Schlachthöfe* has very little in common with Schiller's "romantic tragedy." However, once the audience is willing to engage with the task of searching for the connections between the reworking and the tradition alluded to, the discourse of moral freedom versus political liberty is thrown into relief.

Ironic Reproduction: In a biological sense "reproduction" refers to continuation of a species, to birth and to rebirth. In a more general context the term might stand for repetition and duplication. And this is what Kroetz does in his *Maria Magdalena: Eine Komödie frei nach Friedrich Hebbel.* Hebbel's tragedy and Kroetz's "comedy" closely correspond to one another, and function on the principle of reproduction. Hebbel's nineteenth-century *Kleinbürger* continues to exist but has been recreated in a different age; the conflict is duplicated, and the tragic outcome is repeated. The chapter on Kroetz's *Maria Magdalena* play will show how, in accordance with the pattern described by Marx, Klara, Hebbel's tragic heroine, had to perish once more, this time in a comical fashion; or rather, as even the option of death is denied to her, Kroetz's play introduces an anti-heroine who is completely marginalized and forced into an existence of ever-diminishing prospects.

Fragmentation: Fragmentation is a process by which an existing whole is shattered into diverse and separate pieces and, to use the metaphor of a mirror, the remaining shards and splinters will reflect different and broken images, even if they mirror the same world. Thomas Mann's *Der Tod in Venedig* leads us into Aschenbach's own particular universe, with its unique laws of aesthetics and perfection. Koeppen's *Der Tod in Rom* uses the broken segments of this illusionary realm, and shows a world distorted by ugliness and pain as seen through the eyes of a number of different protagonists.

Integration: In the portrayal of his *Lenz* character Peter Schneider reverses this process of taking an existing whole and shattering it into fragments. Büchner's *Lenz,* itself a fragment, is completed and reworked as a story of re-integration and hope. With Schneider's refusal to clearly define the boundaries between his and Büchner's *Lenz* the twentieth-century *Lenz* gains in stature. On the level of the plot, any parallels or marked contrasts between model and reworking remain minimal. But in Schneider's *Lenz* figure some of the most characteristic qualities of the Büchner model have been absorbed and are integrated into the text to such an extent that without them the new Lenz would remain colorless and insubstantial. As it is, a degree of suffering is suddenly suggested, the depth of which we would not have acknowledged without the explicit link and the constant shadowy presence of the literary predecessor.

Quotation: In contrast to the half-hearted way in which Schneider uses Büchner quotes in order to establish the connection between model and reworking, Ulrich Plenzdorf makes full use of the device. He exploits a whole range of different effects by making "quotation" the most prominent feature of his reworking of Goethe's *Die Leiden des jungen Werther*. In *Die neuen Leiden des jungen W.* the principle of "quotation" operates on several levels. Hutchinson captures the essence of how quotation functions when he says that "in choosing to re-use the words of another, an author is offering a dual challenge to his reader: first, that reader must recognize the quotation, and second, he must seek to relate it to its new context" (107). In this case, however, the Goethe quotations are clearly marked in the text, and are well integrated into the new context. The irony lies in the fact that, although the reader has no trouble recognizing the source and the original context, the protagonist, who uses the quotations so effectively, remains in the dark. Nevertheless, it is still true that "the idea of quotation is linked irresistibly with, above all, a knowledge of sources,"[29] and in Plenzdorf's novel the challenge to the reader lies in contextualizing the quotes, not in the new context, but in the original one. Plenzdorf's use of quotation proves to be the safest — and most subversive — means of expressing far-reaching social criticism in a society subject to systematic censorship.

Constellation: The varied and constantly shifting constellations of initially three and finally four protagonists of *Die Wahlverwandtschaften* form the subject of the investigation of Goethe's novel. In Banville's *The Newton Letter*, the constellation of characters remains constant, except for the arrival and departure of the narrator himself. As it turns out in this case, it is the ever-shifting *perception* of character constellations on the part of the narrator that, first and foremost, creates the link with *Die Wahlverwandtschaften* as inspiration and literary model of *The Newton Letter*, and that moves the plot forward. Once that connection has been established, we are invited to extend the term "constellation" infinitely and apply it to the cosmic constellations of a mechanistic and of a relativistic universe.

1: Allusion to Classicism: Friedrich Schiller's *Die Jungfrau von Orleans* and Bertolt Brecht's *Die heilige Johanna der Schlachthöfe*

> Die radikale Veränderung ist der einzige Weg,
> die Klassik für die Gegenwart zu erhalten.
> *Bertolt Brecht*

Joan of Arc as a Figure in Literature

THE ENIGMA OF JOAN OF ARC (1412–31), saint and sinner, historical figure and legendary, continues to this day to fascinate the church, historians, filmmakers, writers, and readers. The matter of who she really was, and how she achieved what she set out to do, has long been buried under countless layers of literary interpretations of her deeds, directed by feelings ranging from adoration to utter contempt of her person and her quest. This mystification had already started during her lifetime.

The fact that Joan of Arc was a successful woman in the male world of war made her unique in European history. As early as 1429 a poem, *Ditié de Jeanne d'Arc*, by Christine de Pisan appeared, praising her as the bringer of peace. She has been portrayed as the French national heroine, a saintly martyr, an allegorical figure representing the longing for peace and, emphasizing her martial side, an Amazon and a virtuous mixture of courage and piety. Naturally, her enemies portray her as a witch, a whore, and a heretic (for example, Shakespeare's *Henry VI, Part I*). In his poem *La Pucelle d'Orléans* (1759) Voltaire uses her saintly status to mock blind faith in religious superstition. Forty years later Schiller rescues the maiden from ridicule and turns her into a superhuman heroine. In 1921 George Bernard Shaw strips the plot of all supernatural qualities and seeks to explain Joan in psychological terms. Finally, Brecht was so fascinated by the material that he wrote three different plays based on the phenomenon that was Joan of Arc over a period of more than twenty years. Elisabeth Frenzel's encyclopedia, *Stoffe der Weltliteratur* (1992),[1] lists well over fifty literary works about Joan of Arc, but without doubt the two most prominent German dramas about Joan of Arc are those by Schiller and by Brecht. To date, they mark the point of departure and its final destination in the reception of Joan of Arc in German literature.

In *Die Jungfrau von Orleans — eine romantische Tragödie* (1801)[2] Schiller draws his inspiration from the historical figure of Joan of Arc, although he takes considerable liberties with his chronicled sources. At the same time, his stated aim was to rehabilitate Joan from the disgraced status she had received at the hands of Voltaire. In a letter to Christoph Martin Wieland, Schiller writes:

> Sie werden mir zugeben, daß Voltaire sein möglichstes gethan, einem dramatischen Nachfolger das Spiel schwer zu machen. Hat er seine Pucelle zu tief in den Schmutz gezogen, so habe ich die meinige vielleicht zu hoch gestellt. Aber hier war nicht anders zu helfen, wenn das Brandmal, das er seiner Schönen aufdrückte, sollte ausgelöscht werden.[3]

In *Die heilige Johanna der Schlachthöfe* (1931)[4] Brecht ignores the historical sources. Instead he assembles a great number of characters, taken from a variety of social and literary sources, in order to deliver a damning critique of Schiller's work and of the philosophical ideals of the Weimar classical period upon which the romantic tragedy is based.

How is this done? First, we have to ask what are elements that turn Brecht's *Die heilige Johanna der Schlachthöfe* into a Joan of Arc play in general, and a reworking of Schiller's *Die Jungfrau von Orleans* in particular. Are not the differences between Brecht's and Schiller's versions of Joan of Arc's mission greater than the similarities? In Brecht's play we have the story of a contemporary American girl, a member of the Salvation Army, told against the background of the turbulent events of economic crisis and the collapse of the beef market. Brecht sets his play in Chicago rather than France, the time is the twentieth century rather than the late Middle Ages, the characters are workers, industrialists, and members of the Salvation Army. The conflict is between the exploiters and the exploited rather than between two nations. There are no signs of the royal court and its attendant knights. What is more, Brecht uses the elements that he takes over from Schiller to parody the classical drama, and thus undermine their original dramatic function. For example, the *Erkennungsszene* (recognition scene) in which Schiller's Jungfrau proves the divine nature of her powers by identifying the Dauphin hidden among his courtiers, and the final apotheosis of the Jungfrau are both reintroduced by Brecht only to show that his Johanna is neither divine nor redeemed in death. Brecht alludes to the Joan of Arc tradition in the title, he names his central protagonist Johanna, and he quotes, and misquotes freely from Schiller's drama, but he does so primarily to attack his model and to produce an anti-play to Schiller's work.

There are three essential elements that weave together in the life of Joan of Arc: the heroic, the religious, and the romantic-supernatural. All of these emphasize the paradoxical nature of Joan's life. Although Joan was a young, inexperienced girl, she successfully led an army and became an apparently influential figure in royal circles. Being pious and obedient to the church for most of her short life, she was burned as a heretic. In spite of the fact that she was fundamentally humble and modest, her firm belief in the inner voices, which guided her actions, caused her to break the conventions of her social class.

But mysterious as these phenomena may be, they are not tragic in a *literary* sense, because Joan's death is brought about by political circumstance and the change of fortune rather than by a moral dilemma. In order to make the material suitable for tragedy, the tragic situation has to be constructed by the playwright. Schiller's and Shaw's versions are probably the most widely performed Joan of Arc plays, and would have been known to most of Brecht's audience in the early 1930s. In his *Die Jungfrau von Orleans* Schiller creates the dramatic conflict by placing his heroine in the opposition between duty and inclination, between *Pflicht* and *Neigung,* where, according to Immanuel Kant, the moral struggle is fought.[5] Focusing on the right to freedom in the actions of the individual, Schiller concentrates on the moral development of the Jungfrau, and emphasizes the heroic-romantic aspects of the legend. Historical correctness is of little importance, as Schiller stresses in a letter to Goethe: "Das historische [*sic*] ist überwunden, und doch soviel ich urtheilen kann, in seinem möglichsten Umfang benützt, die Motive sind alle poetisch und größtentheils von der naiven Gattung."[6]

When the original records of the trial of Joan of Arc were published in 1841, the reception of her story in literature shifted from her success on the battlefield to her imprisonment and trial. In the light of the growing materialism, the divine revelations, as the source of her remarkable achievements, which had previously been central to the myth that surrounded her life and death, were increasingly replaced by a modern psychological interpretation of her character. The legendary saint was changed into a remarkable woman of this world. The best known example of this trend is George Bernard Shaw's historical play *Saint Joan* (1924), written only four years after Joan's canonization.

Shaw's Joan is a self-confident young woman who is caught between the clear dictates of her conscience and the pressure applied by the authorities that have the power of life and death over her. Supernatural elements of the story appear only in the form of a dream of Charles VII, in which he is part of a ghostly reunion of all parties involved in her trial and execution. In a long preface to his play, Shaw explains away the mythical elements in the legend of the maid:

> She was never for a moment what so many romancers and playwrights have pretended: a romantic young lady. She was a thorough daughter of the soil in her peasantlike matter-of-factness and doggedness, and her acceptance of great lords and kings and prelates as such without idolatry or snobbery, seeing at a glance how much they were individually good for.... All this, however, must be taken with one heavy qualification. She was only a girl in her teens. If we could think of her as a managing woman of fifty we should seize her type at once.... This combination of inept youth and academic ignorance with great natural capacity, push, courage, devotion, originality and oddity, fully accounts for all the facts in Joan's career, and makes her a credible historical and human phenomenon; but it clashes most discordantly both with the idolatrous romance that has grown up round her, and the belittling skepticism that reacts against that romance.[7]

Shaw's psychological-historical portrayal of Joan cannot be regarded as a reworking of Schiller's drama for the simple reason that the earlier play is not relevant to Shaw's stated aims, as he himself explains: "Schiller's Joan has not a single point of contact with the real Joan, nor indeed with any mortal woman that ever walked this earth. There is really nothing to be said of his play but that it is not about Joan at all, and can hardly be said to pretend to be" (24).

Brecht wrote no fewer than three plays on the *Johanna* theme. The first, *Die heilige Johanna der Schlachthöfe*, is one of his *Lehrstücke*, his didactic plays, and although it is set in the United States, it clearly parodies the classical tradition of Schiller and Goethe. It seeks to expose the outdatedness of the German humanist tradition that continued into the twentieth century. The figure of Johanna has not only lost the supernatural qualities she possessed in Schiller's play, but also, to a significant degree, the strong charismatic personality of Shaw's Joan. The second play, *Die Gesichte der Simone Machard* (1941/43), takes an archetypal Joan of Arc figure into the present and deals with the resistance against Hitler's invasion of France. Finally, in 1952, Brecht reworked the radio play *Der Prozeß der Jeanne d'Arc zu Rouen 1431* by Anna Seghers for the stage. As has been pointed out by Joseph Donnenberg, Brecht's continued preoccupation with the Joan of Arc material is significant, not only in the way it evolves from a polemic directed at Schiller's idealistic reception of the Joan of Arc legend to more historical authenticity, and from an uncritical portrayal of the anti-capitalist struggle to a more differentiated presentation of the moral dilemmas of a resistance fighter, but also in the way it uses the "documentary" as a literary form, popular in the 1930s and 1940s.[8]

Nevertheless, I have limited this discussion to Brecht's *Die heilige Johanna der Schlachthöfe* because more important than Brecht's direct references to the Joan of Arc legend are the features that comment directly on Schiller's *Die Jungfrau von Orleans* and the ideals of the German classical period. Both Schiller and Brecht use the material for their own purposes and present the legend of Joan of Arc in an ahistorical fashion. Brecht's *Die heilige Johanna der Schlachthöfe* is conceived not only as a response to Schiller's *Die Jungfrau von Orleans* in particular, but more generally as a challenge to the philosophical foundations of the German classical tradition — namely, the emphasis on individual moral development as an expression of personal freedom. This Brecht presents as the ideological roots of capitalism. Brecht seeks to expose the ineffectiveness and inappropriateness of the bourgeois value system as it attempts to adapt to economic and social change in the early half of the twentieth century. In spite of the dramatists' different focuses — Schiller is concerned with inner freedom and Brecht dreams of liberty and social equality — both share a common belief in the didactic function of the theatre. But just what is it that they want the audience to learn?

Die Jungfrau von Orleans — A Lesson in Obedience

Schiller's *Die Jungfrau von Orleans* was first performed in September 1801, and quickly proved to be among Schiller's greatest stage successes. The romantic tragedy combined a lavish, theatrically effective production of battle scenes, a coronation procession, thunderclaps, special lighting, and musical accompaniment with the mood of a rising national feeling in Germany under Napoleonic rule. The underlying political development of the drama was extremely topical: a country near total disintegration caused by a century of more or less continuous warfare, a country in a state of general moral decline, is being turned around into a fighting nation with a growing sense of national identity, focused on the single figure of the king. With the coronation brought about by divine aid in the shape of an extraordinary young girl, Charles VII takes his rightful place at the head of his nation and thus restores the hope for lasting peace and order. The fifteenth-century legend accurately describes the state of the German nation at the beginning of the nineteenth century, fragmented and politically weakened, and with little sense of a national identity. *Die Jungfrau von Orleans* embodies the hope that miracles can happen, that one day Germany might rise and become a strong and unified nation.

The central question for Schiller concerns the moral consequences of blind obedience to the gods. What happens when a protagonist is sent on a divine mission involving absolute surrender to the cause and is prepared to accept it unconditionally? Schiller places his heroine between *duty* — her mission to save France and to lead Charles VII to his coronation — and *inclination* — her love for Lionel. Two female figures act as foils to Johanna and, at the same time, represent the two extreme positions to which Johanna might be led if she follows either the course of her inclination or that of her particular duty. In her utter femininity and willingness to live only for her lover, Agnes Sorel stands model for one of the temptations Johanna will have to face when Lionel offers her the protection of a strong husband and the "natural"[9] life of a woman, a life in the service of love and a family. Queen Isabeau, on the other hand, has taken up warfare like Johanna. As an "unnatural" woman and mother ("Was ihr am Dauphin tut, ist weder menschlich gut, noch göttlich recht," *JO,* 1399–1400), Isabeau is distrusted by friend and foe alike, a fate that also awaits Johanna on that glorious morning of the coronation when everyone she loves and honors turns away from her. The Queen remains a negative figure throughout the play. Whereas Isabeau's one-sidedness as an embittered goddess of war serves as a warning to what can happen if only the martial aspect of Johanna's personality takes over, Agnes is a natural woman and stands for domestic happiness. But at the same time, Agnes personifies that realm of *inclination* that represents a moral danger to Johanna because of her unique calling. Thus, Johanna finds herself in a particular dilemma, namely, that obedience to her divine voices and fulfilling her duty is perceived to be unnatural by the world, whereas following her female inclination would at the same time be judged as fulfilling a natural role.

Johanna identifies with her mission and believes in her visions absolutely. This inner certainty carries her onto the political stage and convinces the royal court of the genuineness of her voices. Her fall begins with the first stirrings of doubt in the moral justification of her blind obedience to those who guide her and lend her power and victory. Slaughtering Montgomery in cold blood proves to be more difficult for her than breaking the siege of Orleans, and she laments:

> Doch weggerissen von der heimatlichen Flur . . .
> Muß ich *hier,* ich muß — mich treibt die Götterstimme, nicht
> Eigenes Gelüsten — *euch* zu bitterm Harm, mir nicht
> Zur Freude, ein Gespenst des Schreckens, würgend gehn,
> Den Tod verbreiten und sein Opfer sein zuletzt! (*JO*, 1658–63)

Serving the gods in blind obedience carries with it the danger of losing the essentially human characteristic of accepting responsibility for one's actions. As the instrument of something higher, outside her control, Johanna is not only limited in her freedom of choice, but she is also forced to commit cruel and inhuman deeds. She never loses the firm belief in her cause and the justice of the war against England, but she gradually recognizes the moral dilemma of pursuing this course with such single-minded determination. However, by refusing to kill Lionel on the battlefield, Johanna breaks the unspoken vow of subduing all her human emotions in order to succeed as a leader in the world of men, and she is left as vulnerable as any young girl in her situation would be.

The conflict between duty and inclination becomes greater with each of the following encounters: the meeting with Lionel (III, 10), the coronation (IV, 10), followed by the public denunciation at the hands of her father, the darkest hour of Johanna's career (IV, 11). With each episode her supernatural powers are weakened as they affect both her prowess on the battlefield and her ability to persuade, to convince, and to lead. On each occasion ever stronger human emotions, a sign of Johanna's growing maturity, influence her judgment and interfere with the absolute nature of her mission. Johanna's tragic situation is brought about by two incompatible demands in her life: her individual development from girlhood into womanhood versus the claims of the historical moment and her submission to a greater cause. Johanna develops from an unassailable Amazon, almost robotic in her power of destruction, into a young woman of awakening feelings and a corresponding loss of charisma, to the point when she becomes completely silent. She moves from a state of innocence to an entanglement with the forces of good and evil during which she suffers greatly. Eventually, Johanna overcomes this conflict by a renunciation of her rights as a woman and ultimately by sacrificing her life.[10] This development begins when she resists the temptation of a peaceful life with Lionel in England, and thus regains her inner certainty. As an external sign of the victory over her own passions, her fervent prayers are heard, and she is miraculously able to break the bonds of her imprisonment. During the final scene, in a moment of complete freedom, Johanna regains the former state of harmony with herself and with those around her. What is more, the battle is won, and political order has been restored. In an operatic end, in which the stage is lit by a rosy light, her body is covered with the royal flags of a united and victorious French army. Her triumphant final words lift the tragedy from Johanna's death and restore the confidence in the audience that, in spite of the moral failings and political restrictions imposed on the individual, there is order in this world, and that human life, as indeed the fate of a nation, is governed by divine justice.

Contradictions and Questions

Schiller's drama does not correspond to historical fact. His Johanna actually takes part in the fighting, whereas Joan of Arc did not, and she dies a glorious death on the battlefield, rather than coming to a humiliating end on the stake after a lengthy court trial. Schiller's Johanna is a fictional character, placed into an entirely fictional tragic conflict. If we analyze this conflict and her personality more questions and apparent contradictions can be found. As the heroine of a tragedy, Johanna is not really a tragic figure, that is to say, she never finds herself in a situation in which she is compelled by external forces. She takes up her mission, succumbs to weakness — her love for Lionel — but overcomes that passion and regains her inner harmony. Her death on the battlefield is incidental and not necessary. She is a positive, heroic, and noble character, her actions, her decisions, and her moral development are recommended by the playwright and rewarded by heaven. Thus, she should be regarded as exemplary by the audience. But is she indeed a role model to be emulated? Her unique calling, and her blind obedience to the voices which guide her, must keep Johanna in a category to herself, rather than a subject to binding moral laws that apply to everyone alike. Johanna's voices follow their own code of values from beyond good and evil. The cold-blooded murder of Montgomery, as a necessary consequence of keeping faith with her calling, can never be reconciled with any moral code.

A second possible interpretation of the drama is to understand the Jungfrau as representing the spirit of and the yearning for a strong national identity. The question of national identity and the threat posed by Napoleon's invading armies were both issues at the forefront of public discussion in Germany around the beginning of the nineteenth century. Johanna's political success, coupled with her moral superiority, serve as a useful and effective propaganda tool to increase the determination of a small country to rid itself of its enemy. Whichever way the Jungfrau is regarded, the drama draws attention to the cruelty and inhuman behavior that can arise from the single-minded pursuit of a single goal, even if that goal constitutes a worthy cause. A noble end, aided by the saints and the holy Virgin herself, cannot always justify the means. Ironically, at the very moment Johanna begins to act according to the dictates of her own conscience, she falls guilty, and is forsaken by the powers that guide her. As well as being cast in the unnatural part of a war goddess, she is not allowed to develop her own free will and exercise her own moral judgment. Thus, three questions arise, all of which are also relevant in the discussion of Brecht's *Die heilige Johanna der Schlachthöfe*. Is Johanna a role model? Can blind obedience to a single cause ever be reconciled with the humanist ideals of free will and individual moral judgment? How is it possible that one can act according to what seems morally right and at the same time incur personal guilt?

Die heilige Johanna der Schlachthöfe and the Dictates of Conscience

All through his working life, Brecht borrowed freely from other writers and used previous works as a starting point for his reworked versions of older material. Brecht acknowledges this freely, and surprisingly claims that the book that most influenced his thinking and his writing was the Bible.[11] This habit of extensive reworkings and borrowings was not caused by a lack of new ideas or sufficient artistic imagination. On the contrary, it can be seen as proof of a systematic study of the past, and of an ever-changing production and conception of cultural values. Adapting material already fashioned in a literary form proved to be an irresistible challenge to Brecht, who time and again tested his creativity in the particular form of interpreting, reevaluating, and reshaping his perception of the past. Among his better known works, *Das Leben Eduards II von England* (1923–24) can be read as a reworking of Marlowe's play, *Edward II; Die Dreigroschenoper* (1928) is related to John Gay's *The Beggar's Opera,* and later transposed into a novel by Brecht himself; *Die heilige Johanna der Schlachthöfe* (1929–31) constitutes a response to Schiller's *Jungfrau von Orleans; Die Mutter* (1931) is based on a novel by Maxim Gorki; *Mutter Courage und ihre Kinder* (1939) takes as its point of departure *Die Landstörtzerin Courasche*[12] (1670) by Grimmelshausen; *Antigone* (1947) was written after Sophocles; *Der Hofmeister* (1949) borrows its title and plot from J. M. R. Lenz's play; *Coriolan* (1953) takes up

Shakespeare's treatment of the Roman subject matter; and finally, *Don Juan* (1953) deals with Molière's version of the famous lover. All of these works, which appear to be reworkings to a greater or lesser extent, are at the same time original in their own way. Brecht shrugged off all accusation of plagiarism. He adopted the tradition of the poet and writer of the Baroque Age who regarded all existing literary and nonliterary material in its given content and form as suitable raw material for the practice and perfection of the writer's craft.

Brecht is notorious for his biting criticism of the classical age, and he radically predicts: "Das Theater wird in absehbarer Zeit das verstaubte Repertoire eines Jahrhunderts einfach auf seinen Materialwert hin untersuchen, indem es die guten alten Klassiker wie alte Autos behandelt, die nach dem reinen Alteisen-Wert eingeschätzt werden."[13] In his *Die heilige Johanna der Schlachthöfe* Brecht takes those components he regarded as worthwhile for recycling, largely from Schiller's *Die Jungfrau von Orleans* and Goethe's *Faust*. He uses parody and quasi-quotation to establish a firm connection between the ideas and the corpus of the German classical tradition and his own work, with the aim to demonstrate the lack of relevance these concepts have in the context of the political and aesthetic aspirations of his own age.

The title *Die heilige Johanna der Schlachthöfe*, with its mixture of the sacred and the profane, the familiar and the unfamiliar, provides a challenge to the audience and a clue as to the nature of the play. The theatergoing middle classes of the first half of the twentieth century would have been familiar with Schiller's *Die Jungfrau von Orleans,* which firmly belonged to the canon and formed an integral part of the school syllabus. (For example, in Heinrich Mann's *Professor Unrat* [1905], Professor Rath sets the class a test on *Die Jungfrau von Orleans.*) In contrast, abattoirs and meat processing plants would have been less familiar territory to the *Bildungsbürger*. The blood and gore of meat production do not usually feature as a topic of conversation in the bourgeois household, nor do they appear to be an obvious subject matter for the stage. The two opposing elements of the title also point to Brecht's continuing preoccupation with the classical tradition, on the one hand, and the new, revolutionary theater, on the other. Setting aside, for the moment, the complicated genesis of *Die heilige Johanna der Schlachthöfe,* it is clear that Schiller's *Die Jungfrau von Orleans* serves as a model for Brecht's method of reworking. Brecht attacks the ineffectiveness of German humanist idealism as a guide to one's actions, in that it fails to provide a sufficient critique of society and bring about socio-political change. At the same time, Brecht challenges the very idea of the classical drama which, according to him, needs to change from a medium that appeals to the emotions of the audience (fear and pity), to a social product that will induce understanding and critical thought. Then, so the theory goes, the theatergoer will be motivated to action that will change the world into a better place. The classical drama takes as its starting point the attempt of the individual to succeed in the face of adversity, which arises from an abuse of power in the feudal system. Here, the battleground is most commonly the human soul and the victory a moral one. Brecht, on the other hand, seeks to reveal the power structures and interdependencies of capitalist-bourgeois society as a source for social conflict. The aim of *Die heilige Johanna der Schlachthöfe* is to illustrate and explain the laws of the marketplace in a capitalist society; here, the victory would be social and political.

The call for social change lies at the very heart of Brecht's work. The revolutionary theater wants the audience to grasp the *res demonstranda* intellectually, perceive and understand the interrelations and dependencies of social and economic phenomena, and — having understood — to act on them. Brecht's Johanna, a representative of middle-class values, is solely guided by *good will* and as such she is a faithful disciple of Kant's categorical imperative. She follows Brecht's intended path to a gradual understanding of the economic laws that govern a capitalist society. But in her case comprehension comes too late, and she perishes confronted with the ineffectiveness of her actions. The audience, on the other hand, is called upon to learn from the events of the play. Johanna's dying words are an impassioned plea to the audience to act in the world: "Sorgt doch, daß ihr die Welt verlassend / Nicht nur gut wart, sondern verlaßt / Eine gute Welt!" (*HJ*, 222). In *Die heilige Johanna der Schlachthöfe* three thematic strands are woven together. The first strand, the economic theme, is based on Marx's analysis of economic cycles in a capitalist society. The second strand consists of a critique of the social role of religion. The third strand is found in the confrontation with German Classicism. With the introduction of the Joan of Arc theme, focused on Schiller's idealistic version, the play selectively integrates and rejects the language and the ideals of the classical period, particularly, but not exclusively, those of Schiller and Goethe.

Apart from the title, which places Brecht's *Die heilige Johanna der Schlachthöfe* into the Joan of Arc tradition, there are a number of other direct parallels to Schiller's *Die Jungfrau von Orleans*. Like Schiller's Jungfrau, Brecht's Johanna recognizes Mauler, the king of the meat trade, even though he tries to hide himself among his courtiers (*Erkennungsszene*). Both Johanna figures have the charisma and strength to direct the actions of their respective kings when in their presence, but neither is able to greatly influence the decisions or the character of the men. Like the Jungfrau, Brecht's Johanna is also a soldier. As a member of the Salvation Army, she is fighting for God's cause, and initially she feels utterly at one with her mission. As she learns about the laws that govern industrial society, her belief in a God-given order of the world gradually gives way to doubt, until it is eventually replaced by a new understanding of society. In Schiller's drama, we have an account of the last battle between the French and the English given by one of the guards of the Jungfrau, watching from the castle (*Botenbericht*). Brecht too has a messenger, the meat processor Graham, giving an account of a battle; only this battle is being fought on the stock exchange. In his report Graham quotes from Hölderlin's "Hyperions Schicksaalslied"[*sic*]. The poem describes human fate in terms of man destined to fall: "Wie Wasser von Klippe / Zu Klippe geworfen, / Jahr lang ins Ungewisse hinab."[14] In Graham's lament it is the price of oxen which falls: "Wie Wasser von Klippe zu Klippe geworfen / Tief ins Unendliche hinab" (*HJ*, 211–12). Brecht's stage directions for the final moments of *Die heilige Johanna der Schlachthöfe* are almost precisely the same as those of *Die Jungfrau von Orleans*.

Schiller: Man reicht sie [die Fahne] ihr. . . . Der Himmel ist von einem rosigen Schein beleuchtet. . . . Die Fahne entfällt ihr, sie sinkt tot darauf nieder — Alle stehen lange in sprachloser Rührung — Auf einen leisen Wink des Königs werden alle Fahnen sanft auf sie niedergelassen, daß sie ganz davon bedeckt wird.[15]

Brecht: Man reicht ihr die Fahne. Die Fahne entfällt ihr. . . . Alle stehen lange in sprachloser Rührung. Auf einen Wink Snyders werden alle Fahnen sanft auf sie niedergelassen, bis sie ganz davon bedeckt wird. Die Szene ist von einem rosigen Schein beleuchtet. (*HJ*, 226)

The irony is, of course, that Schiller's Johanna dies triumphantly with the words "Kurz ist der Schmerz und ewig ist die Freude!" (*JO*, 3544), and presumably ascends into heaven, whereas Brecht's Johanna dies defeated and in impotent anger, exclaiming: "Es hilft nur Gewalt, wo Gewalt herrscht, und / Es helfen nur Menschen, wo Menschen sind" (*HJ*, 224). Brecht's Johanna has learned from her experiences, but to no effect. Her newly found knowledge is carefully covered up, bit by bit, with each glorious banner that enshrouds her corpse. Both on the economic and on the human plane the ripples of protest and unrest have been smoothed out, and the world continues as before.

The clear references to Goethe's *Faust* are also deliberate borrowings, used on the one hand to illuminate the character of Mauler, and on the other, to emphasize the terrible irony of Johanna's death. Faust dies as a sinner, but angels come to his rescue by cheating Mephisto out of his prey. Carried away by the successful angels, Faust's soul rises higher and higher through the heavenly hierarchies, and he is welcomed into the community of the righteous. Brecht's Johanna, on the other hand, dies as an innocent; her only guilt, if indeed it is guilt at all, is one of omission. But instead of angels raising her soul, the chorus which sings Johanna's requiem is assembled from all those negative forces she has come to reject: Mauler, the dealers, the cattle breeders and her fellow soldiers from the Salvation Army. The hymns they are offering are a justification of their earthly existence and the socio-economic order they represent.

Reaction to the Classical Tradition

What is true of single episodes and particular features taken up by Brecht in his reinterpretation of Schiller's tragedy is also true of the classical tradition in a much wider sense. Like many of Brecht's works, *Die heilige Johanna der Schlachthöfe* was written and rewritten several times, and his appropriation of various literary works and traditions was a gradual process. In her comprehensive study comparing the different versions of *Die heilige Johanna der Schlachthöfe*, Gudrun Schulz has shown clearly how the drama progressed from a first manuscript (*Urfassung*) to the original version (*Originalfassung*) a reworking of Elisabeth Hauptmann's *Happy End*, into which Brecht then introduced fragments of his own works *Joe Fleischhacker* and *Daniel Drew*, to its final version (*Endfassung*) with its confrontation with German classical writers, particularly Schiller's *Jungfrau von Orleans*.[16] The first manuscript focused almost entirely on the economic events, which Brecht wanted to illustrate on stage. The move towards the classical tradition in the final version is particularly clear in the last scene. As indicated previously, the final scene, entitled *Tod und Kanonisierung der heiligen Johanna der Schlachthöfe*, sees Johanna, like Schiller's Jungfrau, dying in the open, surrounded by the soldiers (of the Salvation Army) and the meat king with his courtiers. In verses strongly reminiscent of the end of *Faust II*, the assembled group praises Johanna's good will and charity in loud songs of Hosianna. At the same time they shout her down as she promotes her new gospel of radical change brought about by the class struggle, using violence if need be. Johanna is given her old banner, but she refuses to lift it, and it falls from her hands. The original version ends with a satirical appeal to human generosity. In the final version Brecht adds the ironic reference to Goethe's *Faust*, using the well-known *Zweiseelenmotiv*,[17] the motif of the two souls, to expose the selfish greed of bourgeois/capitalist ideology. There is nothing elevated or spiritual about the final lines of Brecht's *Die heilige Johanna der Schlachthöfe*. On the contrary, they represent sound advice to the shrewd entrepreneur on how to combine economic success with a clear conscience and the reputation of a moral, upright citizen.

Original version:

Mauler:
Ach in seine arme Brust
Ist ein zwiefaches gestoßen
Wie ein Messer bis zum Heft.
Denn es zieht ihn zu dem Grossen
Und es zieht ihn zum Geschäft
Unbewusst!

Alle:
Dass er das Eine dem Andern eine
Sei sein Begehren
Oh dass sie unzertrennlich wären:
Menschengüte und Güte der Schweine![18]

Final version:

Mauler:
Ach in meine arme Brust
Ist ein Zwiefaches gestoßen
Wie ein Messer bis zum Heft.
Denn es zieht mich zu dem Großen
Selbst- und Nutz- und Vorteilslosen
Und es zieht mich zum Geschäft
Unbewußt!

Alle:
Mensch, es wohnen dir zwei Seelen
In der Brust!
Such nicht eine auszuwählen
Da du beide haben mußt.
Bleibe stets mit dir im Streite!
Bleib der Eine, stets Entzweite!
Halte die hohe, halte die niedere,
Halte die rohe, halte die biedere
Halte sie beide! (*HJ*, 227)

The verses are a skilful blend of motifs and metric devices from Goethe's *Faust II*, which sound familiar to the educated audience because of their rhythm and choice of expressions in the classical tradition, but which are at the same time modern and original. The use of this kind of elevated language is reserved for Mauler and his company, creating a linguistic link between the capitalists and the outdated ideals of the classical period.

Mauler is made out to be a direct descendent of Goethe's Faust figure.[19] Their common way of expression and the motif of the two souls establish the parallels between Mauler and Faust. Mauler is torn between the two souls of capitalism as it manifests itself in bourgeois society — the private man is moved to sentimentality, the businessman is driven by ruthless greed. One of the new and outstanding features of Goethe's *Faust* lies in the fact that the active individual is regarded positive *per se*. Although guilty of a multitude of crimes, Faust can be redeemed because he never ceases to strive. Mauler, too, is driven by that restlessness and constant will to create new (business) worlds and to act with feeling in one moment and with utter heartlessness the next. Even if all the odds are stacked against him, Mauler will not resign himself, because the urge to act in the world forms the very core of Mauler's being (*HJ*, 183). Mauler is not only a twentieth-century descendent of Faust, but as a representative of the influential industrialist classes he bears a certain resemblance to a whole cabinet of Schiller's central characters, Wallenstein, Philip of Spain, Maria Stuart and Charles of France, who, according to Schulz, all stood godparent to the figure of Mauler.[20]

Where Mauler is clear-thinking, always a step ahead of his business partners in understanding the current situation, and ready to seize opportunities, Johanna is guided by her instinct without any real understanding of the social and economic interdependencies of the society around her. Her actions are motivated by a deeply felt compassion for the misery of the workforce in the slaughterhouses. At the same time, her religious beliefs cause her to shy away from a revolutionary overturning of the existing social order. She has a strong aversion to any form of violence.

Johanna has joined the Salvation Army to make the world a better place, devoting her life to the poor. But she acts blindly on her impulses and actually promotes the system that causes the misery of the very people she wants to help. During her three descents into the underworld — the repeated subtitle *Gang in die Tiefe* is another motif borrowed from *Faust* — she gradually learns about the social and economic causes of poverty. But only in death, when it is too late to act on the newly found understanding, does she plead for fundamental social change: more important than individual efforts to do good is the active participation in the revolution that will bring about a fairer (socialist) world.

> *Johanna:* Eines hab ich gelernt und weiß es für euch
> Selber sterbend:
> Was soll das heißen, es ist etwas in euch und
> Kommt nicht nach außen? *Was* wißt ihr wissend
> Was keine Folgen hat?
> Ich zum Beispiel habe nichts getan.
> Denn nichts werde gezählt als gut, und sehe es aus wie immer, als was
> Wirklich hilft, und nichts gelte als ehrenhaft mehr, als was
> Diese Welt endgültig ändert: sie braucht es.
> Wie gerufen kam ich den Unterdrückern!
> Oh folgenlose Güte! Unmerkliche Gesinnung!
> Ich habe nichts geändert. (*HJ*, 222)

There is nothing tragic or heroic about Johanna's death. On the contrary, it is rather pathetic: having presumably been brought up in a relatively sheltered environment, she is simply not up to living rough and surviving on her own wits, and she dies of pneumonia. Neither is she a tragic figure. Her personal fate was not governed by compelling circumstances, but in the course of the action she simply changes her mind and adopts new values. All her deeds are guided by good will, and she is always free to act on the dictates of her conscience. In that sense she is much more a role model for someone who lives by the decrees of Kant's *moral law* than Schiller's Jungfrau ever was. And yet she fails. In contrast to Schiller's Jungfrau, whose blind obedience to her voices caused her to commit her greatest moral offence, Brecht's Johanna's greatest guilt is that she gives in to her abhorrence of violence, and does not deliver the fatal letter. By acting independently rather than submitting her moral judgment to a greater cause, Johanna is a true representative of the humanist tradition.

In Schiller's *Die Jungfrau von Orleans* the figure of Johanna is clearly the central protagonist, and all other characters are assembled around her to provide the opportunities for and bear witness to her moral growth and eventual victory. In contrast, Brecht's *Die heilige Johanna der Schlachthöfe* is constructed around two central characters, Johanna and Mauler, and follows the development of two very different fates. Johanna aims to become the voice of the disenfranchised, economically enslaved masses, a mission in which she fails. Mauler stands for the free entrepreneur, who acts on behalf of himself only and, in spite of temporary setbacks, he ends up even richer and more powerful than he had been at the onset of the play. Brecht's Johanna bears the name of the successful historical figure and of Schiller's glorified fictional heroine, but unlike these forerunners she leaves the world without having effected any significant change.

Genesis and Fundamental Critique

In the context of this study, the economic theme and Brecht's attack on religion are relevant only insofar as they demonstrate to what degree Brecht constantly reworks other texts and integrates these into his own work. Three novels on the economic theme, all set in America were particularly important to the genesis of *Die heilige Johanna der Schlachthöfe*: Frank Norris's *The Pit* (1901), which is set against the backdrop of the world grain trade, Upton Sinclair's *The Jungle* (1906), and Bouck White's *Das Buch des Daniel Drew, Leben und Meinungen eines Börsenmannes* (1910; German, 1922).[21] The central plot of the play is the unfolding economic action. The ups and downs of the beef market are shown to follow the economic laws according to Marxist theory. In his detailed study of *Das Kapital* Brecht found the rules that, according to Marx, control the economy. Käthe Rülicke demonstrates how the action of the play runs parallel to the four stages of the capitalist cycle of economic crisis (*Krisenzyklus*) as described in *Das Kapital:* (1) the end of prosperity; (2) overproduction; (3) crisis; (4) stagnation.[22] According to Marxist theory the market forces, which govern periods of *hausse* and *baisse*, are predictable and can be manipulated. Economic disaster does not strike like a natural catastrophe, which a fatalistic workforce has to accept and survive as best as possible, but occurs in man-made cycles, which work in favor of those in power. This power can be taken away from those who abuse it by changing the social and economic conditions of a society. Apart from Mauler, none of the protagonists understands these economic patterns, and the collapse of the beef market overtakes them just as an earthquake or the eruption of a volcano would. At the same time, all characters alike are directly or indirectly affected by the economic developments as they unfold in the plot.

This then is the intention of Brecht's theater: "Das menschliche Verhalten wird als veränderlich gezeigt, der Mensch als abhängig von gewissen ökonomisch-politischen Verhältnissen und zugleich als fähig, sie zu verändern."[23] The great problem for the dramatist is to create an understanding of the economic-political situation by turning it into a lesson palatable for the theater. Brecht was fully aware of the difficulties of using the world of economics as a theme for the stage:

> Es gibt mehrerlei Arten von Leuten: solche, die Geschäfte machen und solche, die Bücher lesen. Diejenigen, die Geschäfte machen, verstehen wenig vom Bücherlesen, diejenigen, die Bücher lesen, wenig vom Geschäfte machen.... Schreibt ein Schriftsteller heute ein dramatisches (oder auch belletristisches) Werk, in dem Geschäfte

vorkommen, so muß er damit rechnen, daß jene, die vom Inhalt des Stückes (oder Buches) etwas verstehen würden, es nicht lesen und jene, die es lesen würden, vom Inhalt nichts verstehen.[24]

Thus, *Die heilige Johanna der Schlachthöfe* becomes an ambitious experiment in which Brecht blends the seemingly familiar dramatic tradition of the human story of the heroine with his real concern: explaining the economic laws which govern the social structure of a capitalist society.

Apart from its attempt to explain economic effects and dependencies, *Die heilige Johanna der Schlachthöfe* also contains an assertive attack on the function of religion in a capitalist society. Elisabeth Hauptmann's *Happy End* is a play about the Salvation Army, which in turn draws on Shaw's *Major Barbara*. In Brecht's play we meet the Salvation Army under the name of *schwarze Strohhüte*, the Black Strawhats. At first they appear to be a religious and nonpolitical movement, merely there in order to relieve suffering. The idealistic and warmhearted Johanna has found a vocation here, and is convinced that she is working for the greater good. She believes in the humanist ideals of compassion and good will. Wanting to alleviate suffering within the existing framework of order, she is against all violence until, in the last scene, she finally understands the mechanisms of power. The Black Strawhats are important to the capitalist system because they legitimize the existing economic structure and lend it a moral base. When the strike threatens to erupt and potentially upsets the balance of power, Mauler appeals to them and suggests that public order will be restored if the religious message of the Black Strawhats is, once more, heard and accepted by the protesting workers (*HJ*, 184). In the end, Johanna herself is hijacked by the establishment, and her inherent good will is used to re-establish and justify the old unjust social order she has learned to hate:

> *Slift:* Das ist unsere Johanna. Sie kommt wie gerufen. Wir wollen sie groß herausbringen, denn sie hat uns durch ihr menschenfreundliches Wirken auf den Schlachthöfen, ihre Fürsprache für die Armen, auch durch ihre Reden gegen uns über schwierige Wochen hinweggeholfen. Sie soll unsere heilige Johanna der Schlachthöfe sein. Wir wollen sie als eine Heilige aufziehen und ihr keine Achtung versagen. Im Gegenteil soll gerade, daß sie bei uns gezeigt wird, dafür zum Beweis dienen, daß die Menschlichkeit bei uns einen hohen Platz einnimmt. (*HJ*, 220)

Some form of religious structure is shown by Brecht to be indispensable to the capitalist system, either in the shape of an organized movement such as the army of the Black Strawhats, or merely in the guise of the "philanthropist" Mauler, who donates generously to public welfare-institutions, thus being seen to alleviate the poverty he himself has created. In Schiller's play the supernatural voices which guide the jungfrau's actions are dubious, because obeying their order leads to murder and warfare. Yet, her guilt is described as disobedience to the voices that demand this violence. Brecht, on the other hand, shows religion to be in the service of the capitalist power structures, and in this case it is the *rejection* of violence on the part of Johanna that makes her suspect and ultimately guilty in the eyes of the people she wants to serve.

The Effect of the Reworking

The genesis of *Die heilige Johanna der Schlachthöfe*, particularly the allusions to *Faust* in the final act, clearly shows the gradual absorption of classical elements into the modern drama. The literary technique of placing *Die heilige Johanna der Schlachthöfe* into the context of the classical tradition changes the impact of a play which would otherwise most likely be shrugged off as a somewhat farfetched socialist propaganda piece. By alluding to not just one, but several of the most prominent works in German literature, Brecht lends his drama weight and status and opens up questions and themes that might not otherwise be raised in the context of this play. At the same time, he attacks the apparently universal value of the classics themselves and questions the usefulness of the ideas by asking: "Was haben die Klassiker gesagt? Wie ist das Bild, das sie von der Welt gaben? Welche Verhaltensmaßregeln gaben sie dem Menschen? Sie gaben ein ungenaues und kleines Bild, und sie lehrten vage und unmögliche Haltungen."[25]

At first glance, Brecht's Johanna play bears little resemblance to Schiller's *Jungfrau von Orleans:* it is concerned with different themes, it is written in a different form and style; time and place do not establish any links from reworking to model; its genesis suggests the influence of numerous other writers and works apart from Schiller; whereas Schiller's chosen genre is a "romantic tragedy" in the form of a prologue and five acts, Brecht's play is *not* a tragedy and is written in twelve subtitled scenes of varying length; there are only few parallel episodes and characters; only Johanna and Mauler correspond in some way to any of the characters from Schiller's *Jungfrau von Orleans;* and finally, Brecht's Johanna is not portrayed as struggling with a moral dilemma between, for example, a clear conscience and promoting violent action, but simply as having made the *wrong* choice.

And yet, in spite of this apparent lack of tangible links between *Die heilige Johanna der Schlachthöfe* and Schiller's drama, Brecht's references and allusions to German classicism are so integral a part of his play that it has become unthinkable to interpret it merely as the story of a contemporary American girl who gradually comes to comprehend the economic laws which determine the capitalist system. Indeed, since Brecht parodies not just Schiller but the whole classical tradition, *Die heilige Johanna der Schlachthöfe* functions as an effective stage play only when the importance of its allusions to classicism is fully recognized. The obscure setting of the meat trade in Chicago gains significance when regarded as a comment on the carnage on the (medieval) battlefield. The language of the protagonists clearly marks their ideological and political background; when the capitalists and the trader's chorus speak in blank verse a clash between the ideal form and the banal content matter is created and turned to comic effect (*Verfremdungseffekt*). Johanna and the workers' chorus use free rhythms typical of Brecht's lyrics, and by this a new age is promised and with it a liberated language.

The use of the chorus, based on the ancient Greek model, introduces yet another traditional element to the play. In Greek theater, the chorus with its solemn dignity and air of mystery creates a link to the divine. In his foreword to *Die Braut von Messina* (1803) Schiller describes the use of the chorus in tragedy as having a twofold effect: a pre-Brechtian application of the *Verfremdungseffekt* on the one hand, and the impact of the sheer physical presence of a representative group on the other. According to Schiller, the interceptions by the chorus ought to destroy the illusion of the reality presented on stage and create a pause for reflection, "denn das Gemüth des Zuschauers soll auch in der heftigsten Passion seine Freiheit behalten."[26] Furthermore, Schiller argues that the theater is effective not only by presenting the content matter, *das Ideale*, but also by operating on the level of the senses, *das Sinnliche:* "Der Chor ist selbst kein Individuum, sondern ein allgemeiner Begriff, aber dieser Begriff repräsentiert sich durch eine sinnlich mächtige Masse, welche durch ihre ausfüllende Gegenwart den Sinnen imponiert" (13). In *Die heilige Johanna der Schlachthöfe* Brecht also introduces a number of different chorus scenes. However, the intention is not so much to interrupt the course of the action, but rather to symbolize the way in which a capitalist society operates in distinct social groups. Passages recited by each chorus state apparently general truths, introducing a comical element to the play at the same time. One short passage might serve as an example:

> *Die Arbeiter:* Wehe!
> Die Hölle selbst
> Schließt ihr Tor für uns!
> Wir sind verloren. Der blutige Mauler hält
> Unsern Ausbeuter am Hals und
> Uns geht die Luft aus! (*HJ,* 132)

The discrepancy between the colloquial language and the sinister and powerful delivery by the chorus is comical, even if the content is desperately serious. It gives rise to laughter, which is caused by inappropriate behavior, or the transgression of social conventions. This kind of laughter is permeated by an initial sense of disbelief, followed by the shocked realization that this is not the way in which one ought to speak or to act. By equating the language of the decadent and selfish elements of society with that of the period of Weimar Classicism, Brecht seems to declare the very core of the German cultural identity, and indeed that of the whole western tradition, as corrupt and evil. However, Jan Knopf argues that Brecht's critique is directed not against the classical or the Greek original, because one cannot fight against the past, but only against the *reception* of the classical tradition in Brecht's own time. Thus, Brecht's reworking does not aim to improve on the model but to re-educate the audience.[27]

Johanna as a Role Model

It was never Brecht's intention to write a tragedy, but the questions which form a link to *Die Jungfrau von Orleans* are still with us and need to be asked again when looking once more at the inner relationship between the two plays: first, the question of Johanna as a role model, and second, the problem of blind obedience versus free will, when obedience means that, in order to act collectively, it is necessary to suspend one's individual moral judgment. Whether in waging a national war or in following the call to a social revolution, the quest for exemplary behavior is always fought out between faith in a just cause, which would justify particular means, and responsibility for one's own deeds.

At first glance Schiller's Jungfrau appears to be a positive heroine — her deeds have an impact in the world and restore order — whereas Brecht's Johanna seems weak, takes the wrong decisions, and her deeds remain ineffectual. As such, Brecht's *Die heilige Johanna* is clearly conceived as an anti-work to Schiller's drama, and the title figure needs to be interpreted in a fundamentally different way. In drama, title figures tend to be either exemplary characters of great strength or moral fortitude — Maria Stuart may serve as an example — or, as tragic figures, who find themselves in situations where they necessarily have to fall victim to particular circumstances, as in the case of Emilia Galotti or indeed Maria Magdalena, who will be introduced in the next chapter. Goethe's Faust, who is neither exemplary in his actions, nor a victim of circumstances, is an exception to the extent that he is portrayed as a positive character in spite of his many failings and fatal mistakes. The reason for his redemption is the very fact that he never ceases to strive, that until the very end he actively tries to make an impact in the world. In contrast, Hans Mayer argues, Brecht in *Die heilige Johanna* has created a title figure who is used to demonstrate how *not* to act, a title figure "an welcher *falsches Handeln* demonstriert werden soll."[28]

Yet, the matter is more complicated than that. The development of Schiller's Jungfrau unfolds in three steps: first we have her blind obedience to the voices, later, with the awakening of her feelings, stirrings of doubt enter her conscience, and she is divided between inclination and duty. In the end she overcomes that conflict by renouncing her love, and thus she gains a moral victory over her passions. But, in the light of the fact that her success does not depend on her own decisions, but on subordinating her will wholly to those voices that guide her, can she ever be a role model? The question is particularly relevant, because the exploration of the concept of free will is so central to Schiller's work that R. D. Miller claims that "Schiller's theory of tragedy is based, not on morality, but on freedom."[29] Therefore, so the argument goes, the task of the dramatist is to give the tragic hero or heroine the opportunity to exercise their free will, even in the face of necessity.[30] This observation gives us the key to understanding the character of Schiller's Jungfrau. The central question is not whether or not she remains an unblemished character, but whether she makes full use of the scope of freedom of will that was given her in her particular destiny. The salvation of the Jungfrau does not lie in the fact that she has successfully accomplished all she had set herself out to do, just as her sin does not lie in the distasteful murder of Montgomery. Her fall begins when she becomes aware of the conflict between the inner voices that direct her actions and her own desires. Paradoxically, this very conflict brings with it the freedom to exercise her moral will. The effort it costs the Jungfrau to overcome her desires shows the extent of her moral strength. The Jungfrau is not a heroine whose actions attain the heights of perfection a human being can aspire to. Rather, Schiller's Johanna demonstrates how, even under the constraints of absolute obedience to an agency outside oneself, exercising her free will is not only possible, but is in fact necessary in order to attain moral perfection.

In contrast, Brecht's Johanna is an example of how *not* to act. She herself condemns the ineffectualness of her actions. Brecht's characters can never be seen in isolation, but they are always intimately woven into their respective social context. The person of Johanna as an individual loses its central position as the title figure and becomes purely functional in the lesson Brecht wants the audience to learn. The prime motive behind most of Brecht's work is to demystify those areas in life that the ordinary person feels powerless to change. In *Die heilige Johanna der Schlachthöfe,* this includes the world of the beef trade and the manipulation of the stock market. At the same time, it is Brecht's aim to reveal the mutual benefit religion and capitalism gain from each other in preventing the creation of a fairer society, and to show that the morally justifiable action of the individual does not necessarily benefit the wider community.

Unlike the Jungfrau, who turned herself into an instrument of the gods, and who committed murder in that capacity, the life of Brecht's Johanna is exemplary for a person following Kant's *Categorical Imperative:* "Handle nur nach derjenigen Maxime, durch die du zugleich wollen kannst, daß sie ein allgemeines Gesetz werde."[31] According to the Kantian ideal, Johanna is a good person who acts according to the dictates of her own conscience and is solely motivated by good will. And in Kantian ethics "good will" is the only thing in the world that can be regarded as unconditionally and universally good.[32] Wanting to take full responsibility for her own decisions, Brecht's Johanna refuses to submit her judgment to an outside agency. Thus, when the call comes to unite for the general strike with the aim to overthrow the existing order, Johanna does not cooperate, for fear of the outbreak of violence, even though she shares the ultimate goals of the strike organizers. This refusal of blind obedience to a higher cause, of the sacrifice of one's own high moral standards for the sake of the well-being of the larger group, is what she denounces so bitterly in her death. The central lesson of the play is its utilitarian message. Is Johanna's idealistic appeal just another form of the dangerous dictum that the end justifies the means?[33] In death, Brecht's Johanna renounces a clear conscience and moral perfection of the individual for the sake of revolutionary change and the struggle for a fairer society. The imperative to give up one's personal judgment in favor of subordinating one's will wholly to a greater cause is qualified only by the appeal to study the underlying causes and the laws governing social and economic phenomena before acting on the desire to liberate the suppressed.

When we compare the moral foundation upon which both Schiller's and Brecht's Johanna figures are constructed, we find that both characters become more complex and neither seems to illustrate the ideals of their creators. We have the paradox that Schiller's Jungfrau, who displays cruelty and who submits her own judgment to external agents, is shown to be successful in her political quest and apparently praised by heaven and earth alike in her glorious death. In contrast, Brecht's Johanna, who is weak and unsuccessful in her eventual political aims, is a good person and one the audience readily empathizes with. Schiller's Amazon Jungfrau and Brecht's dithering Johanna are very different heroines, but through the connection with her literary predecessor, Brecht's Johanna Dark is not merely an insignificant girl who dies after a short exposure to the harsh realities of poverty, but becomes a freedom fighter, the latest in a distinguished line of literary (and historical) forebears.

What is true of the figure of Johanna also holds for Mauler. It is too simplistic to regard him merely as the evil and scheming capitalist. He suddenly becomes an ambiguous character when seen in the context of the classical tradition. Apart from the hard-hearted industrialist, he is also a *Bürger* caught between his sentimental private self and his ruthless business ego. Large parts of Mauler's speech would be meaningless if they were not understood as references to Goethe's *Faust*. This link between the two protagonists puts Mauler in the same category as Faust, insofar as the active participation in shaping the world according to their own will is ultimately a positive characteristic, and one which will be redeemed in the end, even if the deeds have resulted in injustice and crime. The projection of Mauler onto the classical Faust figure adds depth and complexity to the character.

Thus, the reworking operates to the effect that Johanna cannot be fully understood without reference to the Jungfrau, and likewise Mauler must be seen in the tradition of Faust. In spite of his deliberate attack on Schiller's work, Brecht's protagonists are inevitably bound together with those of Schiller, just as the two playwrights share a firm belief in the didactic importance of the theater. In their means of how to bring about social change, Brecht and Schiller are much closer to one another than Brecht's apparently ruthless rejection of the classical tradition would have us believe.

The Ideal of Freedom

When comparing Schiller's and Brecht's appeals to create a better world, we must, of course, take into consideration the different eras these two writers lived in. Schiller's age witnessed the gradually unfolding self-confidence of the middle classes. Much of Schiller's work constitutes a revolt against the tyranny of the absolutist rulers of his time. Following in Lessing's footsteps, Schiller builds on the growing sense of moral superiority of the middle classes, which is also translated into increasing affluence and a gain in political power. This increase in economic and political independence is shown to result from a good education, which in turn leads to the demands for freedom of speech. The ideal of *Freiheit* Schiller strives for is an inner *freedom*, which allows independent thought and the opportunity for free moral choices.

Brecht lived during the moral and economic decline of bourgeois society. Alongside growing urbanization and industrialization, the labor movement was gathering pace, and became a political force to be reckoned with. On their own, worker and laborers were unable to improve their station in life and powerless to prevent economic exploitation. However, according to Marx, the strength of the working class lies in solidarity with one another and in collective action. In his work as a writer, Brecht wants to motivate his readers and his audience to join in the struggle for equality. In Brecht's terms, *Freiheit* stands for *liberty* for the suppressed classes.

Both Johannas are freedom fighters: The Jungfrau strives for *freedom* as a moral force, and for the reform of the individual. Johanna Dark learns that this inner struggle is useless, and advocates *liberty* on a political plane brought about by revolution. Although the Jungfrau is largely a positive heroine, there are aspects to her which we reject because of the inhumanity of her actions and the single-mindedness that does not allow her to realize her full potential as a woman. Brecht's Johanna may be a model for misguided action, as Mayer claims she is, but she has our sympathy. Schiller raises the flag for freedom and reform, Brecht for liberty and revolution, but how do they spread their message? How do we hear their call?

In his essay *Die Schaubühne als moralische Anstalt betrachtet* (1784) Schiller emphasizes both the teaching function and the moral effect of the stage. He points to the potential of the theater to illuminate not only the inner struggles of the individual, but also the ways according to which society functions. Drama must be "Vergnügen mit Unterricht,"[34] *entertainment* to the extent that the emotions on stage affect the audience without being threatening or demanding of any immediate decisions, and *didactic* to the extent that the events on stage are meant to explain human and social conditions. Schiller proclaims this dual function enthusiastically with the rhetorical question: "Wieviel Antheil an diesem göttlichen Werk gehört unseren Bühnen? Sind *sie* es nicht, die den Menschen mit dem Menschen bekannt machten, und das geheime Räderwerk aufdeckten, nach welchem er handelt?" (97). The theater not only causes the release of emotions in the viewer, which ought to lead to an inner development, but it also demonstrates the hidden laws to which human action is subject. The theater, according to Schiller, is a primary source of moral education. Empathy with the suffering and the inner struggles of the character on the stage has a moral effect on the audience. From the examples of the protagonists in a drama, the audience learns of the causes of human action, and is given models who demonstrate how certain decisions are arrived at and what consequences they might have. These models can either be emulated or be avoided. Thus, drama channels and directs the feelings of the audience. At the same time, it depicts rational human behavior on stage, and that, so the argument goes, will teach the audience how to improve their own inner being.

> Die Schaubühne ist die Stiftung, wo sich Vergnügen mit Unterricht, Ruhe mit Anstrengung, Kurzweil mit Bildung gattet.... Der Unglückliche weint hier mit fremdem Kummer seinen eigenen aus, — der Glückliche wird nüchtern, und der Sichere besorgt.... Und dann endlich — welch ein Triumph für dich, Natur! — ... wenn Menschen aus allen Kraisen [*sic*] und Zonen und Ständen, ... herausgerissen aus jedem Drange des Schicksals, durch *eine* allwebende Sympathie verbrüdert ... ihrer selbst und der Welt vergessen.... Jeder Einzelne genießt die Entzückungen aller ... und seine Brust giebt jezt [*sic*] nur *Einer* Empfindung Raum — es ist diese: ein *Mensch* zu sein. (100)

In his philosophical letters "Über die ästhetische Erziehung des Menschen" (1795) Schiller elaborates on the idealistic hope that if enough people enjoy this moral schooling and live and act according to an internalized and individualized moral law, they will have an effect on society. By encouraging the individual to strengthen his or her own moral resolution, the world will become a better place. How else can it be done?

> Sollte diese Wirkung vielleicht von dem Staat zu erwarten seyn? Das ist nicht möglich, denn der Staat, wie er jetzt beschaffen ist, hat das Uebel veranlaßt, und der Staat, wie ihn die Vernunft in der Idee sich

aufgiebt, anstatt diese bessere Menschheit begründen zu können, müßte selbst erst darauf gegründet werden.[35]

Or, as Mauler puts it: "Erst muß, bevor die Welt sich ändern kann / Der Mensch sich ändern" (*HJ*, 146). This is precisely what Schiller's Jungfrau achieves: she overcomes her own desires in the hope that by changing herself she might change the world. With the help of the supernatural voices she is to some extent successful, and indeed leaves behind a "better world," a world in which order has been restored.

Brecht, of course, would not consider a world in which the previous feudal order has been reinstated a better place. But the question is more fundamental: did the moral victory of the Jungfrau really affect those around her, or was the gain wholly her own? Is it ever possible for an individual to change the world? Brecht does not think so. His Johanna fails, not because she is lacking moral strength or willingness to overcome her own weaknesses but because she believes that people are able and willing to improve morally, even within an existing social order based on inequality, in this case the capitalist system. In 1836 Georg Büchner's *Woyzeck* explains for the first time that virtue is not practical for the poor:

> *Woyzeck:* Sehn Sie, wir gemeine Leut, das hat keine Tugend, es kommt einem nur so die Natur; aber wenn ich ein Herr wär und hätt ein Hut und eine Uhr und eine anglaise und könnt vornehm reden, ich wollt schon tugendhaft seyn. Es muß was Schöns seyn um die Tugend, Herr Hauptmann. Aber ich bin ein armer Kerl![36]

Brecht takes up exactly that argument: morality is only for those who can afford it. He draws the conclusion that until the social and economic conditions of the working classes have been fundamentally changed and improved, virtue is too expensive a commodity to be acquired by the poor of this world. Brecht's attacks on Schiller are directed at the — according to Brecht — futile attempt to improve the world through an improved individual. But Schiller was already aware of this vicious circle:

> Aber ist hier nicht vielleicht ein Zirkel? Die theoretische Kultur soll die praktische herbeyführen und die praktische doch die Bedingung der theoretischen seyn? Alle Verbesserung im politischen soll von Veredlung des Charakters ausgehen — aber wie kann sich unter den Einflüssen einer barbarischen Staatsverfassung der Charakter veredeln? Man müßte also zu diesem Zwecke ein Werkzeug aufsuchen, welches der Staat nicht hergiebt, und Quellen dazu eröffnen, die sich bey aller politischen Verderbniß rein und lauter erhalten.[37]

Art, according to Schiller, holds the key to leave this vicious circle.[38] For Schiller, art has the dual purpose of having an pleasurable effect on the individual (*Vergnügung*) and exposing the laws and patterns that govern social relationships within society (*Unterricht*). Because art is subject solely to its own aesthetic laws, it is accessible to everyone, and remains largely independent of political circumstance. Displaying an idealistic faith, which in our more cynical age touches us as largely misplaced, Schiller confidently declares:

> Von allem, was positiv ist und was menschliche Conventionen einführten, ist die Kunst, wie die Wissenschaft losgesprochen, und beyde erfreuen sich einer absoluten *Immunität* von der Willkür der Menschen. Der politische Gesetzgeber kann ihr Gebiet sperren, aber darinn [*sic*] herrschen kann er nicht. (333)

In the twentieth century, Brecht wants to renew the theater, and turn it once more into an instrument which speaks to everyone, and which operates at the center of society. He demands of the theater that it is not only entertaining or educating, but that it mobilizes to action, "[daß es] Gedanken und Gefühle verwendet und erzeugt, die bei der Veränderung des Feldes selbst eine Rolle spielen."[39]

Like Schiller, Brecht uses the theater as the most effective means of getting his message across. What Brecht attacks in his *Die heilige Johanna der Schlachthöfe* is only *one* aspect of Schiller's work, namely the belief that a person can separate him- or herself from the social context, and strive for moral perfection and inner freedom, solely motivated by the wish to do so. This, Brecht holds, is not possible, because we are all tightly woven into a social network and historical circumstance. Nevertheless, the means advocated by Brecht that are to have an effect on the world are the same as Schiller's: both use the theater as a pulpit to preach social change. The different style and differing techniques show each to be a product of his own time. The ancients touched the audience by playing on their emotions — fear and pity; Schiller believes the theater to be most effective when it entertains and teaches at the same time, *Vergnügen und Unterricht,* and Brecht requires this lesson to be put into practice: "Ich wollte auf das Theater den Satz anwenden, daß es nicht nur darauf ankommt, die Welt zu interpretieren, sondern sie zu verändern."[40]

All through his work Brecht draws freely on writers and their works from all ages and numerous cultures. In *Die heilige Johanna der Schlachthöfe* these borrowings may be based more explicitly on one predecessor, namely Schiller, but to talk of a reworking of only one particular literary work would be misleading in this instance. By alluding to both Schiller's and Goethe's aesthetic and philosophical work in a wider sense, Brecht challenges not only *Die Jungfrau von Orleans* but the whole of the classical tradition and its value system. Brecht establishes the link between *Die heilige Johanna der Schlachthöfe* and the classical period by placing his drama into the Joan of Arc tradition, by the styles of language he uses, by the correspondence of certain characters, incidents, and speeches to those in Schiller's *Die Jungfrau von Orleans* and Goethe's *Faust*. Through these allusions, Brecht's contemporary play gains ideological transparency and historical depth.

2: Ironic Reproduction: Friedrich Hebbel's and Franz Xaver Kroetz's *Maria Magdalena*

> The basic principle of Kroetz's re-construction
> is the systematic invalidation of the older work,
> and of the ethical and moral system it reflected.
> *Ingrid Walsøe-Engel*

The Genre

IN HIS REWORKING OF Schiller's romantic tragedy, Brecht made fundamental and sweeping changes on almost every level: the setting, the plot, the subject matter, the emphasis on the individual and the high pathos. Brecht's reworking functions partly by alluding to the Joan of Arc tradition and partly on the level of imitating and parodying the dramatic language of the German classical period. Above all, Brecht does not aim for a realistic representation of his protagonists, particularly when it comes to their manner of speaking. In contrast, the characterization of the *Kleinbürger* by way of their inability to express themselves adequately is precisely what brought Franz Xaver Kroetz to fame. It is also the basis for this second example of an authorial reinterpretation of drama.

On the level of the list of personae and the plot Kroetz keeps the correspondence between his chosen model, Hebbel's *Maria Magdalena*,[1] and his own reworking of the same title extremely close. At the same time, Kroetz's subtitle, *Komödie frei nach Friedrich Hebbel*,[2] indicates an intended change of dramatic genre from tragedy to comedy. This is achieved to a large extent by the comical, sometimes even grotesque effect of the impoverished speech of the protagonists. But Kroetz aims for more than merely demonstrating the absurdity of his protagonists by showing up the depleted language of the postwar petit-bourgeoisie. The uncompromising exposure of the hollowness in the language of the protagonists also carries a political message, and a critique of the utopian nature of Brecht's ideas on reform. In his essay "Liegt die Dummheit auf der Hand?" Kroetz asserts: "Weil Brechts

Figuren so sprachgewandt sind, ist in seinen Stücken der Weg zur positiven Utopie, zur Revolution gangbar. Hätten die Arbeiter bei Siemens das Sprachniveau der Arbeiter Brechts, hätten wir eine revolutionäre Situation."[3]

Kroetz has chosen Hebbel's *Maria Magdalena* for a model for his own critique of society in the 1970s. Hebbel's drama is a prime example of the German "bourgeois tragedy," a dramatic form that originated in the eighteenth century and is generally attributed to Lessing. The first successful examples of the bourgeois tragedy were *Miß Sara Sampson* (1755) and *Emilia Galotti* (1772). Lessing had challenged the hitherto observed convention that noble characters of the upper classes were to be the only worthy protagonists in tragedy, and termed his dramas *bürgerliches Trauerspiel*. Emilia's unnecessary, meaningless death is neither redeemed by a glorious end nor fully motivated by an inner flaw, but instead is caused by social conflict and the abuse of power. Tragedy, according to Lessing, who builds his theory on Aristotle's ideas of tragedy, must stir "compassion and fear" in the audience: "Die Tragödie ... soll Mitleid und Schrecken erregen."[4] Seventy years later, with his *Maria Magdalena* (1843), Hebbel reaches another stage in the history of the *bürgerliches Trauerspiel*. In his foreword to *Maria Magdalena* Hebbel criticizes Lessing for creating the tragic conflict from the clash between the upper and the middle classes with the argument: "Aus dem Zusammenstoßen des dritten Standes mit dem zweiten und ersten in Liebesaffären [geht] unleugbar viel Trauriges, aber nichts Tragisches hervor."[5] Hebbel's *Maria Magdalena* draws its characters exclusively from the lower middle classes. The drama is set at the period of historical transition from the rigid social order of the "corporate state" (*Ständegesellschaft*), wherein every man knew and accepted his allocated place in the class he was born into, to an industrial society that allows a man to break free from his father's trade.

By 1973, the year of publication of *Maria Magdalena*, Kroetz had just begun to take an active interest in Brecht. In an interview with the programmatic title "Ich säße lieber in Bonn im Bundestag" (1973), the radical left-wing playwright Kroetz analyzes his own development from an "angry young man" to a writer with a more analytical approach to his work.

> Wenn man meine Stücke genau untersucht, dann stellt man sehr leicht fest, daß das soziale Engagement, das in ihnen steckt, nicht aus einer gesellschaftlichen Analyse des Autors kommt, sondern aus Erschrecken und Zorn über die Zustände wie sie sind. Und die Stücke fordern auch nicht den Zuschauer dazu auf, Analysen vorzunehmen,

sondern sie fordern dazu auf, Mitleid zu haben. Mitleid ist ein unpolitisches Gefühl. Der Autor Kroetz war wohl ein unpolitischer Autor."[6]

This interest in analyzing the specific circumstances of a particular social group must have motivated Kroetz's creative reinterpretation of Hebbel's tragedy and influenced the kind of effect he was aiming for in his version of this fairly commonplace family tragedy. Aristotelian poetics operate on the principle of *catharsis* effected by empathy with the suffering of the hero or heroine. This concept of tragedy remained largely unchallenged until the early twentieth century. After the First World War, however, Brecht and Dürrenmatt, among others, claimed that tragedy was no longer an appropriate dramatic form for the modern world. They pointed to the fundamental differences between pre-industrial and industrial societies, the latter allowing for much greater social mobility coupled with a new autonomy of the individual. The argument runs thus:

> Uns erscheint von größtem gesellschaftlichen Interesse, was Aristoteles der Tragödie als Zweck setzt, nämlich die *Katharsis*, die Reinigung des Zuschauers von Furcht und Mitleid durch die Nachahmung von furcht- und mitleiderregenden Handlungen. Diese Reinigung erfolgt auf Grund eines eigentümlichen psychischen Aktes, der *Einfühlung* des Zuschauers in die handelnden Personen, die von den Schauspielern nachgeahmt werden.[7]

According to Brecht, empathy is awakened if the audience identifies with the dilemma faced by the central characters. Contradictory demands within an ordered system place the protagonist in an impossible situation, facing impossible choices, and tragedy arises. The tragic hero lives with a sense of destiny:

> Damit wir mit dem Helden verzweifeln können, müssen wir sein Gefühl der Auswegslosigkeit teilen, damit wir erschüttert werden können durch seine Einsicht in die Gesetzmäßigkeit seines Schicksals, müssen wir ebenfalls, was in seinem Fall passiert, als unverrückbar gesetzmäßig einsehen.[8]

Brecht's drama demands a more critical reception on the part of the audience, and argues in favor of the "Verzicht auf die Einfühlung, dem näherzutreten die Dramatik unserer Zeit sich gezwungen sah."[9] In his theory of the Epic Theater Brecht rejects the emotional involvement of the audience that empathizes with the fate of the protagonists. The use of *Verfremdung*, the ironic treatment of his characters, and his particular brand of poetic language (all techniques of the Epic Theater) serve to break with the *cathartic* effect of "fear and compassion" and create an emotional distance to the events on stage with the aim of mobilizing the critical faculties of the audience.

Tragedy presupposes an ordered universe with a fixed value system, and our world has become too complicated and too multifaceted to allow for a clear sense of right and wrong. In his essay "Theaterprobleme," Friedrich Dürrenmatt suggests likewise: "Die Tragödie, als die gestrengste Kunstgattung, setzt eine gestaltete Welt voraus."[10] Once this order disintegrates, and different beliefs and value systems are allowed to stand side by side, so the argument goes, there must be an end to the tragic dilemma. In the transition from a fixed world order with a social hierarchy, in which each subject had its place, to a mass society, the clear knowledge of right and wrong was lost. Writing in 1954, Dürrenmatt analyzes a trend that had already emerged.

> Die Tragödie setzt Schuld, Not, Maß, Übersicht, Verantwortung voraus. In der Wurstelei unseres Jahrhunderts, in diesem Kehraus der weißen Rasse, gibt es keine Schuldigen und auch keine Verantwortlichen mehr.... Wir sind zu kollektiv schuldig, zu kollektiv gebettet in die Sünden unserer Väter und Vorväter. Wir sind nur noch Kindeskinder. Das ist unser Pech, nicht unsere Schuld: Schuld gibt es nur noch als persönliche Leistung, als religiöse Tat. (122)

In this context, any twentieth-century reworking of a nineteenth-century tragedy can no longer be pure tragedy. Franz Xaver Kroetz's reproduction of Hebbel's bourgeois tragedy *had* to appear as a "comedy." The *content* of Kroetz's *Maria Magdalena* is that of the bourgeois tragedy, while the *form* is borrowed from and written in the manner of the *Volksstück*.

Both the bourgeois theater and the tradition of the *Volksstück* were conceived as alternatives to the Baroque theater of the courtly society and, from the eighteenth century, developed along parallel lines. The bourgeois tragedy and the sentimental comedy, the *Lustspiel*, quickly gained popularity also among the upper and educated classes and contributed to the canon. In contrast, the *Volksstück* was able to retain its non-exclusive character, it appealed to broader sections of society, and, unlike the bourgeois theater, saw itself released from any didactic function. Since the beginning of the twentieth century the *Volksstück* has focused on the moral weakness and limited horizon of the urban lower classes (particularly in the works of Ödön von Horváth and Marieluise Fleisser). One of the most marked differences between the conventional drama of the twentieth century and the *Volksstück* lies in the presentation of language peculiar to the respective protagonists as well as to its particular audiences. This function, according to Gerd Müller, becomes the method and the aim of the playwright.[11]

Hebbel's characters are drawn from the lower middle classes but their language is that of their creator, the educated playwright. Kroetz, on the other hand, mercilessly exposes his characters to show their greatest weakness: limited by a language, which consists largely of meaningless phrases and clichés, they are incapable of masking their crass egocentricity. Making full use of the divergence of form and content, the tragi-comedy in the guise of the *Volksstück*, Kroetz exposes the moral weakness of the lower middle classes, the disintegration of social ties, and the complete lack of a social conscience in the urban society of the 1970s.

Acknowledging the intentional transformation of genre from the bourgeois tragedy to the *Volksstück* is essential in the question of the similarities and differences between Hebbel's tragedy and Kroetz's comical reproduction. The deliberate means Kroetz employs to create the desired effect have often been misunderstood. In the largely negative reception of Kroetz's *Maria Magdalena,* the play was described as "a degradation and trivialisation of Hebbel's powerful metaphysical tragedy: a cheap travesty, the analysis of which proved to critics that the prolific Kroetz had sunk into an authorial crisis."[12] It was remarked that Kroetz did not provide the audience with an answer to Hebbel but with "Klischees einer Posse,"[13] replacing Hebbel's emphatic dialogues "durch hilflos geschwätzige [Dialoge] mit zahlreichen vordergründigen Anspielungen aufs Zeitgeschehen,"[14] and thus "die beabsichtigte Satire verkommt zur billigen Parodie."[15]

Georg Kurscheidt qualifies this dismissive criticism by placing the play in the evolution of the German tragedy since Lessing. In the eighteenth century Lessing made it possible for a member of the middle classes to become the protagonist of tragedy on stage in a dignified manner. He constructed the crisis from the differences between the moral corruption of the aristocracy and the enlightened morality of the *Bürger*. In the nineteenth century Hebbel places his tragedy wholly among the lower middle classes, creating characters who live according to a moral and social code that has become narrow and unyielding, but who, nevertheless, are still possessed of a certain dignity. In the twentieth century Kroetz's characters no longer live in a comprehensive social system in which everyone knows his or her place; as a result, they have lost their dignity.[16]

Understanding Kroetz's experimental reworking of Hebbel's *Maria Magdalena* in the larger context of the general development of drama in the twentieth century, a development characterized by the demise of tragedy, will allow us to see the modern play in a more favorable light than is generally the case. While Kroetz's own description of *Maria Magdalena* as a comedy might be misleading, *any* modern reworking of a nineteenth-century tragedy will tend to contain features of the comical, the grotesque, the absurd.

The Problem of Language

The protagonists of plays written before the mid-eighteenth century came from an educated background, which gave them full range of language to express their emotions and bemoan their fate. To some degree, the fact that the lower middle classes of the nineteenth century are so much better able to express themselves than their twentieth-century counterparts can be explained by a thorough acquaintance with and knowledge of the Bible. Although formal education for the small tradesmen — the environment of Meister Anton and his wife — was either inadequate or non-existent, the constant repetition of the catechism and long church services with readings from the Old and the New Testament frequently exposed this generation to a language rich in metaphors and complex thought. The absorption of these readings, so the argument goes, might eventually enable the listeners to speak for themselves. This source of a differentiated and refined language is no longer available to their twentieth-century successors. However, in addition to the linguistic competence through familiarity with the Bible, Hebbel clearly lends his own language, the language of the writer, to his characters and enables them to put their difficulties and their point of view into words. Meister Anton is essentially shaped by the narrowness and inflexibility of his strictly confined social environment. His counterpart in real life would most certainly not have had the ability to declare himself in the way his "double" on the German stage can. Neither would he have been tempted to go and see the tragedy in the theater, preserved for the educated middle classes.

The problem for the twentieth-century dramatist arises from the attempt to depict social and linguistic impoverishment and deprivation realistically because, according to Kroetz, the very hallmark of the subjects portrayed on stage is their inability to use language adequately to analyze a given situation, to express their feelings, or to put their predicaments into words. There are no simple solutions to this dilemma between a new kind of realism and artistic expression. Brecht, who also draws some of his protagonists from the proletariat, does not attempt to reconcile the contradiction. His characters are held in a fine balance between real life situations and an artistic articulation. Thus, the characters, marked by extreme poverty and deprivation, become near-allegorical figures who exist only within the self-contained world of his plays. For example, Frau Luckerniddle in *Die heilige Johanna der Schlachthöfe* uses a simple but poetic language to describe the effect of starvation: "Das ist die Grausamkeit des Hungers, daß er / Wenngleich befriedigt, immer wieder kommt" (*HJ*, 175). Kroetz, on the other hand, wants to depict characters *from* the real world *in* the real world. In the plays leading up to *Maria Magdalena* he succeeded in this and gained a reputation as the "protagonist of speechlessness."[17] The impoverished language of his subjects on stage was taken as an adequate means to symbolize the physical and psychological bankruptcy of the lower middle classes.

However, the difficulties of rewriting Hebbel's *Maria Magdalena* as a comedy within the narrow confines of the self-imposed restriction of language were considerable. Jan Berg argues that the attempt to portray the characters both as realistic figures and as caricatures of themselves was not possible within the chosen linguistic framework.[18] At about the time when Kroetz was working on *Maria Magdalena*, he realized that he had come to the limits of his exploration of "speechlessness" that had gained him fame, and he began to experiment with a more liberated use of language and form. In a short article, "Über *Die Maßnahme* von Bertolt Brecht," Kroetz describes the process himself:

> Brechts Werk war mir bis ins Jahr 1973 hinein ziemlich unbekannt und deshalb gleichgültig. Erst als immer klarer wurde, daß es mit der Fleißer und dem Horváth allein keine Entwicklung geben kann, habe ich angefangen Brecht zu studieren. Inzwischen ist mir Brecht näher als die Fleißer und der Horváth, und ich lerne von ihm fortwährend. . . . Vor allem um den kleinen und (in den Figuren) den kleinsten Bereich meiner Stücke zu verlassen und mehr gesellschaftliche Zusammenhänge, mehr Hintergründe, also größere Flächen zeigen zu können, bedarf es des Brecht.[19]

In this process, the creation of a reworking signifies Kroetz's first steps towards depicting a more widely representative section of society compared to his earlier works, which dealt with largely exceptional characters and in unusual circumstances.

Maria Magdalena establishes a far more intimate relationship between model and reworking than any of the other texts discussed in this study. Compared to the figures in Hebbel's *Maria Magdalena*, Kroetz's characters express themselves by using much shorter speeches, made up from shorter sentences, but a close correspondence between model and reworking in the form of quotes and semi-quotes can be found on every page. The opening scene sets this trend and may serve as an example. Both plays begin with the mother and daughter admiring the mother's wedding dress, which she has also consigned to be her burial shroud. Exactly the same sentiment is expressed by the two mothers, but each uses a distinct linguistic register.

> *Mutter:* Dies Kleid war schon zehnmal aus der Mode und kam immer wieder hinein. (*HMM*, 331)

> *Mama:* Das war schon zehnmal in und aus der Mode. Alles schon dagewesn![20] (*KMM*, 199)

Some images used in the model are reversed in the reworking. Any religious belief that might have strengthened Meister Anton's wife, has dwindled to mere convention in the case of Mama, who proudly lists all the charitable deeds she has done, but only in order to make a good impression on her neighbors. Having just recovered from serious illness, both mothers express their fear of death using the same words: "Man krümmt sich wie ein Wurm" (*HMM*, 332 and *KMM*, 202). But whereas her religious lifestyle allows Klara's mother to draw some comfort from her faith, to Mama death means unredeemed darkness:

> *Mutter:* Der Tod ist schrecklicher als man glaubt ... es wird finster allenthalben, aber im Herzen zündet er ein Licht an, da wird's *hell*. (*HMM*, 331, my emphasis)

> *Mama:* Man denkt zu wenig an seinen Tod. / Alles wird *dunkel* und die Lichter gehen aus. (*KMM*, 201, my emphasis)

Intertextual links of this kind continue throughout Kroetz's text. Some seem significant in their contrast to the original; others merely serve to highlight the empty phrases widely used by most of Kroetz's characters most of the time. For example, Mama, still talking about the wedding dress, proclaims pathetically: "Das könnts mir anziehn, / wenn ich einmal nimmer bin, *weil ich hinüber muß in das Reich der Schatten*" (*KMM*, 200, my emphasis).

Reading a text and seeing a play in a stage production are, of course, two fundamentally different experiences. Apart from the visual effects of the theater, the language heard on the stage has already been given a personal interpretation by the actor. Gesture, intonation — and even silence — all lend expression to the spoken word. The current discussion has to be limited to the texts alone. In the case of

Hebbel's *Maria Magdalena* this matters less, because Hebbel's language is well able to speak for itself. But it makes a large difference to Kroetz's attempt to show us the inability of his characters to speak for themselves. Much of the mostly black humor, any sense of sympathy, or even identification with the characters or their predicaments is not so much inherent in the text, but arises out of an actual stage production. The following analysis of Kroetz's text has to take into consideration the fact that the words on the page tell only half the story, and that the effect on the reader might be quite different from that on the actual audience in the theater.

Hebbel's *Maria Magdalena*

The secondary literature on Hebbel's *Maria Magdalena* is extensive and, bearing in mind the outdatedness of the play's moral and social concepts, it is surprising how much interest to this day the drama stills holds for scholars (and playwrights) alike. Relevant to our discussion is above all Hebbel's notion of *necessity*. Hebbel maintains that all protagonists are in the right, if we consider their character and their social position.

> Ich bin zufrieden, besonders damit, daß sie alle eigentlich recht haben, sogar Leonhard, wenn man nur nicht aus den Augen läßt, daß er von Haus aus eine gemeine Natur ist, die sich in höhere nicht finden und an sie nicht glauben kann, und daß also die Gebundenheit des Lebens in der Einseitigkeit, aus der von vorneherein alles Unheil der Welt entspringt, so recht schneidend hervortritt.[21]

It follows that Hebbel presents his tragedy in such a way that one development necessarily leads to another with deadly consequence.

> Es war meine Absicht, das bürgerliche Trauerspiel zu regenerieren und zu zeigen, daß auch im eingeschränktesten Kreis eine zerschmetternde Tragik möglich ist, wenn man sie nur aus den rechten Elementen, aus den diesem Kreise selbst angehörigen, abzuleiten versteht.[22]

The small-town setting and the financial and social decline of the traditional trades during the industrial revolution provide the framework for Meister Anton's narrow worldview. He lives in the past and cannot accept that changing economic patterns bring about social change. His most highly prized possession is his spotless reputation, and his greatest fear the loss of his good name. "Denn alles, alles kann ich ertragen, und habs bewiesen, nur nicht die Schande! Legt mir auf den Nacken was ihr wollt, nur schneidet nicht den Nerv durch, der mich zusammen hält!" (*HMM*, 356).

Paradoxically, most of the public disgrace Meister Anton fears so strongly is brought about by his own unyielding character. Had Anton not previously snubbed Adam, the town clerk, because of his lower social status (*HMM*, 360) and, as a result of Anton's arrogance, had Adam not borne an ancient personal grudge against Anton, Karl would not have been arrested in such a humiliating, public fashion. As it is, Adam declares: "ich [Adam] hasse ihn, wie ich nur hassen kann ... und auch Er [second clerk] müßte sich beleidigt fühlen, wenn Er Ehre im Leib hätte" (*HMM*, 351). Indirectly, this earlier display of disdain on the part of Anton brings about the catastrophe. Klara never doubts the inevitable logic of one action causing another, and she immediately draws a link between her father's pride and the death of her mother resulting from Adam's grudge. "Was ist nicht alles möglich auf der Welt! Das hat meine Mutter mit einem jähen Tode bezahlen müssen!" (*HMM*, 360). This deterministic outlook even causes her to perceive a connection between her own indiscretion and her mother's illness: "Als ich zu Hause kam [after having given in to Leonhard's demands], fand ich meine Mutter krank, todkrank. Plötzlich dahingeworfen, wie von unsichtbarer Hand" (*HMM*, 338). Not only is Hebbel's plot arranged in such a way that each development is a direct and necessary result of what went before, but even his characters perceive the world in such a deterministic way. Only Karl, in his wish to escape from the world of his father, indicates the possibility that this cycle of inevitability may be broken.

The Title "Maria Magdalena"

Hebbel's choice of title *Maria Magdalena* is a name borrowed from the New Testament figure. Although there is no textual evidence in the Gospels, Mary Magdalene is widely regarded as a sinner, even a prostitute, who was nevertheless allowed to be a member of the inner circle around Jesus.[23] She exemplifies the new gospel of forgiveness. Jesus defends her against the accusing Pharisees with the words: "Her sins, which are many, are forgiven, for she loved much" (Luke 7:47). Where the old faith of the Pharisees condemns, the new Christian belief teaches forgiveness of the repentant sinner. In this sense, the society portrayed by Hebbel proves to be Christian in name only. Hypocrisy, uncharitable narrow-mindedness, and manipulation of others are the order of the day and Klara has become the victim of the sexual and moral prudishness of her social environment. It is ironic that not only the life of the protagonist Klara is threatened, but initially also the very publication of the drama itself. In an answer to

Hebbel's request to sponsor the drama, Auguste Stich-Crelinger, actress in Berlin, has only one major criticism of *Maria Magdalena*.

> Nur *Eins,* eine Kleinigkeit wenn Sie wollen, aber nach meiner Ansicht eine unübersteigliche Schwierigkeit, sobald es sich um die Aufführung handelt, das Hauptmotiv der Handlung, die offenkundige Schwangerschaft der Heldin, stößt Alles [*sic*] über den Haufen.[24]

Stich-Crelinger seems not to have noticed that Klara's pregnancy is, after all, not a mere detail, but the *agens movens* of the plot. Hebbel's Klara, although no prostitute, has "fallen." She has succumbed to the pressure Leonhard bore upon her, slept with him once in order to prove to him (and, more importantly, to herself) that she was no longer in love with Friedrich, a former admirer, and has become pregnant. This circumstance triggers every other development of the plot. The drama itself sets out to demonstrate the essential innocence of Klara — innocence in both meanings of the word. Socially, Klara is shown to be the victim, a helpless pawn to the selfishness of the men around her, and psychologically she has remained the naive innocent, unable to turn the situation to her advantage, in spite of her so-called sexual experience. The society around Klara is shown to be unyielding, but the audience is moved. If Mary Magdalene stands symbolically for the sinner who is forgiven, Klara appears as the innocent who is condemned. In spite of the Christian values proclaimed in the drama, the society portrayed shows itself to be concerned with reputation rather than the truth. Klara is less afraid of the possibility of suffering hellfire for committing suicide and thereby also infanticide, than of confronting her father with the truth. Unlike the death of Schiller's Jungfrau von Orleans, Klara's death is not redeemed in any way. She has not made her peace with the world, nor can she die with the belief in any reward in heaven. The only glimmer of redemption in the whole of the tragedy dies as soon as it is voiced. Friedrich recognizes the shallowness of the social rules that govern all their lives, and exclaims: "nun, ich bezahls mit dem Leben, daß ich mich von einem, der schlechter war als ich, so abhängig machte" (*HMM,* 381). But this understanding comes too late for him to act upon.[25] By the nineteenth century, the Christian faith, which is ideally built on the virtues of forgiveness and hope, has become an empty form with little influence on the actions of the protagonists in the drama. Even God has become a remote terrible figure without mercy, a God to be feared but not loved. Klara appeals to him without believing she is heard: "Gott im Himmel, ich würde mich erbarmen, wenn ich du wäre und du ich!" (*HMM,* 364).

"Sin," "repentance," and "forgiveness" are words no longer part of the vocabulary of Kroetz's family when we meet them in the second half of the twentieth century. Kroetz's title *Maria Magdalena* appears doubly ironic. Neither has Marie retained any of Klara's innocence or willingness to sacrifice herself for others, nor does she share any characteristics with the biblical figure "who loved much." The fact that biblical references are used as an ironic device, not only in the title, but also in a number of subtitles to various scenes, shall be discussed later.

Kroetz's "Comedy"

Both model and reworking are written as three-act plays. Considering how close Hebbel's philosophy is to that of Hegel, the threefold form of exposition, — climax, — catastrophe is an appropriate form for Hebbel, and corresponds to Hegel's *dialectical principle* of thesis, — antithesis, — synthesis as *agens movens* for any historical development. Unlike Brecht, who breaks up the traditional structure of tragedy in his reworking of Schiller's *Die Jungfrau von Orleans,* Kroetz chooses to retain the original three acts, but replaces Hebbel's twenty-four scenes with seventeen, each given a subtitle. The order of the scenes has been preserved, and the variance in number is largely the result of a slightly different subdivision of the acts. Kroetz leaves out some monologues (for example, Klara II, 6; Karl III, 9) or, on another occasion, turns one scene into two (*HMM,* I, 3), each marked with a separate subtitle. The only significant divergence from Hebbel's model is found in Kroetz's last scene. One would, of course, expect a comedy rewritten from a tragedy to end differently, but ironically it is in this last, new scene that Kroetz's somewhat farcical *Maria Magdalena* suddenly turns — almost — tragic. In the end Marie finds herself in the same social isolation, as did her predecessor.

The explicit correspondence between the two plays, initially established by the title, is further continued in the list of characters, but with some significant changes. Hebbel's Meister Anton has been replaced by a mere "Papa." He has lost his autonomy as "master," his secure place in society, and is characterized only by the relationship to his family. Anton's wife, "seine Frau," on the other hand, is no longer defined as the property of her husband but reappears as "Mama," and thus of equal (non-)status as the reduced "Papa." The most notable difference between the two lists is the change of "Klara" to "Marie." Hebbel originally planned to call his play *Klara* after the main protagonist,[26] but eventually he opted for *Maria Magdalena* as the archetypal figure against whom the fate of his Klara could be measured. Kroetz, on the other hand, named his main protagonist after Hebbel's (and his own) title figure, and thus creates an ironic dissonance between the name (and what it stands for) and the character traits of his heroine. The figure of Karl, the son and brother, remains unaltered. Leonhard reappears as Leo, and "ein Sekretär" (Friedrich) as Peter. These changes all signify a loss of status of the characters in the reworking compared to those of the model. The abbreviation Leo is hardly a term of affection, and Peter, still supported by his parents, has not yet attained the financial independence and the relative maturity of Friedrich, the secretary in Hebbel's drama. The minor figures of Adam, the clerk, and Wolfram, the jeweler, have been replaced respectively by the grotesque caricature of a police inspector and the stereotyped jeweler Huber, a change that corresponds to the logic of transferring a play from the closely knit community within "corporate society" of the nineteenth century to the anonymous mass society of the second half of the twentieth century. As with the title and subtitle of Kroetz's *Maria Magdalena,* the character list of the reworking emphasizes the inner link between the two plays, but at the same time the differences already point to the ironic effect, indicating the "Untergang des Bürgertums,"[27] as is intended by Kroetz.

The Subtitles

Apart from the different use of language and the alterations made necessary by the change of genre from tragedy to comedy, everything so far points to a fairly faithful reproduction of Hebbel's drama: the borrowed title is supported by a direct reference to Hebbel; the lists of characters are largely the same in both works; the plot is followed almost pedantically; there are only minor changes in the arrangement of the scenes; even the dialogue does not digress far from that of the model. All of Kroetz's scenes are preceded by subtitles. These titles have the function of shedding an ironic, not to say sarcastic light on the tragic material, and completely undermine the original intention of Hebbel's drama. In his article of 1982, Kurscheidt has rightly identified the key formula for the reworking as following the "principle of inversion" when he argues: "Die enge Anlehnung in formaler Hinsicht hat freilich die Funktion, als Kontrast zu dienen für inhaltliche Veränderungen, die, wie die neue, 'komische' Version des Dramenschlusses andeutet, nach dem *Prinzip der Umkehrung* vorgenommen sind" (408–9). Kurscheidt convincingly applies this "principle of inversion" to the contrasts of genre, to parallel characters and to comparisons of single scenes. It can further be applied to the ironic distance created by the subtitles.

The subtitles can be loosely grouped into subject areas borrowed from: (1) the Bible; (2) fairy tales; (3) the code of chivalry and romantic love; and (4) the language of economics. Each of the subtitles either indicates exactly the opposite of what is actually happening or else casts a deeply ironic shadow over the events of the scene. And, considering how closely the plot of the reworking is based on the model, it is tempting to apply the same subtitles to Hebbel's *Maria Magdalena* as well. By so doing, the absurdity of the morality that rules the world depicted by Hebbel is mercilessly exposed, as is the outdatedness of the tragic conflict. This is immediately apparent already in the first scene subtitled "Hochzeit" (*KMM,* 199).

Should we indeed be preparing for, or even be celebrating a wedding, both plays would have finished before they began. In the biblical context the term "wedding" might also remind us of the miracle performed by Jesus at the "Wedding at Cana" (John 2:1–11). For both Klara and Marie, marriage would mean that the social predicament they find themselves in would not have arisen. Both girls also secretly hope for a miracle that would put an end to their pregnancies. Klara wishes she were a Catholic and could thus hope to be forgiven by doing penance. "Wenn meine Mutter gestorben wäre, nie wär ich wieder ruhig geworden, denn — . . . Aber Du bist gnädig, Du bist barmherzig! Ich wollt, ich hätt einen Glauben wie die Katholischen, daß ich Dir etwas schenken dürfte" (*HMM,* 335). Marie is more direct, and falls into the habit of childhood prayers. The subtitle for this scene "Madonna allein" (*KMM,* 209) is deeply cynical. The two heroines stand under the shadow of Mary Magdalene, the sinner, but that name is, of course, also shared by Mary, mother of Jesus, who begot her only son by immaculate conception. The biblical Mary humbly accepted the pregnancy. But not so Kroetz's Marie, who prays:

> *Marie:* Lieber Gott,
> mach daß das Kind ein Abgang wird.
> Sei vernünftig lieber Gott,
> bitte!
> Wenn du eine Macht hast,
> dann mach,
> daß es weggeht,
> bevor man es merkt!
> Das is eine Kleinigkeit,
> wenn man etwas davon versteht.
> (*KMM,* 209)

The third biblical reference introduces Karl as "Verlorener Sohn" (*KMM*, 203). Unlike the Prodigal Son, who after collecting his inheritance went out into the world and wasted it, apparently Karl comes home regularly asking for more. As in the tradition surrounding Mary Magdalene, in essence the parable of the Prodigal Son is about forgiveness. In both plays, Karl is not so much forgiven as spoilt and overindulged by his mother and sister. Unlike the biblical father who immediately forgives the prodigal, never doubting the inherent goodness of his son, neither Meister Anton nor Papa know a moment of doubt about the supposed guilt of their respective sons who, as it turns out, are both falsely accused of theft. The three biblical allusions in the subtitles highlight the stark contrasts between their inherent meaning and the actual events on the stage. Already in Klara's nineteenth-century world, religious beliefs were less important in decision-making than considerations of a social reputation. In Kroetz's *Maria Magdalena*, the discrepancy between the biblical subtitles and the society that still claims to pay lip service to religious values is bordering on the absurd, and serves to add a grim humor to the situation.

This is also the case with the allusions to the realm of the fairy tale in titles like "Prinz Leo" (*KMM*, 210) and "Prüfung" (*KMM*, 216). A happy ending is not granted to the dilemma faced by Marie, and Leo proves to be anything but a noble prince. In a fairy tale world the prince often has to undergo a number of trials to prove himself worthy of his princess. In this instance, it is Papa (and Anton) who does not pass the "test," namely holding on to the money that could have provided his daughter with a dowry. The "Prüfung" is not a test to examine the courage and quickness of thought of the prince, as is the case in fairy tales, but an audit of the balance sheet. Particularly in this scene, it becomes clear how well the subtitles illuminate not only Kroetz's own but also Hebbel's play. The combination of "Prinz" and "Prüfung" describes exactly how Hebbel's Leonhard sees himself, and how he justifies his actions, but it takes a strong sense of the absurd to describe it thus.

The next group of subtitles describes the rules of courtship. The scene entitled "Was sich gehört" (*KMM*, 206) sees mother and daughter discussing the future prospects of the young couple. Mutter sighs: "Wenn er nur erst etwas wäre!" (*HMM*, 334), and resolves to pray for them, committing their fate in the hands of God: "Und was deinen Leonhard betrifft, so liebe ihn, wie er Gott liebt, nicht mehr, nicht weniger" (*HMM*, 334). Mama is more direct in her advice: "Das war gestern heute und morgen! / Erst die Versorgung dann das Vergnügen, / also der Anstand" (*KMM*, 209). The subtitle "Schäferstündchen" (*KMM*, 224) is a positively grotesque term for the climax of the first act in which Karl is accused of a jewel theft, the mother collapses dead on the floor, and the police ransack the house with the comment: "Machen Sie weiter, meine Herrn, / das is eine Privatangelegenheit" (*KMM*, 226). The sudden death of the mother, although prepared by the talk of disease and burial, is probably one of the weakest points in Hebbel's *Maria Magdalena*. In Kroetz's version it is pure farce. The crucial difference between the two versions of this scene, however, is that, unlike Meister Anton, Papa does not force Marie to take an oath on her virginity. Thus, the whole of Klara's dilemma, the momentous choice between her father's threat of suicide, should she bring shame to the family's good name, and, failing marriage, infanticide as a result of her self-destruction, does not arise for Marie. This loss of tragic motivation for what follows is the most problematic aspect of Kroetz's attempted reworking.

There is one more subtitle, "Duell" (*KMM*, 244), worth mentioning here for its inverted meaning. In Hebbel's drama, Friedrich's sense of honor will not allow him to marry Klara without fighting Leonhard, because Leonhard will *know* that Klara's child is not his. "Darüber kann kein Mensch weg! Vor dem Kerl, dem man ins Gesicht spucken möge, die Augen niederschlagen müssen?" (*HMM*, 366). When both protagonists die in the ensuing duel, they take away Klara's last hope of finding an honorable solution to her problem at the same time. In Kroetz's play the duel is fought out around the kitchen table, and the contest is about who has the greatest influence either to block or to promote Leo's career. The obscure code of honor of the nineteenth century is replaced by barefaced manipulation of contacts, influence, and chances of promotion. The prize is no longer a spotless reputation, but a larger bank account. Leo emerges victorious.

Finally, subtitles, like "Bilanz" (*KMM*, 253), "Amerika I," and "Amerika II" (*KMM*, 247, 248), or even "Haltestelle" (*KMM*, 240), a stop-over to some better place, refer to economic superiority and to the American myth, a motif already introduced by Hebbel. Hebbel's Karl has plans to emigrate to America in order to escape from the confines of his father's world. Even though the subtitle refers to America, Kroetz's Karl merely wants to leave for Munich. In a chapter entitled "The Balance-Sheet," Mary Garland argues that in Hebbel's *Maria Magdalena* "the references to the idea of payment inaugurate a whole range of words demonstrating man's existence, as a struggle for reward, a calculation for the best possible investment or gain."[28] This not only applies to the obvious candidates, Leonhard and Karl, both of whom are dissatisfied with their lot and want to better their prospects, but in particular to Meister Anton. Publicly shamed by the disclosure of Karl's apparent crime, and bereft of his better half, the foundations on which Anton has built his life are shaken. According to Garland, "from this moment on Anton's relationship to his children as well as his self-characterization is marked at points of crisis by words of payment, of credit and debit. The balance-sheet is now blotted for all the world to see; he is bankrupt" (166). What is the clearly stated intention of Leonhard and Karl, their burning desire to break out of their social restrictions and improve their material circumstances, already exits as a potential tendency in Meister Anton, albeit in an indirect way. Anton's decisions and actions might not be driven by considerations of material gain, but his language and his thinking are permeated by economic terms, and his metaphor for guilt and repentance is one of debt and repayment.

In the mid-nineteenth century, at the beginning of the industrial age, the older generation in Hebbel's drama still seeks security and self-affirmation in their social station, while the men of the younger generation want financial independence. Whereas Anton's most prized possession is his reputation, Leonhard's highest goal is the power and influence of a better social position, and Karl's the freedom to choose his own lifestyle, to make his own fortune. The actions of each of the characters are determined by these goals. In Kroetz's version any pretense of ethical motivations has disappeared and, according to Ingrid Walsøe-Engel, "all moral values have been replaced by economic ones, and the only qualifying test of Marie's marital fitness, a test which she cannot pass, is financial, as emphasized by the title of the scene, *Prüfung*" (*KMM,* 146).

The Effect of the Reworking

Freely borrowed from various contexts, the subtitles cast an ironic light on Kroetz's scenes. The subtitles make it quite clear that the action on stage is verging on caricature, something obviously intended by the author as he comments on and judges his creatures every step of the way. But even beyond that, the subtitles also highlight the absurd notions of Hebbel's drama — absurd to our twentieth-century understanding of the moral code and social progress. As soon as the subtitles are applied to the model, something clearly intended by Kroetz himself, they act as an alienation device and create an awareness that Klara and Meister Anton are able to move the audience only if they are understood in their particular historical and cultural context, and not as archetypal figures facing an archetypal dilemma. None of the reasons motivating their decisions and actions, their dubious code of honor driven by the fear of public shame, would be valid today. Nevertheless, Kroetz's drama has a sting. In the end Marie is "aus der Welt verdrängt"[29] as was Klara. The callousness and egotism of the men around the two Magdalena figures has survived a century of social change. But today we have to look for the reasons in a different place. Hebbel's notion of *necessity,* the idea that Anton cannot but act the way he does, which equally applies to the other characters, is given a different slant in the reworking. Kroetz's protagonists are also determined by their age, by their lack of education, and by their class, but as the class system of the 1970s is far less rigid that that of the 1840s, they need no longer be as tied to the social conventions as were the protagonists of Hebbel. Therefore, their coarseness, their ill-mannered conduct and their rude language make Kroetz's characters appear cynical rather than unable to help themselves. In short, the sympathy of the audience, which, in spite of all their shortcomings firmly engages with Hebbel's protagonists, is alienated by the sheer vulgarity of Kroetz's characters. They are no longer portrayed as victims of their own unenlightened social context, but merely appear incongruous. Kroetz's characters are driven exclusively by money. Reputation and moral values are only of secondary importance. The "balance-sheet" which is used as a metaphor for reality in Hebbel's drama has now *become* reality. This tendency emerges clearly when we examine Kroetz's additions to, and omissions from the structure of the plot.

The greatest and most interesting difference between Hebbel's and Kroetz's *Maria Magdalena* is not any variance in the plot, not even the marked contrasts in the language, but the different *motives* that drive the characters — different motives that lead, however, to (almost) the same outcome. At the end of the first act, Anton makes Klara swear over her mother's dead body that she will not bring him any disgrace. There then follows Anton's threat of suicide, which determines Klara's actions from that moment onwards, and which eventually leads her to commit suicide. In Kroetz's *Maria Magdalena* there is nothing corresponding to that oath. On the contrary, Marie remains unmoved by her father's drunken ramblings: "Bring dich um, alter Depp . . . / das ist das beste, was du tun kannst. / Wo es eine Eigentumswohnung ist und der Karl ned erbt, / weil er sitzt. . . . /

Aber das sind ja bloß leere Versprechungen" (*KMM*, 232). Whereas Klara eventually sacrifices herself and her child, Marie only ever dreams of a convenient solution to all her problems. The absence of the father's threat to kill himself, should the daughter disgrace the family, as good as eliminates Papa as an important character from the plot. Marie's fate is in the hands of Leo and Peter, and not influenced by her father's decisions and values. The loss of a dominant father figure leaves the children, Marie and Karl, free to determine their own lives. But, whereas Karl sees new prospects in the anonymity of the big city, and plans to leave for Munich, Marie is not equipped to make her own way either by staying at home in Augsburg or by moving elsewhere. The motivations for the protagonists' decisions in Hebbel's *Maria Magdalena* all involve a potential loss of reputation. Most crucially, Anton's threat to kill himself, rather than see his daughter the object of scandal, no longer plays a part in Kroetz's version, and single motherhood, according to Marie, "is kein Unglück, wie früher, bloß ein Blödsinn" (*KMM*, 242).

In the comparisons between Anton and Papa and between Marie and Klara striking reversals in character have taken place. Anton is marked by his unshakeable firmness and ruthless consistency. Hebbel himself calls him "den eisernen Alten"[30] and commends his "Felsenhaftigkeit."[31] Papa, on the other hand, is a pathetic and whining loser. The subtitle "Suppenkaspar" (*KMM*, 227) refers to Papa, who, full of self-pity, shies away from the scrutiny of others: "Da obn is die Mama und schaut uns zu. / Ich komm mir beobachtet vor. / Schau weg Mama mir denkn an dich und tun dabei / nichts Unrechtes" (*KMM*, 227). He also is afraid of his children: "Du bist jung und ich? / Ein Witwer mit einem Muttermörder im Gefängnis. / Wenn er wieder in die Freiheit darf dann geht er heim / und bringt seinen Papa um" (*KMM*, 228). The self-centered but all-powerful father figure has turned into an egotistical and pathetic parent. And Klara is self-sacrificing to the point of showing strong masochistic tendencies. Not only does she eventually commit suicide for the sake of her father, but her proposal to Leonhard is also extremely self-demeaning. Provided he will marry her, if only for the sake of appearances, she promises:

> Ich will dir dienen, ich will für dich arbeiten, und zu essen sollst du mir nichts geben . . . ich will lieber in meinen eignen Arm hineinbeißen, als zu meinem Vater gehen. . . . Wenn du mich schlägst, weil dein Hund nicht bei der Hand ist, . . . so will ich eher meine Zunge verschlucken, als ein Geschrei ausstoßen, das den Nachbarn verraten könnte, was vorfällt. (*HMM*, 368–69)

The equivalent in Kroetz's *Maria Magdalena* has Marie saying: "Mir wickeln ein Geschäft ab. / In einem Jahr kannst dich wieder scheidn lassn. / Auf eigenes Verschulden. / Zwischendurch brauchn mir uns nie zu sehn, / während der Ehe. / Zumindest ich / leg keinen Wert drauf" (*KMM*, 241).

In the 1970s, a spotless reputation is no longer of prime importance, and comes some way behind personal comfort and financial considerations. Papa is still afraid of scandal and social disgrace, yet this fear no longer arises from a concern with *moral* transgressions. Both Anton and Papa toy with the idea that Klara/Marie intend to poison them. Anton asks Klara cynically: "War Gift in der Suppe, wie ich gestern träumte? Einiger wilder Schierling, aus Versehen beim Pflücken ins Kräuterbündel hinein geraten? Dann tatst du klug!" (*HMM*, 353). Papa tells Marie defensively: "Ich hab geträumt, daß meine Tochter mich vergiftn will. / Mit E 605. / Es war gut leserlich auf der Dosn. / Gedankn und Träume sind zollfrei" (*KMM*, 227). But when it comes to their respective nightmares, Anton's and Papa's worst fears are different. Anton has a dream wherein Karl is turned into a murderer, and a rich one at that. However, there is no corpse. Is it possible that the vision of Karl being rich, and thus having managed to step out of his social environment, is worse than the apparent murder? Papa also dreams of Karl handling a revolver, but more importantly, Marie has become a terrorist, and in his dream he sees her as "ein Mitglied der Baader-Meinhof-Bande" (*KMM*, 229). Unlike Anton, whose ultimate nightmare of Klara's illegitimate pregnancy proves to be a fact, Papa has no reason for any suspicions such as these. Nothing in Marie lets us suppose she has either the brains or the determination to become a terrorist. Yet, even this scenario could be turned into hard cash as Papa's first conscious thoughts are of selling the story of his daughter to the media. Continuing on the theme of reputation, there are two different real perpetrators of the alleged jewel thefts that both Karls are accused of. Hebbel's Wolfram, the jeweler, has tried in vain to deflect attention from the madness of his wife, and thus to avoid the social stigma attached to insanity. Just like Anton, he is obsessed with his reputation. Kroetz's jeweler, Huber, on the other hand, cannot think why his suspicion did not immediately fall on his own son, a law student and left-wing radical: "Wenn mich einer beraubt, / daß ich da nicht sofort an / meinen Sohn denke, / das is direkt unnormal" (*KMM*, 234). That neither Anton nor Papa doubts his son's guilt for a second shows how normal such a suspicion is in the worlds of both plays.

There has been a noticeable shift in the frame of reference Anton and Papa use in the attempt to make sense of the world. Both regard the laws of nature as reliable and permanent and contrast these with the incomprehensible and unpredictable patterns of the human soul on the one hand, and those of the market economy on the other. In contrast, Leonhard and Leo demonstrate the superiority of the younger generation by being able to recognize the current trends in society and turning that knowledge to their advantage by manipulating others. Meister Anton places reliance on the natural laws around him, and he cannot comprehend the working of human nature:

> Wenn ich einen Baum grünen sehe, so denk ich wohl: nun wird er bald blühen! Und wenn er blüht: nun wird er Früchte bringen! Darin sehe ich mich auch nicht getäuscht, darum geb ich die alte Gewohnheit nicht auf. Aber über Menschen denke ich nichts, gar nichts, nichts Schlimmes, nichts Gutes, dann brauch ich nicht abwechselnd, wenn sie bald meine Furcht, bald meine Hoffnung täuschen, rot oder blaß zu werden. (*HMM*, 341)

Leonhard turns this certainty upside down and emphasizes psychological laws: "Meister Anton, Er macht es ganz verkehrt. Der Baum hängt von Wind und Wetter ab, der Mensch hat in sich Gesetz und Regel" (*HMM*, 341). These laws and rules Leonhard refers to are, of course, the general human weaknesses he makes use of in his manipulation of others. He does not shrink from blackmailing Klara into sleeping with him in order to gain a hold over her and her dowry. And he shows himself to be equally ruthless when it comes to promoting his career prospects by making sure his rival was drunk for the interview when he admits: "Es kam auch nicht ganz von selbst, daß der junge Herrmann in dem wichtigsten Augenblick seines Lebens betrunken war" (*HMM*, 339–40). Leonhard is successful in promoting his own interest through his understanding of the human psyche, something which remains a riddle to the hapless Anton.

Kroetz's Papa is not interested in psychology but contrasts the order of nature with the vagaries of the economy. Paraphrasing Meister Anton, he states: "Einfach ist die Natur, / die Wirtschaft nicht. / Ich sehe ein, daß man nichts ändern kann und füge mich" (*KMM*, 217). The connection between the laws of nature and those of the economy has already been made by the chorus of the Packherren in Brecht's *Die heilige Johanna der Schlachthöfe*. In this instance, both are described as unpredictable and unknowable. The chorus bemoans the fact that economic disasters come and go like natural disasters, inevitably and beyond human control:

> *Die Packherren:* Unverrückbar über uns
> Stehen die Gesetze der Wirtschaft, unbekannte.
> Wiederkehren in furchtbaren Zyklen
> Katastrophen der Natur! (*HJ*, 161)

Again, whereas to Papa the laws of the economy remain a riddle, Leo is able to advance his prospects by understanding and taking advantage of one of the fundamental truths of the capitalist economy: "Was klein ist stirbt. / Was groß ist wächst. / Heißt das Gesetz der Stunde" (*KMM*, 217). In both plays the men of younger generation are shown as flexible and ready to adapt to the (economic) spirit of the times. In contrast, the daughters remain within the mindset of the parents and are thus doomed to failure.

The Ending — Different, but Yet the Same

Unlike most other reworkings, Kroetz's *Maria Magdalena* is rarely regarded as a work in its own right. Critics hardly ever provide a plot summary, because the link to the model is made instantly, and Hebbel's drama is taken as generally known.[32] Because Kroetz's play introduces the same characters, all differences collapse into nothing, and even the contrasts described above paradoxically emphasize the resemblance between Hebbel's tragedy and Kroetz's comical reproduction. But the different ending, which is yet so chillingly reminiscent of Klara's fate, still needs closer examination.

For that, it is necessary to return to Dürrenmatt who, in his essay "Theaterprobleme," states: "Die Tragödie überwindet Distanz" (121). In tragedy the playwright aims to awaken in the audience the emotions of fear and compassion. That effect can be brought about even if our actual experience has no longer any part in the dramatic events. A review of a 1956 production of Hebbel's *Maria Magdalena* in Göttingen may stand as an example for this view:

> Das Schicksal der Tischlerstochter Klara entlockt uns zwar keine Träne mehr — dazu ist die innere Distanz zu groß geworden, der Schicksalsbegriff zu eng, die Tragik zu sehr aus Wahn und Vorurteil abgeleitet. Doch die Konsequenz und die durchhaltende Leidenschaft, mit denen Hebbel diese dumpfe kleinbürgerliche Welt und ihre Menschen sprachlich geformt hat, sind immerhin so stark, daß es sich wie ein Alpdruck auf die Seele des Zuschauers legen mag.[33]

Comedy, on the other hand, has quite a different effect, according to Dürrenmatt's theory, which maintains: "Die Komödie schafft Distanz" (121). Right to the very end the audience is alienated by rather than drawn to any of Kroetz's characters, who appear either pathetically stupid, like Papa, Mama, and Peter, or brazenly selfish, like Marie and Leo. The comical moments do not arise from genuine humor, but from the unashamed carelessness of the characters, which either shocks the spectator into stunned silence or gives cause to laugh in disbelief. Marie's pregnancy does not give rise to tragedy, and none of the characters pretends it does. Nevertheless, Marie's situation can be seen as tragic in the sense proposed by Dürrenmatt: "Wir können das Tragische aus der Komödie heraus erzielen, hervorbringen aus einem schrecklichen Moment, als einen sich öffnenden Abgrund" (122–23). At the end of the play, Marie faces just such an abyss, when the sudden isolation she finds herself in approaches that tragic moment.

The last scene of Hebbel's *Maria Magdalena* is littered with corpses. Leonhard has died at the hands of Friedrich, who is himself mortally wounded. Karl leads the dying Friedrich to the back room that harbors the drowned corpse of Klara. Meister Anton, surrounded by the broken shards of his existence, utters the programmatic last sentence "Ich verstehe die Welt nicht mehr!" (*HMM*, 382). In spite of the fact that Anton's unyielding austerity was the cause of the tragic consequences he has just witnessed, the audience cannot but have a degree of sympathy with him, as he faces the utter isolation he has created around himself.

Kroetz's final scene, subtitled "Bilanz," offers the climax of the economic plot that underlies the whole of the "comedy." But it is no longer comical. Marie calls out, "die Komödie wachst mir über den Kopf. / Ganz unbarmherzig" (*KMM*, 254), and she endures an almost ritual declaration that she no longer counts as a person in her own right. One after the other, the men she appeals to for help turn her down and refuse to acknowledge her dilemma. No one shows any interest in her future, and they all laugh off her threat to commit suicide: Papa wants to remarry and has already placed an advertisement in the lonely-hearts column, Karl is off to Munich to start a new life, and Peter has nothing to offer but his verdict on Marie's situation: "Schlechte Aussicht" (*KMM*, 254). After a fleeting pause the men settle down to a round of cards. As is the case with Anton in Hebbel's drama, the sympathy of the audience is suddenly engaged, and flows out to the character who has nowhere to turn to. The distance, as an effect of comedy, collapses into empathy, which, according to Dürrenmatt is the hallmark of tragedy. In all probability, Marie will not die, in spite of the fact that she claims that she has taken some poison. But at that moment her isolation is complete, and she approaches the tragic. Kroetz has given the tale a twist; his heroine does not commit suicide like her predecessor, but the *deus ex machina* has failed to materialize and the farce turns into a tragi-comedy.

For Klara the logical conclusion to her predicament was self-destruction; Marie reaches a single moment in which her complete isolation likewise approaches tragedy. However, this does not turn her into a tragic heroine, because as a person she is far too simple and crude. It is her situation that is tragic: the total rejection on the part of all those around her coupled with the fact that she has no inner or outer resources to help herself. She lacks the language to express her predicament and the education to stand on her own feet. The tragic moment passes and the curtain comes down on Marie's desultory figure, as she goes out to serve another round of beer.

Ironies

Kroetz's reworking of Hebbel's *Maria Magdalena* is fraught with irony, some of which is already contained in Hebbel. The titles of both works refer to the biblical Mary Madgalene whose sins have been forgiven, for she loved much. Klara has loved much, but is not forgiven, and Marie, who loves no one, does not need forgiveness, for she has no concept of "sin." It is also ironic that a tragedy, rewritten as a comedy, should turn tragic once more in the end. In the treatment it has received at the hands of Kroetz, the reworked drama borders on the absurd, but the desperate situation of the heroine has hardly changed in the 130 years that separate Klara and Marie. That is why Hebbel's sentiment, "Mich selbst erschüttert diese Klara gewaltig, wie sie aus der Welt herausgedrängt wird," which Kroetz quotes at the end of his play as a kind of epilogue (*KMM*, 256), is both ironic and deadly serious. The sudden change of register from colloquial language to Hebbel's poetic pathos has, of course, an ironic effect. Should we, however, apply Hebbel's sentiments for his own heroine also to Kroetz's Marie, then the fleeting impression of Marie as a tragic figure in the final scene in Kroetz's play is endorsed and must be taken seriously. Marie as a character does not stir much compassion in us, but the Hebbel quote expresses Kroetz's "Erschrecken und Zorn" with the situation Marie finds herself in. In his essay "Ich säße lieber in Bonn im Bundestag" Kroetz admits that he has no ready answers to offer. "Ich [hätte] meinen Figuren keine Alternative bieten können, wenn sie mich gefragt hätten: Kroetz, unsere Probleme kennst du genau! Was aber sollen wir tun, damit wir rauskommen!" (628). Like Brecht, Kroetz wants to expose and explain the circumstances of his protagonists, and show how their lack of autonomy is caused by the society they live in, in accordance with Marx's dictum: "Das Sein bestimmt das Bewußtsein."[34]

The use of Hebbel's drama as a model lends Kroetz's *Maria Magdalena* a historical dimension. Social attitudes have changed, but basic human prejudices have not. Moral pressure has been replaced by economic considerations, but the choices open to Marie are strictly limited. On the other hand, the criticism leveled at Kroetz's *Maria Magdalena* is justified: the characters are flat, the plot is problematic, and the play functions neither as tragedy nor as comedy. Evalouise Panzner speaks for the majority of the critics when she states:

> Zum anderen ist es Kroetz nicht gelungen, sich so weit von der Vorlage zu lösen, die Figuren wirklich zu von ihm geformten Menschen zu machen; stellenweise sind sie verständlich, sind ihre Reaktionen nachvollziehbar, im großen und ganzen fehlt ihnen aber ein Charakter, eine Geschichte, ein Hintergrund, der sie glaubwürdig erscheinen ließe.[35]

Without knowledge of Hebbel's *Maria Magdalena*, the plot of Kroetz's comedy would lose all its logic. To a certain degree it has done so already, with the omission of Anton's suicide threat. Hebbel's notion of *necessity* no longer applies, as nothing that happens in Kroetz's play is inevitable. Without exception, the characters are selfish and incapable of seeing the world from any other perspective than their own. At the same time, the daughter of the family is still a victim of circumstances, which she can neither avoid nor turn to her advantage.

Hebbel's Klara had transgressed against the moral values of her society and perished. In his reworking, Kroetz shows how little the world has changed for a certain class of people who remain imprisoned by their ignorance and lack of ability to express themselves. At least within the confines of the theater, the prospect of Marie's bleak future can be quite as cathartic as the scene of carnage that concludes Hebbel's tragedy. Like all tragic playwrights before him, but paradoxically using the vehicle of the so-called comedy, Kroetz moves the audience to compassion and understanding. In the final scene the farce momentarily turns into tragedy, but the plot leads *beyond* the tragic climax, and the audience is invited to take a glimpse into the endless vista of desolation, indifference, and helplessness that awaits a girl like Marie.

Rewriting one of the best known "bourgeois tragedies" of the German canon as a "comedy" Kroetz remains exceedingly faithful to plot and structure of his model. Transferring the drama into the twentieth-century milieu Kroetz attempts to portray the linguistic impoverishment of the characters portrayed. By doing so, he loses the psychological depth of the characters and — with the omission of Anton's oath — the single most important motivation for the unfolding of the plot. However, Kroetz's cynical portrayal of provincial mores, when seen against the model of nineteenth-century society, throws into question the notion of progress. And then again, if we work backwards from reworking to model, and apply Kroetz's subtitles to Hebbel's tragedy, something easily done because of the close correspondence between model and reworking, the absurdity of nineteenth-century social conventions, which ultimately drive the individual into utter isolation and death, are highlighted. Thus, Kroetz's *Maria Magdalena* can be described as an "ironic reproduction" of Hebbel's nineteenth-century tragedy that reflects on the social changes that have taken place during the last hundred years, and that likewise demonstrates the changes of attitude that have *not* taken place.

3: Fragmentation:
Thomas Mann's *Der Tod in Venedig* and Wolfgang Koeppen's *Der Tod in Rom*

> *Der Tod in Rom* works as a myth much
> better than as an agglomeration of allusions.
> *Michael Hoffmann*

Criticism and Commentary

IN HIS ESSAY ON *Die Wahlverwandtschaften* (1925), Walter Benjamin makes the distinction between literary criticism and commentary, a distinction between the depiction of lasting truths in a literary work on the one hand, and the presentation of a particular (historical) situation on the other.

> Die Kritik sucht den Wahrheitsgehalt eines Kunstwerks, der Kommentar seinen Sachgehalt. Das Verhältnis der beiden bestimmt jenes Grundgesetz des Schrifttums, demzufolge der Wahrheitsgehalt eines Werkes, je bedeutender es ist, desto unscheinbarer und inniger an seinen Sachgehalt gebunden ist.[1]

Benjamin's line of thought continues with the argument that only over time, when the world portrayed has become unfamiliar and removed from our immediate experience of reality, does it become possible to perceive the universal truths that were previously inseparable from the material content of the novel.

> Dem Dichter wie dem Publikum seiner Zeit wird sich zwar nicht das Dasein, wohl aber die Bedeutung der Realien im Werke zumeist verbergen. Weil aber nur von ihrem Grunde das Ewige des Werkes sich abhebt, umfaßt jede zeitgenössische Kritik, so hoch sie auch stehen mag, in ihm mehr die bewegende als die ruhende Wahrheit, mehr das zeitliche Wirken als das ewige Sein. (126)

Thomas Mann's *Der Tod in Venedig* (1912)[2] and Wolfgang Koeppen's *Der Tod in Rom* (1954)[3] is the only combination of model and reworking in the context of this study in which both works were written in the twentieth century. A mere forty-two years separate the publication of the two narratives. Yet the social and political changes of the twentieth century were so enormous that, even though Mann was only thirty years older than Koeppen, they each represent a different age, and their respective narratives are set in different worlds. Thomas Mann can be seen as personifying the last of the nineteenth-century *Bürger*. *Der Tod in Venedig* became a "classic" even during his lifetime, and the society portrayed in the novella, the leisurely, secure world of near-silent hotels, guests sipping pomegranate juice on the veranda, undisturbed by worldly concerns, the laughter and games of children on nonpolluted beaches, unaware of impending disaster, were swept away forever in the turmoil of the Great War. In contrast, Koeppen's representation of German society in the early 1950s shows a world struggling for a new identity, which is threatened by the shadows of the past and paralyzed by the melancholy of the present; the future holds no hope. The novel suffered a correspondingly hostile reception. The aesthetic merits of the text might have been appreciated by a few, but the content was utterly rejected, and is described by Marcel Reich-Ranicki as "*Zerrspiegel* der deutschen Wirklichkeit."[4]

From the perspective of the twenty-first century, postwar Germany — a country struggling for a new identity, undergoing the process of denazification, attempting to define new values and ideals, and rebuilding destroyed cities — has also truly passed. Given the passage of time, it is much easier for the reader of the present day to confront the uncomfortable truths contained in *Der Tod in Rom* than it would have been for Koeppen's contemporaries, who felt paralyzed by the harsh judgment of German postwar society suggested in the novel, or indeed who judged it to be a "peinliche Störung bei der Bewältigung der Vergangenheit durch Vergessen und Verdrängen."[5] Times have changed. It may be that not many years have passed, it may be that our present contemplation of the past, our current set of values are no more lasting than those of the 1950s, but they are certainly different. Only from this distance in time, so Benjamin argues, can the critic ask the questions essential to recognizing the truth content of the literary work. We can ask with Benjamin, "ob der Schein des Wahrheitsgehaltes [truth content] dem Sachgehalt [material content] oder das Leben des Sachgehaltes dem Wahrheitsgehalt zu verdanken sei" (125). *Der Tod in Venedig* and *Der Tod in Rom* draw two utterly opposing portraits of the human condition: Thomas Mann offers a refined and aesthetic view of life, in which unpleasant truths and fundamental human desires can apparently be almost completely suppressed and denied, while Koeppen insists on a bleak outlook into a world in which we are solely confronted with our own human weaknesses and shortcomings. By allowing the model and the reworking to enter into a dialogue, we can look for the truth content of these two texts in the syntheses that may arise from the differing vantage points. This particular example of model and reworking demonstrates that in our question of what constitutes a creative literary reworking, the prominent parallels and contrasts that exist between the two works on a factual level are less important than the dynamic processes that arise from the discourse between them. Having said that, it should be emphasized again that, just as the discussion of each literary model is limited in this study to the features relevant to the reworking, to understand a work as a reworking should be *additional* to any interpretations of the work itself, should be an enrichment of the understanding, and should never act as a restriction to the appreciation of the literary descendant. Reworkings must also be treated on their own merit; appraising them is not the same as source hunting. This position is also the starting point of Thomas Richner's psychoanalytical analysis of Koeppen's *Der Tod in Rom*[6] in which Richner warns of the danger of seeing Koeppen's work solely in terms of Mann. He argues that in spite of the deliberate references to Mann's novella, *Der Tod in Rom* rightly deserves to be regarded as quite independent of *Der Tod in Venedig*. In this way, the relationship between Koeppen's and Mann's texts is fundamentally different compared to that of Kroetz's and Hebbel's *Maria Magdalena* plays.

Der Tod in Venedig — Complexity and Unity

The title of Koeppen's novel, *Der Tod in Rom*, establishes the first deliberate link to *Der Tod in Venedig*. If that were not enough, Koeppen's novel is preceded by two mottoes, the first of which roots the text, via Dante, in the very creation of man: "il mal seme d'Adamo." The second motto, the final sentence of Mann's novella, "Und noch desselben Tages empfing eine respektvoll erschütterte Welt die Nachricht von seinem Tode" (*TV*, 525), serves as a reminder that death is part of the very condition of life. The explicit reference to Mann is amplified, and at the same time contrasted, by the last sentence of *Der Tod in Rom*, which echoes the sentiment, but contradicts the message of the model: "Die Zeitungen meldeten noch am Abend Judejahns Tod, der durch die Umstände eine Weltnachricht geworden war, die aber niemand erschütterte" (*TR*, 187).

These very obvious devices encourage the reader who is familiar with *Der Tod in Venedig* to search for further correspondences between the two works, and at the same time they offer a challenge, namely, to think ahead and look out for the way in which certain key events and themes from the model may be presented in the reworking. The effect of recognizing certain motifs, which Koeppen takes from Mann and reintroduces in a new, alienated context, adds enjoyment to the reading process, and a new dimension to the text itself. Koeppen not only takes up key themes from *Der Tod in Venedig*, but by its very contrast, the narrative framework and the structure of *Der Tod in Rom* can itself be understood as a rejection of Mann's refined aestheticism. Koeppen's novel constitutes a radical attack on any form of beautifying refinement based on the historical experience of two world wars and National Socialism. According to Oliver Herwig, Koeppen's particular brand of realism is permeated by a deep cultural pessimism, which views history as an eternal cycle of abuse of power and the rule of terror.[7]

Mann's novella and Koeppen's novel present us with two very different points of view as to what the human being might be, and can possibly attain. Furthermore, there are no parallels in the number of characters, the time span, any personal development, or even the narrative style. But contrasts can be just as effective as parallels to establish links between reworking and model. The central protagonist of *Der Tod in Venedig* is Gustav Aschenbach, a successful but burned-out, middle-aged writer who travels to Italy in order to recuperate. For the first time in his life he ignores the call of duty and his almost complete self-discipline, and recklessly follows his inclination wherever it takes him. Or is it his fate that finally catches up with him? Eventually, Aschenbach ends up in Venice, and falls heedlessly in love with what is described in the text as beauty incarnate, "das Schöne selbst" (*TV*, 490) in the shape of a fourteen-year old Polish boy on a bathing holiday on the Lido. The city is in the grip of a cholera epidemic, and, not heeding the ominous warnings about the spreading disease because of his love for the boy, Aschenbach falls victim to the fever and dies.

The novella, ambiguous and multi-layered, full of references to the classical past, is constructed so tightly and skillfully that it has often been interpreted as the artist's quest for beauty and perfection in a purely abstract and metaphorical sense, describing an inner process rather than an external plot, which traces the pederastic and homoerotic desires of a middle-aged man. In mind and in spirit Aschenbach moves in the company of the Greek gods Apollo and Dionysos and the greatest of the Greek philosophers Plato, Socrates, and his lover Phaidros. Yet, it can be argued that aestheticizing the novella to such a degree distracts from the questionable subject matter, the infatuation of a mature man with a young boy. Victor Zmegac's delicate choice of language may serve as an example of this readiness of the readership to ignore the seedy side of the novella: "In Manns Erzählung gerät der Künstler insgeheim in einen Gegensatz zur Gesellschaft, wohlgemerkt nicht durch seine Kunst: der Zwiespalt beruht gerade auf einer Leidenschaft, die, *wie auch immer man die Dinge sehen mag*, eben der Sphäre der Natur zugehört" (162–63).[8]

The plot of *Der Tod in Rom* is far less straightforward. The narrative, which spans two days and nights in the Rome of the early 1950s, is a disjointed description of various meetings involving three families who are all connected by events in the past. Siegfried Pfaffrath, composer (and of similar pederastic tastes as Aschenbach) is in Rome to receive a prize for his music. He is sponsored by a renowned conductor, Kürenberg, who lives in exile with his Jewish wife Ilse. Unbeknown to Siegfried, his father, mother, brother Dieter, and aunt Eva Judejahn have come to Rome to prepare the secret return to Germany of his uncle, Gottlieb Judejahn, an escaped ex-SS officer who had been sentenced to death at the Nuremberg trials and is now living in exile in the Middle East. Apart from meeting up with his relatives, Judejahn has a second reason for having come to Rome: he is involved in an illegal arms deal. Judejahn's son Adolf, a novice in a holy order, is in Rome on a pilgrimage to redeem himself and his family. Old wounds and vulnerabilities are exposed once more, and the novel ends with Judejahn's murder of Ilse Kürenberg, soon followed by Judejahn's own death from a heart attack.

Representation of Venice and Rome

In spite of the title and the motto, there is little on the level of the plot or the character constellation to suggest that *Der Tod in Rom* be understood as a reworking of *Der Tod in Venedig*, although there are, in fact, a number of parallel incidents and motifs that tie the two works together. The first of these is the significance of the location, and the respective role the two Italian cities play in the structure of the two texts. From Goethe's *Italienische Reise* (1816/17) onwards Italy has had a specific meaning in German literature. It epitomizes a place of longing, where beauty and a sense of *joie de vivre* exist in perfect harmony, and where in spite of, or even because of its ancient culture, the German traveler seeks to renew his energies and to find the secret of eternal youth. Both Thomas Mann and Koeppen turn that notion on its head, and in both instances Italy has become a place of dying and decay. However, Venice and Rome signify very different symbolic values. Rome is eternal, whereas the very existence of Venice is fragile and transient. Rome stands for power, Venice stands for beauty and decay. Rome is universal and has always been a meeting point for people from all corners of the world; Venice infects everyone in her vicinity with her uniquely Italian dream of *dolce vita*. In addition, Venice acts as the external mirror of Aschenbach's inner landscape: both have seen times of grace and influence and have enjoyed the admiration of the world, both are riddled with decay and harbor a deadly secret. On arrival in Venice, the hitherto always correct, self-controlled Aschenbach is taken by surprise: "Eine abenteuerlich Freude, eine unglaubliche Heiterkeit erschütterte von innen fast krampfhaft seine Brust" (*TV*, 484).

Bernd Widdig distinguishes between Venice, which he describes merely as a symbolic backdrop to Aschenbach's final days, and Rome, which becomes an independent entity in Koeppen's novel.[9] Herwig contrasts the all-pervading atmosphere of decay in Venice with Rome as a modern metropolis and a place of untamed vitality by day and night, and concludes that the eternal city embodies Koeppen's pessimistic theories on history and society to the same degree that Venice provides an ideal if ambiguous backdrop to the complex and problematic nature of Aschenbach.[10] Again we have the contrast between Rome as an "embodiment" and Venice as a "backdrop" to the respective works. It is true that in these two works we come to know Rome better than Venice. But that difference does not mean that Venice is less important to Mann's text than Rome is to Koeppen's.

As is already indicated by the opening narratives, we are dealing with two very different narrative structures. *Der Tod in Venedig* opens with Aschenbach's name. The narrative focuses solely on Aschenbach, on the development of an individual. We are presented with an account of his inner and outer experiences. Aschenbach concentrates almost exclusively on Tadzio and his own obsession. Time is measured by encounters with the desired boy, the environment becomes real only in as far as it aids or hinders the observation of Tadzio's movements. And yet, Aschenbach's meandering through dark alleyways and along stinking canals are at the same time inner paths he must follow. The silent pestilence that spreads through the city also takes hold of Aschenbach's soul. Just as the Venetians deny and fear the presence of the disease, Aschenbach refuses to acknowledge the infatuation that increasingly permeates his whole existence. Aschenbach's death proceeds as much from the malaise that holds the city in its grip as from the disintegration of his inner being. The open beach, the threshold between land and sea, where Aschenbach has experienced his most peaceful hours in the observation of Tadzio, becomes at the same time the threshold between life and death, when Aschenbach sets out on that final journey. Outer and inner world, the city and the soul, become a unified whole, both carrying the seeds of their own destruction.

By contrast, the opening section of *Der Tod in Rom* describes Rome in its historical-mythological context. Koeppen does not tell us the story of an individual. The central protagonist is replaced by a number of persons all bound together by a common history. For some of them that is the very reason they want to declare their separateness. Rome treats all its subjects with equal indifference, from the perspective of eternity, as it were. At the same time Rome is the one unifying element that affects all of the protagonists. The randomness of characters is also reflected in the narrative structure. The novel is written in loosely connected longer or shorter sections, falling into two chapters covering two days and nights. The narrative focus constantly shifts from one protagonist onto another, only occasionally singling out Siegfried as a first-person narrator. Thus, the nameless faces of Rome are at times given a similar status to those of the named protagonists. We meet young and old women going about their daily chores, we meet ordinary Romans in cafes and thugs on the streets. We even meet some of Rome's countless stray cats (*TR,* 10–11). When taking the different narrative approaches adopted by Thomas Mann and by Wolfgang Koeppen into consideration, Venice is as closely tied to Aschenbach as an individual as Rome arises as a distinct entity in the cross-section of human history we encounter in *Der Tod in Rom*. The inversion of Italy as a signifier of a land of harmony and beauty to a place of decay and corruption as represented by the two cities is further emphasized by the development of character, the single figure of Aschenbach on the one hand, and the extended family of the Pfaffraths/Judejahns on the other.

Aschenbach and the Stranger

Only three protagonists in *Der Tod in Venedig* are given names: Aschenbach, Tadzio, and Tadzio's dark double, Jaschu. Everyone else is described either by their function or by the relationship in which they stand to Aschenbach or Tadzio: the hotel manager, the governess, a clerk of the English travel agency, and so on. The narrator, who describes and comments critically on the events of the novella, speaks exclusively from Aschenbach's perspective, and this device serves to emphasize Aschenbach's almost complete isolation from his surroundings. Aschenbach never gets close enough to other people to learn their names. Even with Tadzio, who occupies his whole heart and mind, he never enters into a conversation. This depersonalization of character is further emphasized by the narrator who, as the novella unfolds and Aschenbach increasingly becomes the victim of his obsession, begins to distance himself from his protagonist and turns ever more judgmental in his attitude.[11] Aschenbach's name is gradually replaced with adjectival nouns such as "der Enthusiasmierte" (*TV*, 491), "der Verwirrte" (*TV*, 503), "der Einsame" (*TV*, 509, 514), "der Starrsinnige" (*TV*, 511), "der Betörte" (*TV*, 504), or "der Schauende" (*TV*, 524). All these allegorical descriptions refer to the single figure of Aschenbach.

On four occasions Aschenbach has unexplained encounters with mysterious strangers who are wholly unconnected to him or to one another. These chance meetings have a surprisingly strong effect on Aschenbach, even causing an altered state of consciousness. The strong impression left by these characters, who are not only strangers to Aschenbach but also seem foreign in whatever location the encounter takes place, merges the four separate men into an archetypal stranger who has two distinct functions: he acts as a warning to Aschenbach, and at the same time he sends the aging adventurer off to meet his fate.

In the first chapter, Aschenbach sees a stranger on the steps of a mortuary chapel, whose appearance suggests an exotic foreigner and widely traveled wayfarer. He has reddish hair, his nose is curiously flat, he wears a yellowish suit (*TV*, 445)[12] and sports a straight-rimmed straw hat (*TV*, 445). Aschenbach stares at the stranger, and "eine seltsame Ausweitung seines Innern ward ihm ganz überraschend bewußt" (*TV*, 446). Suddenly he has the impulse to travel. The false youth in chapter three, who so shocks Aschenbach on the boat from Pola to Venice, foreshadows Aschenbach's own foolish attempts to recapture his lost youth in order to get closer to the beloved. He too wears a bright yellow summer suit and a Panama hat with a cockily turned-up brim (*TV*, 459). The ghastly old impostor even exhorts Aschenbach to remember him, continuing: "Unsere Komplimente, dem Liebchen, dem allerliebsten, dem schönsten Liebchen . . ." (*TV*, 463). The prophetic nature of the exchange is emphasized by its being narrated in direct speech, which is used only sparingly in the whole of the narrative. Again, this meeting has a striking effect on Aschenbach: "Ihm war, als lasse nicht alles sich ganz gewöhnlich an, als beginne eine träumerische Entfremdung, eine Entstellung der Welt ins Sonderbare um sich zu greifen" (*TV*, 460).

If the false youth was an object of ridicule and disgust to Aschenbach, the encounter with the gondolier who takes Aschenbach to the Lido has far more sinister undertones. He, too, appears in yellow and wears a straw hat, has a short nose, and, like the traveler in Munich, seems foreign, and not of Italian ancestry (*TV*, 465). When the will of the gondolier opposes that of Aschenbach, Aschenbach soon gives in with uncharacteristic lethargy. "Was war zu tun? Allein auf der Flut mit dem sonderbar unbotmäßigen, unheimlich entschlossenen Menschen, sah der Reisende kein Mittel, seinen Willen durchzusetzen. Wie weich er übrigens ruhen durfte, wenn er sich nicht empörte!" (*TV*, 466). Once more Aschenbach is transposed into a dreamlike state by the presence of the one who comes in many guises. When Aschenbach wants to settle with him, the gondolier has vanished without trace. Both the false youth and the gondolier herald Aschenbach's and Tadzio's future roles respectively. The way in which the false youth rehearses Aschenbach's attempted transformation under the hands of the make-up artist has already been mentioned. The gondolier, on the other hand, is the one who is explicitly described as the messenger of death. As it turns out, eventually it is Tadzio himself, the pale and charming psychagog, who beckons Aschenbach across the final threshold (*TV*, 525).

Finally in chapter five, we meet a somewhat threatening street musician, snub-nosed and with reddish eyebrows (*TV*, 508), who comes to entertain the guests in the hotel. This time, it is Aschenbach himself who initiates a conversation. He is told what he wants to hear: there is no threat of the fever in Venice. This reassurance is immediately followed by a song of mocking laughter, which spreads hysteria to the whole assembled company with the exception of Aschenbach, who, it seems, is once more in a state of trance.

> Aschenbach ruhte nicht mehr im Stuhl, er saß aufgerichtet wie zum Versuch der Abwehr oder Flucht. Aber das Gelächter, der heraufwehende Hospitalgeruch und die Nähe des Schönen verwoben sich ihm zu einem Traumbann, der unzerreißbar und unentrinnbar sein Haupt, seinen Sinn umfangen hielt. (*TV*, 510)

Invariably these characters, all with a stubby nose, reddish hair, and foreign demeanors, are described as being strangers in their surroundings. Does the dreamlike state they inflict on Aschenbach foreshadow the appearance of *der fremde Gott* (*TV*, 516) of Dionysos, to whom Aschenbach finally falls victim? T. J. Reed suggests: "Die Figur ist überall fremd, was den Begriff des in Aschenbachs Traum gefeierten fremden Gottes vorbereitet."[13] And Matthias Hurst adds: "Diese unheimlichen Begegnungen also werden zu Konfrontationen mit der mythologischen Figur des *Hermes Psychopompos,* des Verkünders des Todes und Begleiters der Seelen in die Unterwelt."[14]

On one level, the meetings with the four strangers are just as incidental to Aschenbach as are those with the hotel manager or the representative at the railway station. Yet, the inner links in the description of these characters, and the effect they have on Aschenbach's consciousness, a device that contributes considerably to lifting the whole narrative into the mythical realm of fate and lending it a sense of inevitability, unify these apparently unconnected appearances. In the traveler, the false youth, the gondolier, and the street musician, Aschenbach is confronted with an eternal mythical stranger who points him on to a course leading ultimately to his death. From four independent characters Thomas Mann has created one unified symbolic figure. The meetings with the strangers are strategically placed in the narrative framework of the novella, which is divided into five chapters. The encounters with the traveler in Munich and the street musician take place in chapters one and five respectively. The false youth and the gondolier both appear in the third chapter. The remaining chapters are free of the shadowy presence of the mythical figure: chapter two is wholly devoted to Aschenbach's character and his past, while chapter four describes the earlier stages of his growing obsession with Tadzio.

Der Tod in Rom — Fragmentation of Character

Different critics have different views as to who the main protagonist of Koeppen's novel might be, but this question will become irrelevant to the present discussion. Koeppen's shifting narrative style represents an attempt of a single author to speak with a multiple voice, a device which, as early 1907, has been described by Sigmund Freud as the hallmark of the modern psychological novel:

> Der psychologische Roman verdankt im ganzen wohl seine Besonderheit der Neigung des modernen Dichters, sein Ich durch Selbstbeobachtung in Partial-Ichs zu zerspalten und demzufolge die Konfliktströmungen seines Seelenlebens in mehreren Helden zu personifizieren.[15]

Leaving aside the psyche of the author and the inner connection between the artist and his creations, we can take up this idea and apply it to examine several of Koeppen's characters as part-representatives of

Aschenbach and also of Tadzio. Widdig suggests that Koeppen's characters are intended as purely allegorical, that is, not as characters with psychological depth but merely assembled in order to stand for certain principles. He argues that this allegorical interpretation of the characters allows Koeppen to protect his narrative from being understood merely as a contemporary comment, particularly on the horrors of National Socialism and its aftermath, by lifting the novel into the realm of general truths and de-historicized conflict. Allegorical representation of a principle or an idea can be achieved by breaking up the complex psyche of an individual human being into more or less stereotypical fragments. In this way, the figure of Aschenbach returns in Koeppen's novel in the form of various literary descendents. Where Mann creates a single mythical figure from four independent characters, Koeppen reverses this process and endows several of the male protagonists of his novel with attributes and characteristics of the single figure of Aschenbach. Like others among Mann's central protagonists, and indeed like Mann himself, Aschenbach lives in a constant inner tension between what he perceives as two conflicting principles: the world of the artist and that of the *Bürger* — overflowing and chaotic creativity *vis à vis* form, order and stability. Koeppen's characters can be designated as belonging to one or the other side of this human divide, but throughout the novel, the representation of the artist and of the *Bürger* is given in extremely negative terms.

The link between Siegfried and Aschenbach is easy to see. Like Aschenbach, Siegfried is an artist. He also shares Aschenbach's hidden homoerotic preferences. But whereas Aschenbach denies this, even to himself, Siegfried indulges in it, albeit in the face of his own self-disgust. Thus, Koeppen's initial attack of Mann's supreme aestheticism is on the level of a brutal and demystifying representation of reality as he sees it. But what about Judejahn, Kürenberg, and Adolf as possible representatives of Aschenbach in *Der Tod in Rom*? After all it is Judejahn, and not Siegfried, who dies in Rome, and thus becomes the title figure of the novel. Kürenberg, on the other hand, is a more refined and established artist than Siegfried, and therefore closer to Aschenbach in age and in renown. Adolf, the priest, is called upon to represent and foster the moral principles of society, a role, which Aschenbach had claimed for himself during much of his career. Clearly more than one candidate would qualify as a literary descendant of Aschenbach in the reworking. Among critics there is no consensus as to which of Koeppen's characters is most closely modeled on Aschenbach. Widdig focuses on the inference of the title and the parallels in the last sentence of the respective texts, and argues that Aschenbach, while he is replaced by Judejahn, at the same time has obvious and numerous connections with Siegfried. And he describes Siegfried and Judejahn as being as closely connected as a perpetrator and his victim. Widdig attempts to trace the process of historical and cultural evolution from Aschenbach and his era to its inevitable conclusion in Koeppen's world, which he summarizes thus:

> Es scheint fast, als könne man aus dieser Verdopplung eine Genealogie der Moderne herauslesen. Am Anfang steht Gustav Aschenbach, der sterbende Vertreter der bürgerlichen Kultur gegen Ende des neunzehnten Jahrhunderts. Sein Erbe verdoppelt sich: Der eine Strang führt in die Avantgarde der Zwölftonmusik, der andere in den Faschismus. (165)

The character of Judejahn is not only an allegory of Fascism and ultimately of death, but he also represents the worst possible caricature of the *Bürger,* while Siegfried is allocated the role of the homosexual artist. Widdig is not the only critic to comment on this fragmentation of the figure of Aschenbach. Also referring to Siegfried and Judejahn, John Pizer claims that "this is not the first time Koeppen took Thomas Mann's portrayal of Aschenbach and divided it between two characters."[16]

Siegfried, the artist, and Adolf, the voice of conscience, comprise a further fragmentation of character. Richner draws particular attention to Adolf, whom he sees as Siegfried's alter ego, and who, according to Richner, even replaces Siegfried as the main protagonist in the novel.[17] Then again, the very contrast between Adolf and his father Judejahn is indicative of the polarity that ties these two together.[18] In relation to Aschenbach as a possible predecessor of the male characters of Koeppen's *Der Tod in Rom,* Siegfried and Adolf, Judejahn, and even Siegfried's father Pfaffrath, are so closely linked with one another, that at times the boundaries between them become blurred.

The Artist

Siegfried comes closest to being Koeppen's main protagonist. He is the first character who is introduced, and more is disclosed about him than about anyone else. The narrational point of view, limited to one person at a time, moves from character to character, and on occasion changes from a third-person to a first-person perspective, though only in the case of Siegfried. Siegfried is Aschenbach's descendant as a creative artist, but his art is the very opposite of Aschenbach's quest for harmony and the perfection of form. Siegfried's music is judged by

Ilse Kürenberg to be full of "Dissonanzen, einander feindliche unharmonische Klänge, ein Suchen ohne Ziel, ein unbeharrliches Experiment" (*TR*, 16). As a person Siegfried is riddled by self-doubt, and his view of the world is deeply skeptical. Even when we first meet him, Siegfried's music seems to him as flawed as his own appearance. Siegfried's choice of words, describing his reaction to his own music, conjures up the deceptive and illusionary appearance of the false youth, "der greise Geck" (*TV*, 461), whom Aschenbach meets on the deck of the ferry to Venice:

> Falsch klang die Musik, sie bewegte ihn nicht mehr, fast war sie ihm unsympathisch wie die eigene Stimme, die man, auf ein Tonband gefangen, zum erstenmal aus dem Lautsprecher hört und denkt, das bin nun ich, dieser aufgeblasene Geck, dieser Lügner, Gleisner und eitle Fant. (*TR*, 7–8)

Under the shadow of a traumatic childhood, dominated by the tough regime of Nazi ideology for the upbringing of promising young boys, Siegfried lives in a state of permanent discontent. His capacity for love and happiness seem destroyed forever. At the same time, just like Aschenbach before him, Siegfried strives for artistic perfection and beauty both in his art and in his hesitant approach to other human beings. Just like Aschenbach, the dedication to the purely abstract pursuit of his work suddenly changes into erotic cravings when he is presented with a suitable object of desire. But whereas the conventional and conservative Aschenbach experiences scenes of unfettered copulation (*TV*, 517) merely in his Dionysian nightmare, Siegfried's sexual encounters are real, ugly, and demeaning. Dietrich Erlach takes this argument one step further and suggests that, in contrast to Aschenbach's pederastic inclination, which can be seen as a symbol for the moral danger of the artist figure as such, the motivation for Siegfried's depravity is psychological, and can be understood in terms of the childhood spent in the Spartan environment of the Nazi boarding school.[19]

On perceiving Tadzio's double, a perfectly beautiful youth on the banks of the Tiber, Siegfried's heart is initially filled with reverential joy, with "Wehmut aus Glück und Trauer und glücklich traurige Einsamkeit" (*TR*, 118). Reality soon shatters this nostalgia when the fleeting vision of the boy is replaced by the real figure of an ugly and streetwise rent boy with whom Siegfried engages in a shameful sexual act. Siegfried's tender emotions turn to self-hatred and disgust. "Ich haßte mich. Der Ekel war mit mir allein in der Zelle. . . . Es war Lust und Vergangenheit, die ich empfand, es war Erinnerung und Schmerz, und ich haßte mich" (*TR*, 118). Aschenbach can lose himself in the intoxicating presence of his beloved, but Siegfried is cheated out of his one fleeting encounter with beauty when the reality of his homoerotic desires presents him with an unattractive urchin. While Aschenbach never gets as far as that sexually, he is also spared these bouts of extreme self-hatred. Aschenbach's mythical quest for perfect beauty keeps him firmly entrapped in self-delusion. At his lowest point — Aschenbach is lost in a filthy Venetian backyard, near physical collapse, his made-up face disintegrating into a horrid mask — any comment on the part of the narrator is ironic but restrained, merely hinting at the depth of degradation to which the venerable artist has sunk:

> Er saß dort, der Meister, der würdig gewordene Künstler, . . . Überwinder seines Wissens und aller Ironie entwachsen, . . . dessen Ruhm amtlich, dessen Name geadelt war und an dessen Stil die Knaben sich zu bilden angehalten wurden, — er saß dort, seine Lider waren geschlossen, nur zuweilen glitt, rasch sich wieder verbergend, ein spöttischer und betretener Blick seitlich darunter hervor. (*TV*, 521)

The narrator will not commit himself to elaborate on Aschenbach's self-esteem. Even in the face of death, Aschenbach is still not clear about the reality of his situation. The narrator describes Aschenbach laboring under feelings of "Auswegs- und Aussichtslosigkeit, von dem nicht klar wurde, ob es sich auf die äußere Welt oder auf seine eigene Existenz bezog" (*TV*, 522–23).

Koeppen utterly rejects this aestheticized self-delusion. In 1980, almost thirty years after writing *Der Tod in Rom*, Koeppen still proclaims his disgust of such willful blindness with great passion. He condemns Mann's novella and demands more realism: "Kein Platon, kein Streben nach der Welt der Idee, kein Phaidros mehr. Realität!"[20] His own protagonist, Siegfried, has to live out the morbid side of Aschenbach's passions to the full. Unlike Aschenbach's lofty communion with the gods and Greek philosophers, the focus of Siegfried's life is on the mean and ugly realities of the world. Only once does he let his fancy take him into the realm of Aschenbach: like his predecessor he visits the barber, not in order to regain lost youth (he is still young himself) but from mere boredom. Yet, under the treatment of skilful hands, he begins to dream of a previous era: "Ich war Petronius, der Dichter, und ich sprach im öffentlichen Bad mit Weisen und mit Knaben, wir lagen auf Marmorstufen in der Dampfkammer und sprachen über die Unsterblichkeit der Seele" (*TR*, 174).

Siegfried is destined for loneliness. Whereas Aschenbach's self-inflicted isolation stems largely from a feeling of moral superiority, it is

Siegfried's low self-esteem and deep-seated world-weariness that are the cause of his solitude. Kürenberg encourages him to turn this isolation into a source of inspiration: "Um Gottes willen — kein Leben für die Kunst! Gehen Sie auf die Straße. Lauschen Sie dem Tag! Aber bleiben Sie einsam! Sie haben das Glück, einsam zu sein" (*TR*, 52).[21] Siegfried uses his outsider status almost exclusively to listen to the voices of misery and suffering (*TR*, 52). Any love he expresses is for abstract ideas, never for a particular person. In a passionate "ode to Rome" Siegfried professes his love for the city, for her buildings, for her history but the inhabitants remain impersonal and Siegfried himself has no part in their existence:

> Aber noch mehr liebe ich Rom, wie es lebt, . . . ich liebe das Volk am Abend vor den Haustüren, . . . ich liebe die Kinder auf dem Brunnenrand aus Marmelstein, . . . ich liebe das Drängen, Reiben, Stoßen, Schreien, Lachen und die Blicke auf dem Corso und die obszönen Worte. (*TR*, 48–49)

Herwig argues that Siegfried's pederasty is a reaction to a childhood regime obsessed with power and domination of others, and that, as a result of this early abuse, his homosexuality expresses a refusal to engage in any relationship that might result in producing a child.[22] In contrast to Aschenbach, who is respectably widowed and father of a distant daughter, Siegfried will die without founding a family. We are told: "Der Gedanke, ein Leben zu verursachen . . . entsetzte ihn wahrhaft und verdarb ihm den Umgang mit Mädchen" (*TR*, 160). His brother, the opportunist Dieter, on the other hand, who has his public career already mapped out, will doubtlessly have children and continue the succession — thus perpetuating the shallow and self-centered society of Koeppen's postwar Germany, which has already forgotten the horrors of the past. But it is not only Siegfried who has this deeply pessimistic and melancholy view of life. In fact, the novel is permeated by despondency. Siegfried's sole glimmer of hope is the faint possibility of a new start in Africa. But then again, this is precisely what Judejahn had tried to do, only to return to Europe, and die in the very city that had witnessed his greatest triumph.

Kürenberg, the conductor, is not a major character in the novel, but there are some important parallels with Aschenbach. He is an established, successful artist, much of the same age as Aschenbach. Being possessed with a similar temperament and education as Aschenbach but without any suggestion of homosexuality, Kürenberg proves to be a caring mentor of the younger colleague. He is described as a spiritual person who is self-reliant, always in control of his feelings, never showing impatience or disdain. His life is solely focused on his art and his wife Ilse (*TR*, 18). Ripe strawberries, symbols initially suggesting the first signs of sweet indulgence on the part of Aschenbach (*TV*, 477), but later described as overripe and associated with cholera and the spread of the deadly disease (*TV*, 520), are enjoyed by the Kürenbergs in the form of "wollüstige rote Riesenerdbeeren" (*TR*, 18), and become an image for their satisfying sexual fulfillment. Theirs is the only harmonious and unselfish love between two people described in either work. "Sie waren *der* Mensch" (*TR*, 43, my emphasis). This *ecce homo* motif finds its terrible inversion in references to Judejahn. All other mention of "der Mensch" allude to the *Unmensch* Judejahn ("Judejahn als Mensch unter Menschen," *TR*, 33, 56, 57). Ultimately, a love like that of the Kürenbergs has no place in Koeppen's world. The price they have to pay for this unusual bond is a rootless, wandering existence, and eventually the union is broken by the pointless murder of Ilse Kürenberg.

The Bürger

Mann's title "Der Tod in Venedig" refers both to the cholera epidemic claiming hundreds of lives in the city, and to the moral decline and eventual death of an individual staying there. "Der Tod in Rom," on the other hand, alludes to the all-pervading presence of death, particularly in a city with a history like Rome, "auf Erschlagenen aufgebaut" (*TR*, 155), which has been a seat of secular and religious power and influence over the last twenty-five hundred years. Here, both Ilse, of Jewish extraction, and Judejahn, Nazi-officer incarnate, suffer a sudden and violent death. At the same time death is personified, even allegorized, in the character of Judejahn himself, of whom it is said: "er selber war ein Tod, ein brutaler, ein gemeiner, ein plumper und einfallsloser Tod" (*TR*, 15).

Gottlieb Judejahn is driven by a deep-seated inferiority complex, which started developing with the contempt shown him by his father. The older Judejahn, an overbearing and tyrannical primary teacher, was of a generation that might even have taught from Aschenbach's improving books. The scorn shown by his father drives Judejahn to hate and subordinate what he most fears, but cannot disassociate himself from: the better-off middle classes and the priesthood (*TR*, 54). In contrast to Siegfried, who remains permanently inhibited from reaching into the fullness of life, Judejahn, representing the worst perversion of the *Bürger,* leads a life that takes him from excess to excess. He is driven by the permanent fear of being found out as the miserable little Gottlieb he knows himself to be, "eine Null, die aufgeblasen wurde" (*TR*, 41). This weakness he hides in brutality and the fear he arouses in others.

Why then is Judejahn associated with the *Bürger* in Aschenbach, when neither his attitudes nor his career are in any way comparable to those of that worthy citizen? There are more textual links between Aschenbach and Judejahn than to any other of Koeppen's characters: Judejahn's car, "lackglänzend, schwarz, geräuschlosen Getriebes, ein funkelnder dunkler Sarg," with "schwellenden Polstern" (*TR*, 15), is the Roman equivalent to the Venetian gondola, "dieser sargschwarz lackierte, mattschwarz gepolsterte Armstuhl, der weichste üppigste, der erschlaffendste Sitz von der Welt" (*TV*, 464). Both Judejahn and Aschenbach think about leaving Italy and, had they done so, they would have escaped death. But both are too caught up in their respective passions to take this step.[23] Richner maintains that the motifs of intoxication followed by a sudden onset of weakness serve as a forewarning of the approaching death of Aschenbach as well as that of Judejahn.[24] Pizer examines Aschenbach's motto "Durchhalten" and describes it as "a characteristic common to both: their will to persevere."[25] Herwig points to a connection between Judejahn's exotic and foreign looking appearance, and the various descriptions of Thomas Mann's symbolic messenger of death.[26]

Aschenbach merely dreams of lewdness and the frenzy of surrender (*TV*, 517); nevertheless, these dreams "ließen seine Existenz, ließen die Kultur seines Lebens verheert, vernichtet zurück" (*TV*, 516). Judejahn, on the other hand, lives these orgies whenever the opportunity arises: "er wollte fressen, saufen, huren, er hatte Lust dazu, Unruhe zwickte seine Hoden, warum nahm er sich nicht, was er haben wollte?" (*TR*, 66). Once more, Thomas Mann's Apollonian/Dionysian symbolism, which remains only fantasy in the mind of Aschenbach, is actually lived by one of Koeppen's characters.

Like Siegfried in *his* sexual encounter, Judejahn realizes what is only a potential in Aschenbach's Bacchanalian dream by the near-rape of Laura and the murder of Ilse Kürenberg. Judejahn is a monster of destruction, but in the end he destroys himself without leaving any progeny. Eva, his wife, has become a living ghost, and his son, Adolf, will never provide him with any grandchildren. Even Judejahn's death, although newsworthy, "erschüttert niemand" (*TR*, 187). Although Judejahn is no direct descendant of Aschenbach, he is nevertheless tied very closely to Aschenbach on a textual level, and represents the modern bringer of death: common, brutal, and mindless, real and allegorical at the same time, all-powerful and yet constantly defeated.

Koeppen's portrait of ordinary German citizens, the "decent" *Bürger,* is almost as loathsome as that of Gottlieb and Eva Judejahn. The opportunism of the elder Pfaffrath and of Siegfried's brother, Dieter, adds to Koeppen's pessimistic picture of Germany's future. Are not the Pfaffraths of this world, the respectable and successful representatives of the *Bürgertum,* almost as dangerous as the Judejahns, because they will prevail? According to Richner, the terrifying caricature of the German *Bürgertum* in the shape of the Pfaffrath family, suggests that the roots of the dangerous nationalism, having resulted in the horrors the Third Reich, remain unaffected.[27] The dichotomy of the artist and the *Bürger,* which runs through all of Mann's work, finds its representation in various characters in *Der Tod in Rom.* Besides Siegfried as the artist and Judejahn as the one who dies, we should add the Pfaffraths, upright citizens and survivors, to the list of the true heirs of Aschenbach's nineteenth-century middle-class culture.

The Innocent

Aschenbach dies a peaceful death before the horrors of two world wars. His soul crosses the threshold to the "Verheißungsvoll-Ungeheure" (*TV,* 525) under the gentle guidance of his beloved. His reputation is preserved, the world is "erschüttert" (*TV,* 525). In his reworking, Koeppen utterly rejects Aschenbach's unique moral struggle, "ein Leben der Selbstüberwindung und des Trotzdem" (*TV,* 504). Are there then no redeeming features in Koeppen's novel?

The role allocated by Richner to Adolf as the alter ego of Siegfried allows us to include Adolf as one of the characters created from the fragments of Aschenbach's whole. In fact, of all of Koeppen's characters only Adolf, Judejahn's son and novice priest, attempts a life of renunciation, thereby laying himself open to the contempt of his whole family. Adolf is as deeply affected by a traumatic childhood as Siegfried is, but, unlike Siegfried, who withdraws into opposition and isolation, Adolf seeks to serve and redeem the world. He does so with great devotion. Yet, in an inner monologue Siegfried judges this as arising not from inner strength but from weakness:

> Du bist nicht berufen, und du weißt, daß Gott dich nicht gerufen hat; du warst frei, eine einzige Nacht lang bist du frei gewesen, eine Nacht im Wald, und dann ertrugst du die Freiheit nicht, du warst wie ein Hund, der seinen Herrn verloren hat, und du mußtest dir ei-

nen neuen Herrn suchen; da fand dich der Priester, und du bildest dir ein, Gott habe dich gefunden. (*TR,* 80)

In that same inner monologue Siegfried maintains that he is the one who is truly free (*TR,* 80). This is a statement at best open to debate and at worst a sign of gross self-delusion. But whereas the shifting narrative perspective gives the reader greater insight into Siegfried's thoughts and feelings, allowing for quite an intimate knowledge of his strengths and weaknesses, Adolf is given no such voice, and only rarely is the reader offered a glimpse into his soul. Regardless of the answer to the question whether Adolf's devotion is born out of weakness or strength, there can be no doubt as to Adolf's sincerity and deep sense of humility.

Siegfried's negative assessment of Adolf's motivation remains largely unchallenged by the text. In spite of his skepticism (or because of it?), Siegfried wants to make a match between Adolf and Laura. Apart from a beautiful boy, briefly glimpsed by Siegfried on the banks of the Tiber, Laura is the only character in the novel who can be seen as having some resemblance to Tadzio who so bewitches Aschenbach by "jenes, tiefe, bezaubernde, hingezogene Lächeln" (*TV,* 498). Surrounded largely by homosexual men, Laura is likewise renowned for her smile, "ihr liebliches Lächeln" (*TR,* 36), which is not only the hallmark of her good nature and artlessness, but it also has its commercial uses: she attracts customers. Beautiful, naive, but at the same time intuitively seductive, Laura possesses all the qualities that make Tadzio an object of desire. Siegfried's motive for introducing Laura to Adolf is a mixture of mischievousness and momentary kindliness. Laura is willing: "es freute sie, daß sie etwas zu verschenken hatte" (*TR,* 162). But as events unfold, it is not Adolf but Judejahn who takes advantage of that gift, and robs it of its innocence.

Adolf can be seen as a successor to Tadzio because he is pure and humble. Laura, on the other hand, shares with Tadzio that bewitching smile. And the appearance of the rent boy, representing the more mischievous side of Tadzio, is another instance in which the fantasy in *Der Tod in Venedig* is lived out in *Der Tod in Rom.* Once more, Koeppen's fragmentation of character and his disjointed narrative style, arranging unrelated parallel events side by side, highlights the underlying unity of the novel.

The Effect of the Reworking

Writing in essentially different eras, Thomas Mann and Wolfgang Koeppen started from very different positions, which are reflected in both content and form of the two texts. Dieter Kafiz provides us with good reasons why this is necessarily so: in the latter half of the twentieth century, writers and poets have lost their privileged position of the detached observer, which allowed them to create and direct the fictional world of their imagination, because that safe distance of uninvolved insight is no longer sustainable.

> Der Dichter steht nicht mehr außerhalb dieses Stromes, um ihn zu ordnen und zu gestalten, wie sich die traditionelle Dichterposition umschreiben ließe, sondern auch er ist ihm ausgesetzt. Die geschichtlichen Erfahrungen der Vergangenheit und die naturwissenschaftlich-technische Entwicklung der Neuzeit haben die Weisheit des Dichters in Frage gestellt.[28]

The guiding principle of *Der Tod in Venedig* appears to be perfection of form and harmony. In contrast, *Der Tod in Rom* is permeated by fragmentation and discordance. Aschenbach's journey follows a direct, almost necessary route to his eventual fate, while the characters of *Der Tod in Rom* could well fit the motto that Koeppen proclaimed for his own life: "mein Ziel war die Ziellosigkeit."[29] Yet, we have found significant thematic and structural connections between the two works: both deal with the problems of the artist in relation to society, with death and the destructive forces in life, and with homoeroticism and pederasty. Both works are inseparably interwoven with their respective settings, Venice and Rome, and the explicit link to the model in *Der Tod in Rom* serves to widen our understanding of the reworking predominantly by the fundamental contrasts in outlook between Thomas Mann's attempt to create harmony and Koeppen's inclination to fragment and show discordance in the world.

Koeppen's own reception of Mann's works was largely enthusiastic. In 1955, one year after the publication of *Der Tod in Rom,* he addresses Mann on the occasion of his eightieth birthday with unusual warmth: "Herzlich ergeben und wahrhaft begeistert möchte ich den Meister der Kunst und des Lebens ehren und preisen."[30] But Koeppen was to lose this enthusiasm. Twenty years later, in a short article, "Die Beschwörung der schweren Stunde," he writes: "Irgend ein Zugang, eine Leidenschaft, die mich hinreißt, fehlte und fehlt mir zu seinem Werk, das ich bewundere, ohne von ihm begeistert zu sein."[31] In the same article, he expresses his disappointment with Mann for not being radical enough in his criticism of society, and for the conformity of his conventional lifestyle.

> Der Verfasser denkt an eine Gesellschaft im konservativen Sinn der Zugehörigkeit zur guten Gesellschaft. Seine Menschen sind Leute,

die miteinander verkehren, die, selbst wenn sie sich nicht mögen, stolz sind, sich zu kennen, hineingeboren oder emporgekommen zu sein, dazuzugehören. (107)

These comments are, of course, just as revealing about Koeppen himself as they are a comment on Thomas Mann. In spite of Aschenbach's evoked presence in *Der Tod in Rom,* Koeppen was always conscious of the fundamental philosophical differences between himself and Mann. Aschenbach, and indeed Mann himself, see themselves on the fringes of society, artists who observe the world, but at the same time they long to be part of a group, and indeed *are* members of the society they describe and ironize. Subject and object overlap to a large degree. Koeppen's characters, on the other hand, are the genuine outsiders, and those who are closest to the author, Siegfried and Adolf, *do not want* to be integrated into their surroundings for reasons of their own. They seek the distance and endorse the differences that separate them from their social environment.

Both texts transcend their historical frameworks and give the topical content matter an archetypal-mythological slant. Where Mann created four independent characters in such a way that they seem to merge into one, Koeppen took the principle of narrative fragmentation so far that he created several independent characters as descendants of Aschenbach. *Der Tod in Rom* is in every respect an anti-work to *Der Tod in Venedig,* but by this very contrast, the reworking is firmly tied to the model. In spite of the differences in the plot, the contrast between a single focused narrative and a fragmented perspective, the lack of a main protagonist in the reworking, and the thematic divergence between love in *Der Tod in Venedig* and death in *Der Tod in Rom,* a number of key parallels and counterparts operate both in opposition to and as endorsement of the literary model. The search for an inner relationship to *Der Tod in Venedig* is initiated by Koeppen's explicit references to Thomas Mann's novella in the title, the motto, and the last sentence. As a result, the reader becomes aware of intertextual links and echoes between individual features of the two works, but aware also of the contrasts. Koeppen's fragmentation of the character of Aschenbach is likewise the overarching principle of Koeppen's segmented narrative style. All characters in Koeppen's novel bear the heavy burden of an individual and isolated fate, which is tightly interwoven with a violent and unredeemed human history that ultimately ends in destruction and death.

The process of reading *Der Tod in Rom* as a reworking of *Der Tod in Venedig,* and of thereby allowing the two texts to enter into a dialogue, enriches and widens the understanding of both. It not only lets us see Koeppen's characters in a less stereotypical light — Judejahn, the utterly evil Nazi, Siegfried, the homosexual artist, Adolf, the ascetic, inhibited and naive beyond belief — but as aspects of a greater whole. In turn, this treatment gives Aschenbach a less elevated status and forces us to remember that he, too, must be understood in a social context, that is, as a lonely, middle-aged man in pursuit of a growing boy.

Allusions to the Classical World

From the first encounter with the mysterious stranger who has such an unexpected effect on Aschenbach, the transparent language of *Der Tod in Venedig*, always pointing beyond itself, invites the reader to pay particular attention to a great number of mythological references. Aschenbach first notices the traveler as he stands on the steps of the mortuary chapel in Munich, surrounded by apocalyptic beasts, and this image triggers an immediate effect: Aschenbach, a man who lives by routine, becomes restless and finally diagnoses a whole range of unexpected feelings: "Es war Reiselust, nichts weiter; aber wahrhaft als Anfall auftretend und ins Leidenschaftliche, ja bis zur Sinnestäuschung gesteigert" (*TV*, 446–47). Although his impulse is initially tempered by reason and habit, overwhelming emotions soon send him on a journey of self-discovery.

There are frequent intertextual links with Homer, Plutarch, Erotikos, and above all with Plato. Most interpretations comment on the Apollonian and Dionysian elements in the language and construction of the novella.[32] Aschenbach is the very image of the *Bildungsbürger*. We know next to nothing of his emotional life before we meet him, a man in his fifties, but his thinking and his taste move along "classical" lines. He lives in an idealized world and seems not to recognize the mundane present of his surroundings when he sees it. At the first sighting of Tadzio, Aschenbach's hitherto well-trained mind wanders off. But his aesthetic musings could not be further from his true emotional state, and from what is about to happen to him:

> Müde und dennoch geistig bewegt, unterhielt er sich während der langwierigen Mahlzeit mit abstrakten, ja transzendenten Dingen, sann nach über die geheimnisvolle Verbindung, welche das Gesetzmäßige mit dem Individuellen eingehen müsse, damit menschliche Schönheit entstehe, kam von da aus auf allgemeine Probleme der Form und der Kunst. (*TV*, 472)

Has he ever looked at boys before? It seems not. The narrator would have us believe that all of Aschenbach's creative energy had gone into his work. But such an absolute repression of an emotional life cannot be sustained forever, and eventually the forces of life claim what is rightfully theirs. But even now, the narrator insists, it is the *educated artist* in Aschenbach who responds to Tadzio's beauty in terms of ancient Greek custom:

> In aufschwärmendem Entzücken glaubte er mit diesem Blick *das Schöne selbst* zu begreifen. . . . Das war der *Rausch;* und unbedenklich, ja gierig hieß der alternde Künstler ihn willkommen. Sein Geist kreiste, seine *Bildung* geriet ins Wallen, sein Gedächtnis warf uralte, seiner Jugend überlieferte und bis dahin niemals von eigenem Feuer belebte Gedanken auf. (*TV,* 490, my emphasis)

Modeling himself and Tadzio on the ancient Socrates and Phaidros, his pupil and lover, Aschenbach effectively silences his conscience and banishes all moral doubts a conventional middle-aged German living in the early twentieth century might have about fantasizing about a half-grown boy. Aschenbach is a visitor in a country that had by then itself become the embodiment of classical values to the educated German reader. Aschenbach's awakening takes place on the boundary between land and the sea, which connects Italy with ancient Greece. The Greco-Roman ideal of classical beauty and the timeless philosophical canon is ever present and alive, both in Aschenbach's mind and in the new environment.

In Koeppen's world, on the other hand, the gods are displaced and dying. *Der Tod in Rom* begins like a German fairy tale and immediately refers to classical myth: "*Es war einmal* eine Zeit, da hatten *Götter* in der Stadt gewohnt" (*TR,* 7, my emphasis). Then we move to the realm of the mortals and meet Rafael, the favorite offspring of Apollo. But the former gods themselves have learned to conform or else lead a miserable existence on the fringes of human society: "Die Meduse behält ihr Haupt und richtet sich bürgerlich ein. Und Jupiter? Weilt er, ein kleiner Pensionär, unter uns Sterblichen?. . . Oder haust er hinter Mauern am Stadtrand, in die Irrenanstalt gesperrt und von neugierigen Psychiatern analysiert?" (*TR,* 7). The opening section, which starts in a mythological, golden age, ends in the prosaic present in which the tourists are both onlookers and subject to the mythological and the historical forces that have molded the city. "Die Gesichter der Touristen sind in dem Licht des Pantheons wie ein Teig. Welcher Bäcker wird ihn kneten, welcher Ofen ihm Farbe geben?" (*TR,* 7). Indeed, what are the new forces which shape human destiny? Who are the present-day gods? The world Koeppen describes to us is devoid of all ambiguity or redeeming ideals. It shows the ugliness of human thought and deed in all its perversity. Nevertheless, the mythological subtext has the effect of giving the particular historical period in which the novel is set a greater, more timeless frame of reference. The discussion of the difficult and highly problematic postwar German society is thus dehistoricized and becomes a depiction of the eternal human condition.

Truth Content and Material Content

This raises the question of whether we should read the text as *Zeitgeschichte*, firmly tied to the political and historical period it is set in, or rather as an archetypal-mythological work. Initial reaction to the novel certainly reflects the former interpretation. Marcel Reich-Ranicki remembers that part of the press simply ignored the novel, whereas the rest understood it only in terms of a polemic against Fascism, neo-Fascism, and the economic miracle, with a highly unnecessary aggressive tone.[33] Over the decades this topical reception of the novel has given way to a more general reading. Walter Benjamin's *Sachgehalt*, the material content, has given way to the *Wahrheitsgehalt*, the truth content of the novel.

We also find different opinions as to how *realistically* the characters and the plot are presented by Koeppen. Kafitz argues that Koeppen's novel does not describe the world as it really is, but that the novel *is* reality in all its chaos and its dependence on chance. Therefore, he continues, the language used is not the guiding principle by which the world of the novel is arranged, but merely recreates the sounds of the world.[34] In contrast, Widdig reads the novel as an allegorical text. Rome represents human history and Judejahn becomes death personified. "Als allegorische Figur wird Judejahn im Laufe des Textes von der Stadt Rom einverleibt. Er findet sein Ende in den Ruinen des Thermenmuseums, ein weiterer Leichnam der Geschichte" (165). For Richner, Judejahn is himself partly human and partly mythical, the pathetic little Gottlieb who can be explained with the help of psychoanalysis and an incarnation of Hades, the god of the underworld himself.[35]

From these widely different interpretations as to the nature of the Koeppen's text, its degree of realism, and its construction of character, it becomes obvious that there are very different levels at which the text functions. In the context of this study, in which the focus rests on the links to *Der Tod in Venedig*, the specifics of time and place are transcended, and likewise give rise to a wider, more universal interpretation. This brings us back to Benjamin's observations on the relationship between the material content of a work of art, which is tied to the period of its creation, and the truth content, which emerges only over time. *Der Tod in Venedig* was originally received as a beautified quest for perfection in a world not yet ready to discuss the murky and physical aspects the novella raises. It was left to Koeppen in the 1950s to take issue with the whitewashed account of pederasty, and to highlight the misery of hidden and partly suppressed homosexuality, thus drawing attention to other aspects of the truth content of *Der Tod in Venedig*. *Der Tod in Rom*, on the other hand, which was received by its contemporary readers as merely topical, and uncomfortable at that, has transcended its material content and can now be read in more general terms, transcending the boundaries between specific historical periods. The truth between two opposing views, between thesis and antithesis, is usually found somewhere in the middle. The synthesis between the two extreme positions taken up in *Der Tod in Venedig* and *Der Tod in Rom* respectively appears when the two works are read in conjunction. Each one is modified and opens up hitherto hidden aspects of meaning.

In contrast to Kroetz's almost pedantically faithful reproduction of his chosen literary model, Koeppen merely hints at the connection between Thomas Mann's novella and his own novel *Der Tod in Rom*. In vain, we search for sustained parallels in the plot, the character constellations, or the language. Only when we look at the structural relationship between the two texts do we come upon the close affinity between *Der Tod in Venedig* and *Der Tod in Rom*. The overriding principle of the reworking is one of fragmentation and contradiction, the dissolution of character, of place, and even of the narrative stance itself. But when seen together, both texts are somewhat relativized and open up to new interpretations. Thomas Mann's myth of a perfect aesthetic victory over the grimness of death is shattered by the merciless portrayal of human suffering and, indeed, the brutal depiction of the death of Ilse and Judejahn. Koeppen's bleakness, on the other hand, is relieved by the clear allusions to *Der Tod in Venedig* which resonate with memories of idealist aspirations and the quest for beauty.

4: Integration: Georg Büchner's and Peter Schneider's *Lenz*

> Die Welt des tradierten Sinnes erschließt sich
> dem Interpreten nur in dem Maße, als sich
> dabei zugleich dessen eigene Welt aufklärt.
> *Jürgen Habermas*

The Subject

FEW WORKS IN GERMAN LITERATURE have had such an influence on generation after generation of readers and writers as Büchner's *Lenz* (1835).[1] The opening and the closing sentence of the novella have entered the common language and cause an immediate and persistent association with the plight of the protagonist. Lenz's flight into the mountains is associated with mental crisis and the journey becomes one of no return; thus "Durch's Gebirg gehen" renders the dark counterpart to the German Romantic love for walking in the mountains as a process of rejuvenation and finding communion with nature. The closing sentence, "So lebte er hin," provides the antithesis of the happily-ever-after and signifies the final breaking of the spirit, leading to an existence in which all hope is abandoned. Never before had the perspective of the disturbed person been related in quite such a way, that is, from the point of view of the sufferer. Büchner invented a new language, a new syntax, in which the voice of the narrator mingles with that of the suffering protagonist to the effect that the boundaries between inside and outside, between related speech and inner thoughts begin to merge. In his study of the same title, Roy Pascal describes that effect as "the dual voice."[2]

The influence of this particular text is proved not only by the continued fascination with the subject matter but also by a constant stream of writers imitating Büchner's style. In the context of the East German novel Dennis Tate particularly mentions five novels upon which Büchner's *Lenz* had "a crucial bearing."[3] The revival of Büchner's *Lenz* is not limited to the novel of the GDR, although it is, of course, particularly striking that the subject of mental crisis should have become so prominent in a socialist context. In fact, there has been a steady stream of works in the *Lenz* tradition almost since it was first published. In his book *Lenz — Erzählungen in der deutschen Literatur* (1984) Timm Reiner Menke analyzes four "Lenz" narratives: Starting with Büchner's *Lenz*, he moves on to Gerhard Hauptmann's *Der Apostel* (1890), Robert Walser's *Kleist in Thun* (1907), and finally Peter Schneider's *Lenz* (1973).[4] The central theme of all of these texts is the onset and progression of mental illness in a writer or intellectual. Ever since Büchner's *Lenz*, this particular form of insanity has been described not as the result of a heightened artistic sensibility, as the Romantics tended to treat the subject, but rather as derangement of reason caused by the discrepancy between idealistic inspiration for social reform and the prevailing social and economic reality. This, according to Christa Wolf, is an ever recurring dilemma:

> Ein Konflikt in dem sich die tausendfache Bedrohung lebendiger, entwicklungshungriger und wahrheitstüchtiger Menschen in Restaurationszeiten gesteigert spiegelt: der Dichter, vor die Wahl gestellt, sich an unerträgliche Zustände anzupassen und sein Talent zu ruinieren oder physisch zugrunde zu gehen.[5]

Menke also looks at the effect on the individual of the socio-political circumstances that are destructive enough to lead to insanity in characters with a certain disposition and concludes that the psychological damage of the modern person is caused to a considerable extent by the contradictory demands — in the widest possible sense — of society on the individual. This socially induced suffering was initially *lived* by Jakob Michael Reinhold Lenz (1751–1792), *recorded* by Oberlin, a pastor who cared for Lenz for some time during his illness and who kept an extensive diary, and *put into literary form* by Büchner.

The categorization of the above mentioned *Lenz* narratives is based on the possible causes and similar symptoms of insanity as shown by the central characters. That in itself does not mean that any narrative related to Büchner's novella can immediately be regarded as a reworking of the *Lenz* model in the sense we want to define it. The *resemblance* between Büchner's *Lenz* and any of the above mentioned texts is undeniable. But in the context of this study, it is the *intention* of the author that is of crucial importance. Is the new work written as a deliberate response to the model? Does it comment on the text? Does it endorse or reject particular aspects of the original? A narrative thematically linked with Büchner's *Lenz* does not necessarily aim to be read in conjunction with the former. But this is precisely the level on which we are invited to read Peter Schneider's *Lenz*.[6] Schneider not only discusses his chosen theme, in this case a temporary experience of mental illness, but does so with direct reference to Büchner as a *literary model*. The title itself proclaims the affinity between the two narratives. The publisher's blurb on the back of the book draws attention to Büchner with the claim: "Peter Schneider erzählt Büchners gleichnamige Novelle neu." The text is preceded by an acknowledged quote from Büchner's *Lenz*. As is the case with Koeppen's *Der Tod in Rom*, the reference in the title and the motto preceding the narrative establish a clear link to the literary model. The final sentences of the two *Lenz* narratives illuminate one another, although in a different way compared with Koeppen's *Der Tod in Rom* in relation to Thomas Mann's *Der Tod in Venedig*.

Three Revolutions — Three Writers

Each of the last three centuries has seen a wave of revolutionary idealism in Germany that heightened social awareness and gave rise to intense political debate. These were periods of great hope, filled with aspirations to build a better and fairer world. But each time, although powerful and charismatic voices inspired a multitude of people, attempts to bring about political change failed. The impulse of the call for social reform were carried by the intellectuals of the time, but they did not achieve in political terms what they set out to accomplish, and all that remains of the idealism and the suffering of the respective periods are manifestations in literature. J. M. R. Lenz, Georg Büchner, and Peter Schneider were all writers whose work inspired and motivated their readers. However, whether the resulting campaigns made any real difference in the world remains an open question. Menke, for instance, argues that it is a historical illusion, which revolutionary movements of the twentieth century repeatedly succumbed to, that intellectuals either can or will initiate and sustain a social revolution.[7] Likewise in the eighteenth century, J. M. R. Lenz, whose plays *Der Hofmeister* (1776), and especially *Die Soldaten* (1776) contain all the social criticism of the *Sturm und Drang* period, fell victim to the unbridgeable gap between his idealism and the political reality, which eventually drove him to suffer a mental breakdown, followed by a life of exile and obscurity. Eighty years later, Büchner's *Der hessische Landbote* (1834) turned out to be one of the programmatic political pamphlets to anticipate the *Vormärz* revolutions in Germany. Büchner was motivated by a deep sense of compassion for the poor and showed a very early understanding of the connection between deprivation and the economic system. This was recognized in 1878 by Karl Emil Franzos, who welcomes Büchner's polemic with great relief:

> Zum erstenmale in Deutschland tritt darin ein Demokrat nicht für die geistigen Güter der Gebildeten ein, sondern für die materiellen der Armen und Unwissenden; zum erstenmale ist hier nicht von Preßfreiheit, Vereinsrecht und Wahlcensus [sic] die Rede, sondern von der "großen Magenfrage"; zum erstenmale tritt hier an die Stelle der politisch-demokratischen Agitation die sozial-demokratische Klage und Anklage.[8]

Because of his political activism Büchner had to flee Germany, and withdrew into the private realm. Exiled in Strasbourg, Büchner was preoccupied with the problem of failed revolutionary impulses and feelings of guilt, questions that arise for everyone who aims to bring about radical social change by way of revolutionary politics. In contrast to his *Landbote*, Büchner's *Lenz* is not a political text, but an account of what happened to an individual whose deeply felt social inspirations came to nothing, and who gradually breaks down under the strain that arises between his idealism and the futility of his efforts.

The student movement of the 1960s rebelled against the existing social order, and wanted to bring about another kind of society. Once more, Germany saw an intellectually led revolution aiming for social, rather than political reform, this time based on the teachings of Marx, Engels, and Mao. Peter Schneider's *Lenz* is set at a time when the activists among the students, one after the other, begin to realize that their rhetoric of social reform is not leading to change, and that many of the campaigns and demonstrations, the boycotts and street violence, result more in the destruction of their own lives than in the renewal of social structures.

The *Sturm und Drang* movement of the 1770s is remembered purely as an aesthetic revolution. The high hopes of the *Vormärz* reformers, which came to a culmination in 1848, some time after Büchner's premature death, were not fulfilled. Likewise, the initial enthusiasm and idealism of the student movement of the late 1960s ended in a withdrawal of contemporary writers and essayists from the political arena into private life. On a *literary* level, however, all these movements were of considerable importance: the *Sturm und Drang* movement set the emotions free from the constraints of the Enlightenment; Büchner's realism overcame and rejected the idealizing world-view of German Classicism, and created a new literary language — that of the people; similarly, Peter Schneider highlighted the hollowness of the politicization of literature during the 1960s, which had completely lost touch with the emotional needs and personal fulfillment of the individual. The socio-political essays of these authors tied them very closely to the needs and historical specifics of their times. But J. M. R. Lenz and Büchner are remembered chiefly for their *literary* works. Whether or not Schneider's works will be remembered is a question yet to be determined.

Büchner's *Lenz* — Ideal and Reality

Büchner's *Lenz* is a tightly constructed narrative with a logical progression of character development and a consistent unfolding of the main themes. The contrasting language, the constantly shifting narrative perspective and the uneven tempo in which the narrative moves, all result from the instability of Lenz's mental state. Writing with Spartan economy and discipline, Büchner gives us no prehistory of Lenz's life, nor a description of the circumstances leading to the desperate journey to Oberlin. Apart from the brief respite Lenz enjoys immediately after his arrival in Waldbach, the symptoms of his insanity grow steadily worse, and eventually lead to the total destruction of his mind. The development of Lenz's illness corresponds to his own journey from north to south and at the same time to Oberlin's movements. During he initial period spent in Oberlin's presence, Lenz temporarily recovers and hopes to lead a peaceful life in the isolation of the mountain community. During Oberlin's absence Lenz develops the delusion that he can change the course of nature and overcome death, and after Oberlin's return he enters a last phase, in which he is actually becoming a danger to himself and potentially to others. Thus, Büchner's narrative style reflects a careful blend between structure and content, internal and external progression. While this correlation provides a certain stability for the construction of the plot, Büchner's narrative style is at the same time marked by a transience that has best been described by John Reddick:

> It helps for us to recognize what is perhaps the paradox of paradoxes in Georg Büchner: his disjunctive mode with its relentless insistence on fragments and particles is always the product of a radiant vision of *wholeness*. Again and again, in every area of his existence — his politics, his science, his aesthetics, his art — we find an ardent sense of wholeness, but a wholeness that is almost always poignantly elusive: it *was* but is no longer; or *will* be but isn't yet; or — most poignant of all — it *is* in the present, but can be perceived or possessed only partially or transiently.[9]

Oberlin's diaries, describing the onset and the course of J. M. R. Lenz's mental illness, stood model for Büchner's *Lenz*, albeit not as *literary* model.[10] The novella still retains the quality and chronology of a diary, but the text has been thoroughly transformed. Büchner's skill as a writer is demonstrated not by the changes he introduces to his source, but rather by the fact that with a slight accentuation here, or a description of the surrounding landscape there, he turns the raw material into a literary, poetic text. Christa Wolf reckons this process is akin to magic: "Zwar benutzt er für seine Lenz-Novelle in horrend unverfrorener Weise den Krankenbericht des Pastor Oberlin, [doch] die Verwandlung dieses Materials in Kunst riecht nach Hexerei" (204).

In Büchner's novella Lenz's condition evolves in three distinct stages: (1) his arrival at Oberlin's house where he enjoys a temporary recovery in the peaceful surroundings, climaxing in the arrival of Kaufmann and the *Kunstgespräch;* (2) the period of Oberlin's absence, which sees a decline of Lenz's mental state, culminating in the attempt to raise a child from the dead; and (3) the events after Oberlin's return: Lenz cannot throw off the delusions he suffers from, eventually his hold on reality becomes so brittle that he has to be put under constant supervision, and Oberlin decides he has to send him away. The narrative is framed by the two journeys through the mountains. On his way to Waldbach, Lenz is on his own, walking uphill to his chosen refuge. In contrast, on his enforced departure from the mountains Lenz sits motionless on a cart, and is attended by two watchful guards. The surrounding landscape is described as breathtakingly beautiful; Lenz's inner state is one of utter desolation.

The time covered in Oberlin's diaries suggests that Lenz spent a period of two and a half weeks in Waldbach. Although Büchner's text also starts with a date, albeit not very precise ("Den 20.[11] ging Lenz durch's Gebirg," *BW,* 79), it is difficult for the reader to keep track of the passing of time. New paragraphs are often introduced by adverbial phrases of time like "den anderen Tag" (*BW,* 81), "um diese Zeit" (*BW,* 86), "gegen Abend" (*BW,* 92), or merely "unterdessen" (*BW,* 92). This technique is a characteristic way of describing Lenz's confused mind, distanced from everyday routines, and has been copied by Schneider and others in their own *Lenz* narratives.[12] The ordinary course of time does not seem to touch Lenz's life in Waldbach. Lenz lives only in the present; the reader can never be sure how much time has passed between incidents. Instead, time appears as a continuum which stretches infinitely between the mountaintops, and is only punctuated here and there by those events which gain some clarity in Lenz's mind.

Three Systems of Reference

The indicators of Lenz's world falling apart manifest themselves in three great themes that have traditionally given meaning to life on earth: nature, art, and religion. By the nineteenth century each one of these was beginning to lose its central function as a result of the gulf gradually opening up between the worlds of metaphysical meaning and empirical reality. In the course of Büchner's novella, Lenz tests out these three systems of reference, and finds that all of them fail to help him in his desperate struggle for sanity. Nature proves to be indifferent to his suffering, art no longer has the purpose of building a bridge to the world of ideals, and personal faith is powerless to prevent the breakdown of his sense of identity. Lenz's mental state gradually deteriorates to the same degree as these external agents lose their significance. This is what makes Büchner's *Lenz* a very modern text.

In the early 1970s, neither the realm of nature, nor those of art or religion are so essential to the protagonist that the loss of faith in any one would normally undermine his mental stability. The reference systems that once provided a sense of meaning and direction in life, and that were disappearing from Lenz's grasp in Büchner's novella, are not even relevant to Schneider's. And yet, the growing sense of alienation from the world that destroyed Büchner's Lenz reappears transformed. In Schneider's *Lenz*, nature is conspicuous by its almost complete absence. We find ourselves in the cityscapes of Berlin, Rome, and Trento: but this environment, created by humans for humans, is as indifferent to the suffering of its creatures as is Büchner's majestic but aloof realm of nature. According to Büchner's Lenz, new art shall be judged by the one criterion of *life*, yet Schneider's Lenz despairs that he and his friends cannot master the art of living. Religious faith has been replaced by political ideology in Schneider's narrative. Nevertheless, the gulf between theory and practice, the problem of how convictions can be turned into deeds that transform the lives of ordinary people, is still one of the central themes of the reworking.

In our post-Freudian age, we no longer look to external phenomena in order to grasp our own psyche. Büchner's narrative voice, however, frequently links the person of Lenz with the surrounding landscape, but gradually it becomes very clear that there is no real correspondence between Lenz's state of mind and the mood of the nature descriptions. Menke draws attention to the absolute loss of faith in the healing powers of nature and provokingly claims: "Das Wort von der Entzauberung der Natur dürfte in diesem Zusammenhang nicht zu stark gewählt sein" (122). Nature is still as magnificent as it ever was, but unlike the narrator, who describes this splendor in unforgettable images, Lenz is unable to respond adequately and becomes the subject of a confusing kaleidoscope of random impressions. This is made clear in the opening passage in what must be one of the longest and most compact sentences of German literature. The main clause of the sentence seems to indicate moments of clearer self-awareness. In contrast, all other descriptions serve only to emphasize the distance between Lenz and his surroundings.

> *Nur manchmal,* wenn . . . die Stimmen an den Felsen wach wurden, bald wie fern verhallende Donner und dann gewaltig heranbrausten, in Tönen, als wollten sie in ihrem wilden Jubel die Erde besinnen . . . oder wenn der Sturm das Gewölk abwärts trieb und einen lichtblauen See hineinriß und dann der Wind verhallte und tief unten aus den Schluchten, aus den Wipfeln der Tannen wie ein Wiegenlied und Glockengeläute heraufsummte . . . und alle Berggipfel, scharf und fest, weit über das Land hin glänzten und blitzten, *riß es ihm in der Brust.* . . . (*BW,* 79, my emphasis)

As the sentence continues with a series of main clauses, the focus shifts from nature descriptions to Lenz himself. One of the first symptoms to befall Lenz, together with most of his literary successors, is a separation of body and mind, which manifests itself in a strangely distorted sense of vision and in the loss of ability to perceive the world in relative proportions.

> . . . er stand, keuchend, den Leib vorwärts gebogen, Augen und Mund weit offen, er meinte, er müsse den Sturm in sich ziehen, alles in sich fassen, er dehnte sich aus und lag über der Erde, er wühlte sich in das All hinein, es war eine Lust, die ihm wehe tat; oder er stand still und legte das Haupt in's Moos und schloß die Augen halb, und dann zog es weit von ihm, die Erde wich unter ihm, sie wurde klein wie ein wandelnder Stern und tauchte sich in einen brausenden Strom, der seine klare Fluth unter ihm zog. Aber es waren nur Augenblicke, und dann erhob er sich nüchtern, fest, ruhig, als wäre ein Schattenspiel vor ihm vorübergezogen — er wußte von nichts mehr. (*BW,* 79–80)

During these momentary flights of fancy, Lenz not only loses all sense of his physical body but also touch with the earth itself, which supports his existence. Frequent descriptions of the surrounding countryside form an integral part of the text. But whereas in the opening passage at least the sentence structure still unites Lenz and his surroundings, by the end of the novella there is no longer any correlation between the state of the human mind and the natural realm. Lenz finds no comfort or reassurance in nature; on the contrary, the chasm between him and his environment cannot be bridged anymore. He no longer responds to the natural world, and nature no longer acts as a mirror to the human soul. With this separation from his environment as an extension of his soul, Lenz loses his first lifeline. As we shall see, in Schneider's *Lenz* the indifference *of* nature has turned into an indifference *to* nature.

Structurally and thematically the *Kunstgespräch* with Kaufmann, who so distresses Lenz by reprimanding him for his inactivity, lies at the very heart of the novella. Lenz argues passionately for an art form, for a new realism, which depicts life as it really is:

> Ich verlange in Allem — Leben, Möglichkeit des Daseins, und dann ist's gut. Wir haben dann nicht zu fragen, ob es schön, ob es häßlich ist, das Gefühl, daß Was geschaffen sey, Leben habe, stehe über diesen Beiden und sey das einzige Kriterium in Kunstsachen. (*BW*, 86)

The quality of *life* as a criterion for art challenges the beholder to an emotive response that to some extent allows for, even demands, an identification with the subject of art. The perfection of Apollo of Belvedere or a Raphaelite Madonna exists in the realm of ideals, and is therefore not directly accessible to the viewer. Lenz declares that the encounter with this kind of art, created along classical lines, leaves him cold, and that only art produced in the new spirit of realism can evoke an emotional response in him. "Der Dichter und Bildende ist mir der Liebste, der mir die Natur am Wirklichsten giebt, so daß ich über seinem Gebild fühle" (*BW*, 88). A further sign of Lenz's extreme alienation is his loss of emotional connection with the greatest of human artifacts, and its replacement by terrible inner emptiness and disorientation. As we will see, Schneider's *Lenz* also shares this sensation of utter detachment from the world of feeling.

The growing estrangement between thought and deed, between belief and perceived reality is most marked in Lenz's religious development. His loss of faith, which is highlighted in three experiences, is closely connected with his growing insanity. After preaching to the congregation of Waldbach, Lenz experiences a state of religious ecstasy symptomatic of his diminishing sense of proportion. Pain and rapture are inextricably mingled: "er konnte kein Ende finden der Wollust; endlich dämmerte es in ihm, er empfand ein leises tiefes Mitleid mit sich selbst, er weinte über sich" (*BW*, 85). The overwhelming strength of these emotions bears no relation to the event that triggered them. Some time later, Lenz attends the bedside of a sick girl in the company of an enigmatic old man who has the reputation of a healer. This night, spent in the shadow of death, unsettles Lenz deeply and threatens to overthrow that temporary state of equilibrium he had been granted. "Ahnungen von seinem alten Zustande durchzuckten ihn und warfen Streiflichter in das wüste Chaos seines Geistes" (*BW,* 91). Finally, the attempt to bring into life what has already died is a reflection on the vain struggle that takes place in Lenz's inner life. He himself feels completely numb, and cannot get in touch with his inner self. With the apparent refusal of God to manifest Himself by allowing Lenz to call the dead girl back to life, Lenz loses his faith and turns against God. "Lenz mußte laut lachen, und mit dem Lachen griff der Atheismus in ihn und faßte ihn ganz sicher und ruhig und fest" (*BW,* 94). Has Lenz reached a point of no return, at which the revival of his ailing sense of self is as impossible as raising a child from the dead? With the loss of his faith Lenz has also lost the last external source of help that could give orientation to his life. He is overcome by an all-pervading sense of *ennui,* the beginnings of that utterly hopeless state of numbness that characterizes his final departure from Steintal: "die Welt, die er hatte nutzen wollen, hatte einen ungeheuren Riß, er hatte keinen Haß, keine Liebe, keine Hoffnung, eine schreckliche Leere und doch eine folternde Unruhe, sie auszufüllen. Er hatte *Nichts*" (*BW,* 98).

Schneider's *Lenz* — on Theory and Practice

Schneider's *Lenz* was published in 1973, a time when the mass-demonstrations, sit-ins, and bold political demands of the student movement had already passed into history. The narrative offers a personalized view of the political events and focuses on the needs of the individual at times of social revolt. Schneider's first fictional work was extraordinarily successful, and soon became the "iconic text of the student movement."[13] The text is preceded by a quote from Büchner's *Lenz:* "Er ging gleichgültig weiter, es lag ihm nichts am Weg, bald auf- bald abwärts, Müdigkeit spürte er keine, nur war es ihm manchmal unangenehm, daß er nicht auf dem Kopf gehen konnte" (*SL,* 5).[14] Already at this point, we have the first divergence between the two Lenz figures. As we will find, Schneider's Lenz is never indifferent. He always reacts to his surroundings. He never gives up trying to communicate with the people he meets, albeit sometimes in a fairly idiosyncratic fashion. Although he is often quite self-absorbed, he does not cease in his attempts to be fully integrated into the society he finds himself in. That in itself indicates that his mental crisis at no stage reaches the severity of that of his predecessor's.

Unlike the Büchner model, Schneider's *Lenz* is not written as a narrative unfolding gradually, with one development followed by another in a necessary sequence. The text is divided into forty-three sections of unequal length and set in three different cities: Berlin (sections one to twenty-four), Rome (twenty-six to thirty-four), and Trento (thirty-six to forty-two). Sections twenty-five and thirty-five are descriptions of the journeys to the respective cities, and the last section sees Lenz back in Berlin. The narrative describes the gradual healing process, which sets in as soon as Lenz gets to Italy. The order of events in the three different locations is fairly random, and could readily be arranged differently without changing the plot. Thus, we have an assortment of snapshots of Lenz's emotional and social life. On the surface he conforms to normal accepted behavior most of the time, while mentally he increasingly feels estranged from his own emotions and alienated from his surroundings. Rhys W. Williams describes this crisis Lenz has fallen into as existential and "reminiscent of Handke's *Die Angst des Tormanns beim Elfmeter,* and via Handke, of Sartre's *La Nausée* and a tradition of German literature stretching back to Hofmannsthal's so-called *Chandos Letter.*"[15] We may add that by placing the text in the *Lenz* tradition, Büchner's *Lenz* should be included in this list, and can, in this context, be regarded as the forerunner of all of the above-mentioned twentieth-century works. The connection with Hofmannsthal's *Chandos Letter* (1902) shall only be hinted at here. We will examine the text in greater detail in the chapter on John Banville's reworking of *Die Wahlverwandtschaften*. But it is important to note how, in his existential struggle for retaining a sense of reality, the *Chandos* figure relates to both Schneider's and Büchner's *Lenz* narratives. Like Schneider's Lenz, Chandos suffers from an almost archetypal breakdown of meaning between words and their representation in the world. Like Büchner's Lenz, he has moments of visionary insights into the nature of ordinary objects, revelations that threaten to overwhelm him.

Schneider's *Lenz* begins with Lenz waking up "aus einem seiner üblichen Träume" (*SL,* 5):

> Er war mit L. kilometerlang in einem Förderkorb durch ein Gebäude ohne Türen und Fenster gefahren. Um sie herum nichts als Wände. Dann war er einen dunklen Schacht hinuntergefallen, viele hundert Meter tief, ohne aufzuschlagen. Ein Fließband hatte ihn aufgenommen, das seinen Sturz in einen waagrechten Flug nach vorne verwandelte. Am Ende des Fließbandes wurde er aufgefangen. Er war erwartet worden: Frauen mit riesigen Brüsten, Zauberer, Clowns, saltoschlagende Kinder, die ganze kaputte Fellinitruppe. Ein Mann

in einem flimmernden Kostüm drückte ihm einen Kuß auf den Mund. (*SL*, 5)

The dream is as a metaphor for all that is about to happen to Lenz. It anticipates Lenz's rebirth from the lifeless functionality of the German setting into the exotic abandonment of Italian society. The words "shaft," "cage," and "conveyor belt" all suggest a man-made environment, hollowed out, dark and utterly hostile to life. In a sudden change of set, which is so typical of dreams, Lenz then finds himself in a totally different world, full of people, colorful, and bursting with life. Still in the opening section, we are introduced to Lenz's present dilemma, and the causes of his *Lenzian* condition: he is caught up in the problem of reconciling the subordination to a greater cause, namely a Marxist revolution, with the pursuit of personal happiness. On waking from his dream, Lenz's first glance falls on the portrait of Marx hanging over his bed. Lenz, who can no longer bear the wise face of that great theorist of ultimate universal happiness, and who had already previously attempted to hang the picture upside down, "um den Verstand abtropfen zu lassen" (*SL*, 5), begins to ask questions about the personal dreams and desires of the man with all the answers. "Was waren deine Träume, alter Besserwisser, nachts meine ich? Warst du eigentlich glücklich?" (*SL*, 5). The Büchner quote at the beginning of Schneider's text speaks of the unpleasantness of not being able to walk on his head. In 1960, on the occasion of being awarded the Büchner Prize, Paul Celan warned us of the dangers of seeing the world upside down, because: "Wer auf dem Kopf geht, der hat den Himmel als Abgrund unter sich."[16]

As for linguistic parallels between the two texts, Schneider reproduces Büchner's device of introducing paragraphs with nonspecific adverbial phrases of time. There are also several unmarked Büchner quotes or near-quotes, which occur largely in the first part of the narrative, before Lenz's departure for Italy. For example, we find Schneider's Lenz sitting on the banks of a canal, shattering the reflection of houses by throwing stones into the water. The passage is reminiscent of a similar moment in Büchner's *Lenz*. Resting on his approach to Waldbach, Lenz sits down. It is evening.

Büchner: Das Gewölk lag fest und unbeweglich am Himmel, so weit der Blick reichte, nichts als Gipfel.... es wurde ihm entsetzlich einsam, er war allein, ganz allein, er wollt mit sich sprechen, aber er konnte nicht, er wagte kaum zu athmen, ... es faßte ihn eine namenlose Angst in diesem Nichts, er war im Leeren.
(*BW,* 80)

Schneider: Als er aufschaute, konnte er die Grenze zwischen Dächern und Himmel nicht mehr erkennen. Soweit er schauen konnte nichts als gewaltige Klötze ... und alles so kalt, so steinern. Es wurde ihm entsetzlich einsam, er war allein, er wollte mit sich sprechen, er konnte nicht, er wagte kaum zu atmen. (*SL,* 18)

Büchner's Lenz breaks out in a panic and begins to run. The passage continues: "Es war ... als jage der Wahnsinn auf Rossen hinter ihm. Endlich hörte er Stimmen, er sah Lichter, es wurde ihm leichter" (*BW,* 80). In contrast, Schneider's Lenz makes an effort after a while and takes himself off into a pub. On some other night, he is running through empty streets until he is utterly exhausted. The text continues: "Als Lenz zurückging war die Angst weg, er fühlte sich leicht" (*SL,* 12). The resemblance between these two running incidents is clear. But we have to question Schneider's justification for these near-quotes. In the above example there has been no initial mention of this fear, which Lenz now loses so suddenly. Another of Schneider's borrowings describes some of the symptoms of mental instability Schneider's Lenz displays:

Büchner: Gegen Abend befiel ihn eine sonderbare Angst, er hätte der Sonne nachlaufen mögen; ... Der rettungslose Gedanke als sey Alles nur sein Traum, öffnete sich vor ihm, er klammerte sich an alle Gegenstände, Gestalten zogen rasch an ihm vorbei, er drängte sich an sie, es waren Schatten, das Leben wich aus ihm und seine Glieder waren ganz starr. Er sprach, er sang, er recitierte Stellen aus Shakespeare.
(*BW,* 82)

Schneider: Eine sonderbare Angst befiel ihn, er hätte der Sonne nachlaufen mögen.... Er klammerte sich an alle Gegenstände, Gestalten zogen rasch vorbei, er drängte sich an sie.... Er fing an zu laufen. Es war ihm plötzlich als stecke er nur noch mit den Füßen bis höchstens zum Knie in der Stadt, ... er schrie, er sang, er wollte sich kleiner machen.
(*SL,* 33)

The Büchner text invites the reader to enter into Lenz's confused mind, join his desperate struggle of clinging onto reality, and experiencing his walk on the tightrope between sanity and insanity. Illusions and shadows appear consistently throughout the narrative. In contrast, the passage from Schneider's *Lenz* stands out from the main body of the text. The images are not integrated into the rest of the narrative, nor is the language consistent with Schneider's usual style. In fact, it is not particularly difficult to spot the expressions or phrases borrowed from other sources. The use Schneider makes of Büchner's language, largely restricted to references of Lenz's emotional state, appears somewhat random, and is not fully absorbed into the linguistic register. Büchner's style, which is so molded by the moods and fancies of the protagonist, fits ill with Schneider's use of rather factual and distanced language.

Descriptions of nature, which are so integral to Büchner's text, are largely replaced by impressions of city life. The only exception is the view of Trento from a nearby mountain. Lenz surveys the panorama, and the narrator illuminates Lenz's inner state. "Kein Geräusch, keine Bewegung, in dem Licht stand alles ruhig und fest da, die Ruhe machte Lenz keine Angst" (*SL*, 79). The choice of words is once again reminiscent of Büchner's text where we find the contrasting, but sadly corresponding sentence: "Sein Zustand war indessen immer trostloser geworden, alles was er an Ruhe aus der Nähe Oberlins und aus der Stille des Thals geschöpft hatte, war weg" (*BW*, 97). The description of the valley and the city is seen in relation to Lenz's emotions, but there had never been an indication why Schneider's Lenz should have been afraid of the stillness in the first place. Once more the imported sentiment is not properly integrated into Schneider's narrative.

The Nature of the Crisis

The symptoms of mental illness suffered by both Lenz figures and other protagonists in that tradition[17] can be grouped into three categories: (1) the loss of or unexpected enrichment of meaning in connection with ordinary objects and events, a conceptual problem; (2) the distortion of the relative proportion of things, a question of perception; and (3) some degree of violence against oneself, and potentially against others, a symptom which is particularly strong in Büchner's Lenz. The first symptom, the *Chandos* syndrome, is described by Williams as "a disruption of the relationship between signified and signifier."[18] During the morning rush hour Lenz watches the crowds around him. He notes minute details about people's clothing and their movements, but he can no longer identify with their purpose. "Sie gehen zur Arbeit, dachte Lenz. Er verband mit dem Satz keine Vorstellung" (*SL,* 6). Lenz experiences a world in which the connection between the external signs of an action and the meaning, which that action signifies, have been severed.

> Ich kann mich auf die Sätze, die hier gesagt werden, nicht konzentrieren. Ich verstehe sie schon, ich kann nur nichts mit ihnen verbinden, jedenfalls nicht das, was mit ihnen gemeint ist. Zum Beispiel bleibt mir bei den Wörtern "die vollständige Beseitigung der Finsternis in der Welt" nur das Wort Finsternis hängen. (*SL,* 30)

Schneider uses the camera as metaphor for his description of the next symptom, the sudden strangely subjectivized vision. Random objects, such as industrial cranes in the harbor scene, suddenly stand out, appear particularly highlighted, and assume an apparently immanent significance. Along with this sudden insight into the nature of material objects, there are numerous incidents during which Schneider's Lenz loses his sense of proportions as to the relative size of things, a phenomenon we also had in Büchner's *Lenz.* Büchner's Lenz can transport himself over huge distances, particularly in the opening passage when he sees the Earth as from space:

> Es war ihm alles so klein, so nahe, so naß, er hätte die Erde hinter den Ofen setzen mögen, er begriff nicht, daß er so viel Zeit brauchte, um einen Abhang hinunter zu klimmen, einen fernen Punkt zu erreichen; er meinte, er müsse Alles mit ein paar Schritten ausmessen können. (*BW,* 79)

Schneider's Lenz distorts the relative size of objects: "Als er die Zeitung aufschlug, sah er die Zähne des Reißverschlusses an seinem Mantel. Sie kamen ihm zu groß vor" (*SL,* 6). Or: "Als er die Münze eingeworfen und gewählt hatte, kam ihm die Bahnhofshalle plötzlich viel kleiner vor" (*SL,* 54). In his imagination Schneider's Lenz interchanges the fixed points with those that move. "Eine Zeitlang stellte er sich vor, daß die Häuser und Straßen auf Schienen an ihm vorüber rollten" (*SL,* 6), a thought somewhat reminiscent of Büchner's Lenz in the later stages of his illness: "Er amüsierte sich, die Häuser auf die Dächer zu stellen, die Menschen an- und auszukleiden, die wahnwitzigsten Possen auszusinnen" (*BW,* 98).

The third symptom suffered by both Lenz figures involves self-inflicted pain as a means of holding onto normality. Büchner's Lenz takes repeated plunges into the cold water of the well in order to hold on to his sense of reality. As the disease progresses these masochistic attacks become more and more desperate:

> Die halben Versuche zum Entleiben, die er indeß fortwährend machte, waren nicht ganz Ernst, es war weniger der Wunsch des To-

des, für ihn war ja keine Ruhe und Hoffnung im Tod; es war mehr in Augenblicken der fürchterlichsten Angst oder der dumpfen, an's Nichtseyn gränzenden Ruhe ein Versuch, sich zu sich selbst zu bringen durch physischen Schmerz. (*BW*, 99–100)

Schneider's Lenz, too, is subject to sudden attacks of fear, and a need to run or to dance until it hurts, in an attempt to keep in touch with his physical body at a time when the mind is threatening to spiral out of control. But, unlike Büchner's Lenz, he is self-consciously aware of what he is doing. Did he, or did he not, yell out in his inner and physical pain? "Er schlug mit dem Kopf und den Fäusten gegen die Wand. Gleichzeitig erschien es ihm blödsinnig, wie er sich benahm. Er wollte sich mit Gewalt von den Bildern befreien. Er begann zu brüllen, merkte dann, daß er es sich nur vorstellte" (*SL*, 12). Finally, when a comparison is made between the symptoms of mental illness displayed by the protagonists of various narratives written in the Lenz tradition, it is important to realize that they all suffer from the same malaise, but to very different degrees of severity. This leads to different outcomes in the fate of the central characters in Büchner's, Hofmannsthal's, and Schneider's narratives: Büchner leaves the reader in no doubt that Lenz's condition is irreversible; Hofmannsthal does not tell us whether Chandos ever overcomes his sense of alienation. In contrast, Schneider's Lenz never loses his grip on reality altogether, and eventually he recovers.

Knowledge of the authenticity provided by the nonfictional framework of Oberlin's diaries and the historical facts known about the figure of J. M. R. Lenz, implicitly place Büchner's narrative firmly into a historical context. Schneider's narrative, too, is given a specific time and place, namely Germany and Italy in the spring and late summer of 1970.[19] In both cases the specific historical and geographical background provides the reader with an additional perspective outside the subjective experience of the two Lenz protagonists. At the same time, the narrative style of Büchner's *Lenz* allows the reader to enter into the highly subjective world of the panic-stricken protagonist who, in his suffering, increasingly loses touch with the passing of time and the natural rhythms of days and weeks. Likewise, Schneider's Lenz lives in that state of flux wherein the flow of time has somehow been suspended. As already mentioned, Schneider copies Büchner's technique of starting new sections with adverbial time phrases such as "an einem anderen Tag" (*SL*, 8), "am anderen Morgen" (*SL*, 20), "mitten in der Nacht" (*SL*, 11), and "an einem Samstag abend" (*SL*, 37). This impression as regards the passing of time, taken together with the fact that the incidents described in these sections can easily be interchanged, suggests that Schneider's Lenz also lives in a time curiously his own, continuous but never changing. The device is most frequently used during the period in Berlin, when Lenz's state of mind most closely resembles that of Büchner's Lenz. Williams has pointed out that nineteen sections of the first twenty-five section in the narrative begin with these loose references to time; in contrast once Lenz has left for Rome, only eight of the remaining eighteen sections do so.[20]

In addition, Schneider's narrative contains a second significant aspect concerning the passing of time, a feature that is only briefly touched upon in Büchner's novella. Lenz's recovery is attributed to the process of coming to terms with his personal past. The first time we accompany Lenz on his aimless ramblings through Berlin, teenage memories of his awakening sexuality rise to the surface (*SL,* 7). On the journey across the Alps more childhood memories erupt (*SL,* 52). But eventually his experiences in Rome reveal to him the importance of acknowledging his past, and thus freeing himself therefrom. An eccentric Italian friend and lover, Pierra, is passionate about her regular psychotherapy sessions. She shows Lenz her native city, but she only takes him to places that hold personal memories for her. In spite of the purely subjective, random selection of locations to visit, Lenz finds a wholeness in the experience, the typical in the specific, and he comes to understand an essential concept: "Er sagte, er könne sich zum ersten Mal vorstellen, daß dieses angstlose Zusammenleben mit der Vergangenheit es einem erleichtere, sich in der Gegenwart einzurichten" (*SL,* 69–70). The Italians teach Lenz to make use of the past instead of obliterating it. This discovery triggers a process by which Lenz begins to explore his relationship with his parents: the pain caused to the eight-year-old by an absent father, and the final row with the mother that was soon followed by her death (*SL,* 85). Memories, long suppressed, rise to the surface, and Lenz is suddenly able to share his recollections with the newly found friends in Trento. He finds that his traumatic past no longer holds him in its grip: "durch das Erzählen rückte alles wieder weit weg. Er merkte, daß er das Erlebnis, das er beschrieb, dadurch hinter sich ließ, daß er es beschrieb" (*SL,* 86). The earlier Lenz has no such opportunities. Oberlin is not Sigmund Freud. The possible healing process by exploring and coming to terms with one's personal history is not explored in Büchner's *Lenz.*

The well-integrated theme of clothes, which stand for Lenz's sense of self, is a motif that does not appear in Büchner's *Lenz*. In Schneider's narrative clothes are mentioned time and again as an image for Lenz's lacking a sense of identity. For the past two years his girlfriend L. had chosen all his clothes, and Lenz has lost his instinct of what suited him best. A friend, Walter, needs a new pair of shoes and finds it difficult to make a choice. Lenz lends him his coat and finally they find a matching pair, but in reality it is not the borrowed coat that matters. Lenz acknowledges: "Sie passen nicht zu dem Mantel, sondern zu dir" (*SL,* 16). In Rome he is robbed of his coat and wallet but instead of becoming frightened or annoyed, he feels relieved and happy (*SL,* 60). It is as though with the loss of his coat, the burden of his own fixed personality has been taken from him. At a party in Rome Lenz finds himself in a suit, the trousers of which are too short. He seems literally ill-suited to the whole affair (*SL,* 66). In Trento, which incidentally has a large textile industry, he is offered clothes from friends and neighbors as the summer comes to an end, and initially he is content to accept these gifts. The well-worn clothes of his newly found friends offer ready access to the well-integrated and harmonious community, and "in kurzer Zeit war er neu eingekleidet und nur noch durch seine holpernde Sprache von seinen neuen Bekannten zu unterscheiden" (*SL,* 82). But towards the end of the narrative, when he feels more certain of himself once more, he suddenly realizes that he no longer needs these borrowed attributes:

> Plötzlich war ihm, als säße er neben sich und sähe sich da sitzen. Die braunen Cordhosen gehörten dem Stotterer Massimo, den Mantel hatte er von einem Marxisten-Leninisten, mit dem er immer häufiger Streit bekam, den Pullover hatte eines Abends sein Arbeiterfreund aus dem Schrank geholt. 'Was machst du bloß in all diesen fremden Sachen?' fragte Lenz den, der am Tisch saß und ungezuckerten Capuccino trank. (*SL,* 89)

In the very next section Lenz is forcibly deported to Germany.

The mental breakdown suffered by Schneider's Lenz is far less severe than that of Büchner's. As it turns out, it is not so much an existential crisis as a temporary withdrawal from a life of campaigning and action, caused by the breakdown of his love affair with L. and his disillusionment when he realizes how difficult it is to put social theory into practice. The structure of Schneider's narrative progresses in three dialectical steps: from the overtheoretical intellectual community in Germany in which personal relationships are sacrificed for the sake of the future goal of social revolution, to Roman society, which focuses almost entirely on personal matters and shows little concern for wider social issues, to a utopian scenario of harmony and balance, which Lenz experiences in Trento. Parallel to this socio-political vision is the development of Lenz's mental state. His sense of physical and conceptual displacement takes him from the crisis point in the present, via the acknowledgement of his past, to a fresh beginning. Furthermore, judging by its wide reception at the time, Schneider's *Lenz* is an important document of the *Neue Subjektivität*, describing the inspirations and problems of the final phases of the student movement in Germany. At the same time, it also creates the bridge between the politicized literature of the 1960s, and the newly found focus on the individual in the German literature of the 1970s.

The Effect of the Reworking

On one level, the relationship between reworking and model in this case is not unlike the fairly loose connection between Koeppen's *Der Tod in Rom* and Mann's *Der Tod in Venedig*. Rather than a set of explicit parallels or contrasts between the two narratives, we have a set of allusions by Schneider to the Büchner model, which operate predominantly in terms of: (1) the name of the respective central protagonists; (2) the hope of both to find relief from their suffering by moving into new social settings; and (3) the narrative styles.

The underlying meaning of model and reworking is contrasted sharply by the different fates that befall the two protagonists. Considerations like these have caused Menke to reject the use of the concept of *Neuerzählung* in connection with Schneider's *Lenz*.

> Im Licht der im Grunde in den beiden Texten radikal unterschiedlichen geschichtsphilosophischen Haltungen kommt dem Rekurrieren Schneiders auf das Vorbild Büchner ein eher problematischer Zug zu. Der Anspruch auf Gleichartigkeit, durch den Titel formuliert und vom Verlag durch die Plakatierung "Neuerzählung" postuliert, muß dann als ein wenig hochgegriffen bezeichnet werden. Sprachliche und thematische Übereinstimmungen dürfen nicht über wesentliche inhaltliche und philosophische Unterschiede hinwegtäuschen. Die Widersprüche zwischen beiden Texten sollten vielmehr sichtbar gemacht werden und stehenbleiben. (116)

Menke is right that on closer examination there is less correspondence between the two narratives than at first appears. Since the publication of Büchner's *Lenz* the name "Lenz" has become the byword for a person of great sensibility who cannot, or will not, integrate into society and is destroyed as a result of it. His suffering is of a psychological nature. Schneider's text, on the other hand, focuses on the political convictions and revolutionary aims of his protagonist, which are proven to be unattainable and need to be modified and softened in order to allow the individual to lead a constructive life.

However, some of the philosophical differences between model and reworking might well be smaller than is apparent at first glance, in spite of the fact that Büchner's Lenz perishes and Schneider's Lenz recovers. It would be hasty to ignore Büchner's deep involvement with social matters, and indeed his clear insight into socio-economic processes, somewhat hidden in the psychological study. Büchner's *Lenz* also has a political dimension. Writing long before Marx, and without the terminology, Büchner has, nevertheless, developed a clear understanding of the values and laws of the emergent capitalist system. His Lenz falls victim to the contradictions between his own set of values and those of the predominant economic ideology. By his refusal to enter into the economic cycle, Lenz also rejects the value system of his society, which attributes such a high place to the virtue of productive work. In comparison, the values he has adopted for himself are not recognized and are deemed worthless. The encounter with Kaufmann, in which Lenz is reprimanded for "wasting his time" in the obscurity of Waldbach, is a turning point in the development of Büchner's Lenz. The temporary arrest of the progressive illness comes to an end with the arrival of this representative of the competitive world Lenz has left. Kaufmann admonishes Lenz for wasting his time in the obscurity of Waldbach, and reminds him of the demands of society, particularly those of his father, who challenges Lenz to return to work. Lenz answers passionately, and shows signs of a deep panic at the thought of being forced to re-enter the paradoxes of a "productive" life:

> Hier weg? Ich verstehe das nicht, mit den zwei Worten ist die Welt verhunzt. Jeder hat was nöthig; wenn er ruhen kann, was könnt' er mehr haben! Immer steigen, ringen und so in Ewigkeit Alles, was der Augenblick giebt, wegwerfen und immer darben, um einmal zu genießen; dürsten, während einem helle Quellen über den Weg springen. Es ist mir jetzt erträglich, und da will ich bleiben; warum? warum? Eben weil es mir wohl ist; was will mein Vater? Kann er mehr geben? Unmöglich! Laßt mich in Ruhe! (*BW*, 89)

In the context of this debate on the relative merits of a Utilitarian ethics in pursuit of happiness versus the intrinsic value of work, Menke draws attention to Max Weber's essay "The Protestant Ethic and the Spirit of Capitalism" (1905). Here Weber shows a deep affinity to

Büchner when it comes to the paradox of Protestant work ethics, wherein riches may be accumulated but not enjoyed. Weber then draws a startling conclusion that "waste of time is thus the first and in principle the deadliest of sins."[21] Thus in this view, Lenz's determination not to become part of the commercial world, bent on producing wealth, would constitute not only a social but also a moral sin. The incident with Kaufmann has a counterpart in a conversation Schneider's Lenz has with his friend B. "B. setzte ihm zu, er habe mit Freunden aus seiner Gruppe gesprochen, sie seien über Lenz' Unzuverlässigkeit verärgert, er verschleudere sein Leben, er solle sich ein Ziel stecken und dergleichen mehr" (*SL*, 49). Unlike the model, in which the meeting with Kaufmann results in the deterioration of Lenz's mind, B.'s censure has the effect of sending Schneider's Lenz to travel to Italy and thus to his eventual recovery.

In the context of the special relationship that exists between model and reworking, the preoccupation of Schneider's Lenz with Marxism and Maoism highlights the socio-political dimensions of Büchner's text, which are often overlooked in psychological readings. In the same way, the critique of Büchner's Lenz on the current notions of art illuminates particular aspects of the malaise suffered by Schneider's protagonist. Art, according to Büchner's Lenz, has to contain *life*, it has to inspire feelings. In the *Kunstgespräch* he uses examples from the visual arts, but does not the imperative "Ich verlange in Allem — Leben" (*BW*, 86) apply equally to Lenz's own literary works and the political essays of Schneider's Lenz? Schneider's Lenz describes the emotional distance he had suffered from in Berlin: "Ich kann . . . einer Idee, die ich mir gebildet habe, erst folgen, wenn ich ihr durch die Anschauung das Gefühl hinzufüge, das ihr entspricht" (*SL*, 38). In an accusation reminiscent of the attack by Büchner's Lenz on manifestations of art, which leave him cold ("ich fühle mich dabei sehr todt" *BW*, 88), Schneider's Lenz refuses to enter into a conversation with the art critic Neidt on the grounds: "Weil ich nichts spüre, wenn Sie reden" (*SL*, 39).

Finally, the religious disillusionment of Büchner's Lenz can be said to have been replaced by a corresponding loss of political idealism on the part of Schneider's Lenz. The possible relationship between theory and practice, ideals and reality, has already been foreshadowed in the first section by Lenz's question about the personal happiness of Karl Marx, the master of theoretical concepts. There follow several quotes from Mao's works, which Williams has traced back to the essay

"On Practice: On the Relation Between Knowledge and Practice, Between Knowing and Doing" (1937). For example:

> Indem sich die gesellschaftliche Praxis fortsetzt, wiederholen sich mehrmals die Dinge, die bei den Menschen in ihrer Tätigkeit Empfindungen und Eindrücke hervorrufen. Dann tritt im menschlichem Gehirn ein Umschlag im Erkenntnisprozess ein und es entstehen Begriffe . . . Das ist die zweite Stufe der Erkenntnis. (*SL,* 28)[22]

Schneider's use of this and other quotes from Mao works on two levels. Structurally they are appropriate in the context: a study group described in the section discusses readings by Mao. On a deeper level, the content of the quotes themselves, the nature of the relationship between sense impressions and the formation of abstract concepts, formulate one of the central themes of the narrative as a whole, namely the relationship between knowledge and action, theory and practice. As an intellectual with little practical knowledge of life, Lenz has to follow the path from idea to experience, from knowing to doing. After having defined and discussed the problems of the working classes for years, he eventually finds a job in a factory. But as it turns out, his concern for the well-being of the workers has more to do with Lenz's search for his own identity than springing from purely philanthropic principles. Wolfgang, a genuine member of the working class, who has also read Marxist theory, exposes this side of Lenz:

> Du möchtest gern glauben, daß wir Arbeiter auch Menschen sind, mit denen man reden kann, aber du glaubst es noch nicht. In Wirklichkeit stellst du dir unter mir so jemanden vor, wie du selbst gern sein möchtest. Zum Teil jedenfalls, denn dein ganzes Leben lang akkern möchtest du nicht. (*SL,* 33–34)

Having suffered from the extremes of the overtheoretical German approach to social problems, Lenz is surprised at the noncritical, nonpolitical attitudes he encounters in Rome. Roman society is wholly preoccupied with personal affairs: "Redeten sie von Politik, so nur über einzelne Politiker, von denen sie ein Charakterbild zeichneten. Sie interessierten sich nicht für gesellschaftliche Vorgänge, aber für ihre Träume fühlten sie sich verantwortlich" (*SL,* 70). As he did in Berlin, Lenz suffers from moments of disorientation, of estrangement from his surroundings in Rome, but the symptoms are receding. In Trento Lenz finally feels reconciled with the need for an intellectual basis for reform, "Die theoretischen Kentnisse, die er sich früher angeeignet hatte, erschienen Lenz plötzlich unentbehrlich, er wunderte sich, warum sie ihm früher so oft wie hohles Gerede vorgekommen waren" (*SL,* 81). Here we have another sign that Lenz's mental disorientation and his feelings of alienation have been overcome. Ideals that had seemed unattainable in the societies of Berlin and Rome are realized in the life Lenz finds in Trento. This healing process is eventually borne out by the open ending of the narrative.

The final passage of Schneider's *Lenz* resembles that of the model very closely, but this time the meaning contrasts sharply with last passage of Büchner's *Lenz*, which reads:

> Er saß mit kalter Resignation im Wagen, wie sie das Thal hervor nach Westen fuhren. . . . er blieb ganz ruhig sitzen; er war vollkommen gleichgültig. . . . es war aber eine entsetzliche Leere in ihm, er fühlte keine Angst mehr, kein Verlangen; sein Dasein war ihm eine notwendige Last. — So lebte er hin. (*BW,* 100–101)

Like Büchner's Lenz during his enforced passage to Strasbourg, Schneider's Lenz is indifferent and calm. The text reads: "Er sah ruhig hinaus, die Berge waren ihm gleichgültig, keine Erinnerung, keine Spur von Angst" (*SL,* 90). Lenz returns to Berlin and finds that society has remained the same in all its essentials, while at the same time the lives of his friends have undergone important changes: everyone has their own cross to bear. Lenz is content and quietly confident. His stated intention for the future and the final world of the narrative is "Dableiben" (*SL,* 90). Büchner's hollow "So lebte er hin" (*BW,* 101) is replaced by a positive decision of the later protagonist. Just as the last sentence of Koeppen's novel, taken from the final passage of *Der Tod in Venedig,* reconnects the reworking with the model by its very contrast, the programmatic "Dableiben" emphasizes the fact that Schneider's Lenz has come to a point when he can once more accept life as it really is.

It is difficult to make out precisely on what level Schneider's *Lenz* functions as a reworking of Büchner's novella. Schneider's demonstrative title, and the textual and atmospheric allusions to the Büchner model, raise an expectation in the reader that the text will be intimately related to the well-known model. But, as it turns out, Schneider has merely absorbed and integrated a fairly random selection of elements. Furthermore, Büchner's novella is only one among a number of other literary traditions that have been integrated into Schneider's text. Compared to Büchner's *Lenz,* the story of Schneider's *Lenz* begins much earlier in the onset of the personal crisis, and suggests some possible causes for Lenz's alienation from his surroundings. It also covers a longer period of time: several months, rather than weeks. Apart from the two protagonists there are no parallel characters in the two texts, although some correspondence can be found between the guiding influence of Oberlin and the catalytic role of B. Büchner's Lenz seems to stand alone in the world. There is hardly a reference to his past except for a brief mention of his parents and his former fiancée, Friederike. In contrast, Schneider's Lenz is surrounded by a multitude of friends and acquaintances most of whom we meet no more than once. Encounters with friends, conversations with fellow Marxists, chance meetings with strangers — all these happen in a bewildering variety of places, in the street, in shops, on the factory floor, in pubs, at parties, in private flats. But again, only a few of these characters, and next to none of these settings, recur in any meaningful way.

If we look for textual links in the descriptions of Lenz's mental illness, we find most of the parallels with the model in the first half of Schneider's text, the period set in Berlin. However, on the level of Lenz's movements in the reworking, the parallels with the Büchner model begin *after* Lenz's departure from Germany. The journeys of Schneider's Lenz, and the way in which they affect his mental state, *seem* to remind us of the model, but the similarity dissolves as soon as we try to grasp it. If we look for corresponding settings within the two narratives, we could argue that the parallel with Büchner begins with Lenz's sudden impulse to leave everything behind him and escape to Italy. The episodes in Berlin could then be regarded as a kind of prehistory of the protagonist, and the reworking of Büchner's text would set in with Lenz's journey across the Alps. From there we would contrast the opposing fates of the two Lenz figures: Büchner's Lenz has to endure the disintegration of his mind to the bitter end; Schneider's Lenz passes through different stations and learns to come to peace with himself and his surroundings. But the healing process does not take place during Lenz's stay with the peasant family in the mountains above Rome. The idyll, which shares its sense of timeless peace with the mountain community of Waldbach, is found not there, nor in Rome itself, but in Trento, a small industrial city, where Lenz arrives only after a *second* important journey. Unlike Büchner's Lenz, whose mind deteriorates with relentless inevitability on his journey from north to south (with only the brief respite of his sojourn in Waldbach), Schneider's protagonist recovers while traveling a circular route, from Berlin, across the Alps to Rome, north again to Trento, and back to Berlin. Geographically and psychologically Trento lies halfway between the poles of Berlin and Rome. Büchner leaves us with a vision of Lenz's life stretched out before him in infinite bleakness. Schneider's Lenz recovers after his experiences in Italy, and he is ready to re-integrate into the life he had left behind.

Other Literary Influences

Using merely the plot as a starting point, it would be questionable to speak of a Büchner reworking at all. Peter Laemmle's skepticism is justifiable when he asks:

> Wäre dieses Buch unter einem anderen Titel und ohne das vorangestellte Zitat erschienen, hätten seine Kritiker mehr darin gesehen als einen ausgezeichneten Erfahrungsbericht der Zeit von 1968 und danach? Hätte man das Buch noch gut gefunden, wenn man zugegeben hätte, daß es außer dem Namen seiner Hauptfigur kaum etwas mit Büchner gemeinsam hat?[23]

Or, indeed, had it not been for that name, would the narrative even have been *recognized* as a self-declared literary successor to Büchner's *Lenz*? In addition to the integration of the Büchner model, other literary influences on Schneider's *Lenz* are of a somewhat bewildering variety. Schneider uses quotes and near-quotes from a great variety of sources, he borrows linguistic and structural features, he comments on and reworks general literary themes, and his character re-lives experiences of other, previous literary characters. Apart from the explicit affinity to Büchner's *Lenz*, there are striking similarities between the symptoms displayed by Schneider's Lenz and Hofmannsthal's Chandos. In addition to this, Schneider's *Lenz* can also be linked, directly or indirectly, with two more important literary traditions: Germany's continuing love affair with Italy, and the genre of the *Bildungsroman*.

Just as Büchner's fictional account of historical events produced the literary tradition of *Lenz* narratives, some of which have been listed at the beginning of this chapter, Goethe's dramatic flight to Italy in 1786 started a literary tradition, the most famous example of which is probably Thomas Mann's *Der Tod in Venedig*. Like most of his fictional successors, Goethe traveled to Italy in order to escape from pressures in Weimar, in order to seek inspiration from the classical spirit, and to regain an inner balance that had been upset. In German literature, Italy is not just any foreign country, but "traditionally the land which has for Germans represented a flight into an unrelated past."[24] Italy stands for a place of transformation, a country with a catalytic effect on those who seek it. This fact, according to Williams, has led to "the tendency of newspaper reviewers to read Schneider's text in the light of the Büchner model, only to have sudden recourse to parallels with Goethe's *Italienische Reise* for the second half of the book."[25]

Goethe is also the best-known exponent of the classical *Bildungsroman*, the genre that traces the development of the protagonist as he or she moves from place to place and is formed and educated by meeting other societies and encountering different cultures. It has been suggested by Leslie Morris that Schneider's "*Lenz* can be read as a latter-day *Bildungsroman,* where Lenz fits the archetype of the restless wanderer."[26] This brings us to the final question as to whether the interpretation of the reworking gains in significance by reading it in the light of the acknowledged literary model, and likewise, whether our reading of Büchner's *Lenz* is revived as a consequence of revisiting it from the perspective of Peter Schneider's work?

The Historical Perspective

As was the case in the earlier chapters, particularly those on Brecht and Kroetz, it can be argued that the allusions to the literary model add a historical dimension to the reworking that it would not otherwise possess. The link between the political aims of Schneider's *Lenz* (by way of the revolutionary figure of Büchner himself) and the social ideals of J. M. R. Lenz embeds Schneider's narrative in a historical tradition of social reformers. And again, as in the case of Kroetz, Schneider does not necessarily gain overall from the association with Büchner's novella. In his assessment of Schneider's *Lenz* as a reworking of Büchner's novella Gordon Burgess concludes:

> The events and characters of Schneider's text gain in historical perspective: the reader is being invited to use the past as an aid in creatively interpreting the present, just as Schneider's own Lenz learns to do from Pierra and others. . . . It may be argued, though, that the price Schneider pays for such historical perspective is a qualitative comparison with the earlier work, in which his own is the loser.[27]

Büchner's *Lenz* has found its established place in the ranks of universal literature, and is no longer tied to any specific political or historical context. In comparison, Schneider's text already possesses a flavor of reading like a historical document, a mere thirty years after its publication. But even in this instance we have to remember that the dialogue between reworking and model is not only a one-way communication from model to reworking. In his essay, "Tradition and the Individual Talent" (1919), T. S. Eliot describes the ideal order of all great works of art:

> What happens when a new work of art is created is something that happens simultaneously to all works of art that preceded it. The existing monuments form an ideal order among themselves, which is modified by the introduction of the new (the really new) work of art among them. The existing order is complete before the new work ar-

rives; for order to persist after the supervention of novelty, the *whole* existing order must be, if ever so slightly, altered; and so the relations, proportions, values of each work of art toward the whole are readjusted.[28]

Schneider's *Lenz* is deeply committed to the anticapitalist ideology of Germany's Left at the time. At first glance, Büchner's *Lenz* seems to be a wholly apolitical text, concerned with the psychological disintegration of an individual. The comparison with Schneider's text has highlighted the elements of a radical criticism of what we now call capitalist values, and the pressures that are borne on the individual — that prove to be an important aspect of Büchner's text as well. Not only does the reworking gain in significance when being read together with the model, but it is also possible that new aspects of interpretation of the model are highlighted when read in conjunction with the reworking, or, as Eliot puts it: "The past should be altered by the present as much as the present is directed by the past" (39).

If the underlying principle of Koeppen's reworking was one of fragmentation, Schneider's *Lenz* could be described as having absorbed and integrated its literary model. This integration functions on several levels. First, the narrative structure incorporates textual features in form of style and near-quotes into the text; these elements are initially highlighted by the title, synonymous with that of the model, and the Büchner quote which precedes the narrative. Second, on the level of the plot we follow the protagonist in his progressive mental disarray but, in contrast to the model, Schneider's protagonist eventually recovers. Finally, within the German literary tradition Schneider's work is, on the one hand, a typical example of the early 1970s, the withdrawal of the writer from the political scene into the private realm — the so-called New Subjectivity — and on the other hand it contains enough elements of the *Lenz* tradition, the *Chandos* experience, the "Italian tradition," and the *Bildungsroman* to be ascribed to either genre.

5: Quotation: Goethe's *Die Leiden des jungen Werther* and Ulrich Plenzdorf's *Die neuen Leiden des jungen W.*

> Zitiertechnik und Erzählstruktur lassen sich
> aus den politischen Umständen erklären.
> Die Verschlüsselung des kritischen Potentials
> kritisiert die Verhältnisse, die sie nötig
> machen, schärfer als jede direkte Kritik.
> *Franz Peter Waiblinger*

The Reception

THE PUBLICATION OF A NOVEL only rarely becomes an item on the social and political agenda of the day. The possibility is even slimmer if the author of such a book is virtually unknown, even in literary circles. But one such novel was Goethe's *Die Leiden des jungen Werther,* first published in 1774.[1] This comparatively short narrative captured the imagination of the times and sent moral shock waves throughout Europe. It started a new *Werther* fashion, and is even reputed to have caused a wave of suicides. *Die Leiden des jungen Werther* was original in more than one way: in the form of the epistolary novel written from the perspective of only one person, in the powerful use of language as a means of expressing personal feelings, and in the unconditional character of the protagonist who, without making any concessions to the conventions of the society he lives in, acts according to the dictates of his heart alone. Werther protests against the stifling rationality of an insensitive age in which creativity, originality, and sensibility are restricted by functionality and the need to conform. The hero speaks from the soul, from *his* soul. The reader is drawn into *his* world and empathizes with *his* feelings. The subjective account of Werther's life disregards the demand for objectivity and a balanced perspective, the central literary conventions of the times.

The publication of *Die Leiden des jungen Werther* in the 1770s became the hallmark of the Age of Subjectivity. Two hundred years later, in the 1970s, Goethe's *Die Leiden des jungen Werther* has lost none of its original fascination for the reader. In March 1973, the publishing house *Insel* launched its paperback edition of *Die Leiden des jungen Werther*. Two years later it had sold sixteen thousand copies, a remarkable phenomenon.[2] Not only does this prove a genuine interest in a canonical writer that goes well beyond the usual *ennui* with a prescribed text, it also shows an extraordinary empathy for and preoccupation with a character who would normally be regarded as lunatic at a period of political tension when great things are at stake. Over the centuries Goethe's *Die Leiden des jungen Werther* has been the subject of countless imitations and anti-works, "Wertheriaden" and "Anti-Wertheriaden." More than 140 reworkings, written both by German and foreign authors, are listed in Goedeke's bibliography. Most of these works have long since disappeared from the bookshelves, such as, for example, W. Alexis: *Ein englischer Werther* (1843), Narkissos: *Der neue Werther, eine hellenische Passionsgeschichte* (1902), or Hermann Jaques: *Der neue Werther* (1915).[3] All descendants of Werther follow the same path of human yearning for unattainable goals, and when they do not find a new preoccupation, they perish in the face of this eternal longing. One notable exception to this list of unremarkable and forgotten *Werther* successors is Plenzdorf's *Die neuen Leiden des jungen W.*[4] In fact, this short work had an impact on German society very similar to that of its distinguished predecessor.

Published in 1973, the same year as Schneider's *Lenz, Die neuen Leiden des jungen W.* is a work of the *Neue Subjektivität*, a tradition generally regarded as a reaction to the political commitment of the writers of the 1960s. What Schneider's *Lenz* meant to the student population, *Die neuen Leiden des jungen W.* signified to the apprentices and older school pupils. The text found an enormous echo among the youth in both halves of the divided Germany. It caused a political storm in the German Democratic Republic (GDR), and a wave of moral outrage in the Federal Republic of Germany (FRG). The critics were divided as to its literary merit; the public was stunned by the affront of using the revered Werther as a model for the proletarian, down-to-earth Edgar. Plenzdorf's recognition arises almost exclusively from *Die neuen Leiden des jungen W.*, which won him the prestigious Heinrich Mann Prize from the East Berlin Academy of Arts in 1973. Like its model, *Die neuen Leiden des jungen W.* has even left its mark on later literary works of the GDR: Edgar, "der junge W.," appears briefly in Rolf Schneider's *Reise nach Jaroslaw* (1974), and in Volker Braun's *Unvollendete Geschichte* (1977) both *Werther* narratives are compared and discussed by the central character. The publication of Goethe's *Die Leiden des jungen Werther* and Plenzdorf's *Die neuen Leiden des jungen W.* is separated by two centuries, but the similar circumstance of their reception is merely the first of the parallels that tie the two works together.

Goethe and His *Werther*

Much has been written about the genesis of Goethe's *Die Leiden des jungen Werther*, about the biographical details that led to the writing of the novel, about the real-life characters who merged into literary characters and thus gained immortality. Goethe himself had some regrets about the overzealous identification with Werther, and the inappropriate forms of source-hunting that started almost immediately after the publication of the novel — prying into his own life and that of the unfortunate Karl Wilhelm, an acquaintance who had committed suicide just before Goethe began work on the novel. Goethe himself describes how the writing process, which had enabled him to rid himself of the past, had the opposite effect on some of the readers.

> Ich fühlte mich, wie nach einer Generalbeichte, wieder froh und frei, und zu einem neuen Leben berechtigt. Das alte Hausmittel war mir diesmal vortrefflich zustatten gekommen. Wie ich mich nun aber dadurch erleichtert und aufgeklärt fühlte, die Wirklichkeit in Poesie verwandelt zu haben, so verwirrten sich meine Freunde daran, indem sie glaubten, man müsse die Poesie in Wirklichkeit verwandeln, einen solchen Roman nachspielen und sich allenfalls selbst erschießen; und was hier am Anfang unter wenigen vorging, ereignete sich nachher im großen Publikum und dieses Büchlein, was mir so genützt hatte, ward als höchst schädlich verrufen.[5]

In the framework of this discussion, we have to restrict ourselves to the elements of Goethe's *Die Leiden des jungen Werther* that have been taken up in the reworking. Much of the existing criticism analyzes the relationship between model and reworking on the level of the plot, of the character constellation, and the effect of the *Werther* quotes.[6] But there are also important parallels in the narrative structure that shed a new light on both the model and the reworking.

Goethe's *Die Leiden des jungen Werther* is an example of the epistolary novel, the *Briefroman*. Although the epistolary novel existed as a literary form at the time — for example, in J. J. Rousseau's *Nouvelle Héloïse* (1759) — *Die Leiden des jungen Werther* is unique in that all letters are written by the same writer, Werther, and sent to the same recipient, Wilhelm. The only exceptions are four notes addressed to Lotte. By far the most substantial part of the novel consists of these letters and diary entries. In *Dichtung und Wahrheit* (1831) Goethe draws attention to the unique qualities of the letter form as a sophisticated medium for telling a story:

> Einem schriftlichen Erguß, er sei fröhlich oder verdrießlich, setzt sich doch niemand unmittelbar entgegen; eine mit Gegengründen verfaßte Antwort aber gibt dem Einsamen Gelegenheit sich in seinen Grillen zu befestigen, einen Anlaß sich noch mehr zu verstocken. Jene in diesem Sinne geschriebenen Wertherischen Briefe haben nun wohl deshalb einen so mannigfaltigen Reiz, weil ihr verschiedener Inhalt erst in solchen ideellen Dialogen mit mehreren Individuen durchgesprochen worden, sie sodann aber, in der Komposition selbst, nur an *einen* Freund und Teilnehmer gerichtet erscheinen.[7]

Werther's apparently impulsive outpourings have already undergone a filtering process through these inner dialogues. This never-ending internal forming and reforming of thoughts and feelings is an important characteristic of Werther's introvert nature, and an integral element of the narrative technique. It lends the novel a certain transparency, and suggest that the final version of events, the one eventually put on paper, could have been written quite differently and is only *one* possible rendering of the story. Each new variation, composed in the mind of the fictional Werther, moves the written account further away from the factual events and deeper into the realm of the subjective.

The novel is preceded by a short preamble in which a fictional editor appeals directly to the reader to be sympathetic to Werther's sufferings. This narrative framework provides a kind of pseudo-objectivity for the novel as a whole. It is, however, swept away as soon as we meet Werther himself, speaking to us directly in his letters. Nevertheless, the fictional editor claims he has selected and ordered the material, and transferred the events into the past. He distances himself from his protagonist, and makes an attempt to record the story in a factual manner. Single capitals or asterisks are used to hide the identity of a person or a place, such as "der Amtmann S." (*GW*, 20) or "daß ich mit dem Gesandten nach *** gehen soll" (*GW*, 40), a device that aims to lend authenticity to the work. On several occasions the editor adds explanatory or apologetic footnotes, which further emphasize the apparent genuineness of the text.[8] When Werther's own voice, in the form of letters and diary entries, dries up during the last few days of his life, the editor finds it necessary to continue the narrative himself, carefully justifying this process (*GW*, 92–93). Werther's final days, his actions and his feelings, are reconstructed by the apparently disaffected narrator who, nevertheless, seems to be much more intimately acquainted with Werther than Werther's best friend Wilhelm is. Although the narrative perspective changes from the first to the third person at this point, this does little to alter the character of the narration, which invites the reader to look straight into Werther's soul.

Borrowed Meaning

When we first meet Werther, he is inspired by the literature of classical Greece, and carries a pocket edition of Homer wherever he goes. On his return from the court, he is preoccupied with the mythology of northern Europe and ponders over long passages from James Macpherson's *The Poems of Ossian*. This change of preference on the part of Werther reflects on the mental state of the protagonist, and also serves as a narrative device. Goethe himself complained that apparently "it was never perceived by the critics, that Werther praised Homer while he retained his senses, and Ossian when he was going mad. But reviewers do not notice such things."[9] *The Poems of Ossian*, a Scottish/Gaelic epic, which reached Germany in 1760, was hailed as another archetypal myth from time immemorial, a northern Homer. As it turned out, it became "the most famous literary hoax in the English language, which sent shock waves rippling through Europe in the last quarter of the eighteenth century. So convinced were the early Romantic critics of the genuineness of Macpherson's *Poems of Ossian* that they were universally referred to as the works of Ossian, the name Macpherson rarely being mentioned."[10] The integration of long passages from the *Poems of Ossian* serves a dual function. In the second half of the novel, the pace and the atmosphere change. Werther and reader alike are influenced by the mood of the *Ossian* epic, with its ceaseless lament of heroes betrayed and lovers perishing, and its descriptions of an untamed and unyielding nature. More importantly, we experience how literature can have a direct effect on life (at least on the life of a fictional character) when the shared reading of the *Poems of Ossian* triggers the passionate kiss exchanged between Werther and Lotte.

Thus, we find that Goethe's *Die Leiden des jungen Werther* is composed of four distinct narrative elements: (1) the preamble and the editor's attempts to disguise the personages and the location of Werther's account, which are aimed at lending the work authenticity; (2) the letters which form the major part of the narrative — here Werther speaks directly to the reader, and the account is immediate and confiding; (3) the narrated final part, which completes the record of Werther's life at a time when his own voice is no longer heard; and (4) the long passages of borrowed literature that reflect on the mental state of the protagonist, and serve as *agens movens* in the flow of the narrative.

Many of the details of Werther's death were taken from Christian Kestner's letter to Goethe, describing the circumstances surrounding the suicide of Jerusalem, a mutual friend. Most strikingly, we find that both the historical Jerusalem and the fictional Werther had a copy of *Emilia Galotti* lying open on the table in the room in which they had shot themselves. Jerusalem apparently died because of unattainable love. Werther's sufferings and eventual suicide also stem from a love without prospects, but equally from a lack of purpose in life, and from the consciousness of our human limitations. Emilia, who accompanied them both during their last moments, died to protect her moral integrity. When faced with the passionate wooing by the prince, she chooses death rather than what she feared would be a life of gradual moral disintegration. By leaving the open book on his bedside table, Werther seems to plead that his death should be regarded likewise as a moral choice in the face of the gradual disintegration of his personality. Thus, Emilia's shadowy presence is not incidental, but adds a moral dimension to Werther's death.[11] The integration of literature read and discussed by the protagonists is an essential characteristic of Goethe's novel and adds significance and meaning to the events of Werther's living and dying. As we shall see, Plenzdorf also employs this technique, and thus we have some justification to look for in Goethe's work, what has not been explicitly expressed in Plenzdorf's novel. Just as Emilia's presence lends meaning to Werther's death, Werther's *Weltschmerz* bears silent witness to Edgar's suffering.

The new *Werther*

The publication of Plenzdorf's *Die neuen Leiden des jungen W.* falls in a period of gradual liberalization of the arts in the GDR, later called the *Tauwetter* period. Only two years previously, Erich Honecker had encouraged a more open-minded approach to literature in the GDR with his landmark speech of 1971, stating: "Wenn man von den festen Positionen des Sozialismus ausgeht, kann es meines Erachtens auf dem Gebiet von Kunst und Literatur keine Tabus geben."[12] But by his irreverent treatment of Goethe's classic, by the casual language and, most importantly, by the failure to reintegrate the protagonist into society at the end of the novel, Plenzdorf had gone too far. Honecker's displeasure at so negative a portrayal of socialist society amounted to complete rejection of *Die neuen Leiden des jungen W.* on the grounds that the novel did not measure up to the aesthetic standards expected of a literary text produced in a socialist state.[13] Robert Weimann, one of the leading critics in the GDR, is more pragmatic in his judgment, paying tribute to Plenzdorf's huge popular success. He tries to justify the impact of the novel by giving Edgar a place among the socialist literary heroes of the time. He acknowledges the social criticism contained in the work, but writes it off as a critique of particular details in the development of the socialist state, and not fundamental to the ideology as a whole.

> *Die neuen Leiden des jungen W.* haben Furore gemacht. Diese rasche Wirkung hat mancherlei Ursachen, vor allem aber die eine: daß widersprüchliche Haltungen in der jungen Generation, kunstvoll aufgezeichnet und konfliktreich zugespitzt, Aufnahme in unserer Literatur finden. Dabei geht es nicht um die Geschichte eines Gammlers; dies ist die Geschichte eines Ausreißers, aber doch nicht eines Ausreißers aus dem Sozialismus.[14]

Naturally, the stronger and more public the condemnation of the novel became, the higher it rose in profile, gaining immense popularity on both sides of the German divide. West German reaction was mixed as well, and tended to emphasize Plenzdorf's critique of the socialist state. Marcel Reich-Ranicki's remarks are typical for this view:

> Was wollte nun Plenzdorf zeigen? Daß in der DDR für einen jungen Menschen mit Charakter das Leben im Kollektiv eine Qual sei?... Oder wollte Plenzdorf mit Schiller predigen: Ans Kollektiv, ans teure, schließ dich an, das halte fest mit deinem ganzen Herzen, hier sind die starken Wurzeln deiner Kraft? Ich meine: Beides ist unzweifelhaft in seiner Erzählung, und man sollte sich hüten, nur eine der beiden Seiten zu sehen.[15]

Just as a number of critics question the validity of Schneider's *Lenz* as a literary reworking of Büchner's *Lenz,* Ilse H. Reis wonders whether the connection between Werther and Edgar is as close as the title proclaims it to be, and indeed whether the references to Goethe's *Die Leiden des jungen Werther* would have been understood, had it not been for the title.[16] But as we shall see, in this instance the inner relationship between the two *Werther* characters is much closer than that between the two *Lenz* texts and figures.

After an argument at the factory where he is apprenticed, Edgar runs away to Berlin and lives illegally in a garden shed on an allotment. Being short of toilet paper, he takes what he finds, and uses the title page and the notes at the back of a small paperback. Bored and lonely in his new existence, he begins to read the now titleless book, which he initially finds totally incomprehensible.

> Nach zwei Seiten schoß ich den Vogel in die Ecke. Leute, das konnte wirklich kein Schwein lesen. Beim besten Willen nicht. Fünf Minuten später hatte ich den Vogel wieder in der Hand. Entweder wollte ich bis früh lesen oder nicht. Das war meine Art. Drei Stunden später hatte ich es hinter mir. Ich war fast gar nicht sauer. (*PL,* 36)

Like Werther and his obsession with Charlotte, Edgar falls in love with a girl he calls "Charlie." Just as Werther's Lotte is engaged to Albert, Charlie is engaged to a worthy young man named Dieter. Like Werther, Edgar tries to free himself of his passion for Charlie and looks for work as another outlet for his energy. Both Werther and Edgar are frustrated by the monotony and lack of creativity in the workplace, and they opt out of the productive cycle of formalized employment. Then comes the great difference between them: Werther focuses increasingly on his hopeless feelings of love for the now married Lotte, a process leading to his mental breakdown and eventual suicide. By committing suicide, he finally actualizes "das süße Gefühl der Freiheit, . . . daß [der Mensch] diesen Kerker verlassen kann, wann er will" (*GW,* 14). Edgar, on the other hand, is increasingly possessed by the desire to build an automatic spray gun on his own, a venture his *Brigade*[17] of painters and decorators had all but abandoned after a long series of collective attempts to overcome the technical difficulties. Edgar dies of an electric shock. Whether his death is an accident, or the inevitable end to an ever-growing alienation from society, remains undecided.

In short, despite the industrial setting of East Berlin in the 1970s and a very different assembly of minor characters in the respective works, we can reduce *Die Leiden des jungen Werther* and *Die neuen Leiden des jungen W.* to the same plot: a young man moves to a new town and meets a girl. Gradually he falls in love with her, although she is already engaged to another man. When the situation becomes unbearable, the young man leaves to find employment. He fails to find satisfaction and fulfillment in his job and returns to the girl, who is now married. Unable to exist in a society that stifles his individuality, he dies just before Christmas.

In addition to the common plot, there is a significant number of analogous situations and constellations between the two texts. Both Werther and Edgar regard themselves as artists. They paint or draw, albeit in a dilettante fashion, and they each produce a silhouette of the beloved, Lotte and Charlie respectively. Lotte is surrounded by her younger brothers and sisters; Charlie is a kindergarten teacher, a role that equally emphasizes a motherly side to her character. Lotte's fiancé Albert and Charlie's fiancé Dieter share many characteristics: they are fully integrated into society, they are both methodical and hardworking, but lack the impulsiveness, the teasing nature, and the lust for life of their prospective brides. Albert and Dieter both own a gun, but whereas Albert's gun, passing through Lotte's hands, is instrumental in Werther's death, Edgar uses Dieter's gun to get closer contact with Charlie, and the "gun" which kills him is of his own making.

In both novels other literature is discussed and has a direct effect on the lives of the (fictional) characters. The importance of Homer and Ossian on Werther's emotions and actions has already been mentioned. Likewise, before Edgar comes across *Die Leiden des jungen Werther*, he also has two books that play an important role in his imagination: Daniel Defoe's *Robinson Crusoe* and J. D. Salinger's *The Catcher in the Rye*. Edgar's love for these books is passionate: "Wenn ich gewollt hätte, hätte ich mich hinhauen können und das ganze Buch trocken lesen können oder auch den Crusoe. Ich meine: ich konnte sie im Kopf lesen" (*PL*, 34). But of course, the greatest influence on Edgar comes from Goethe's *Die Leiden des jungen Werther*, which he internalizes to the degree that he readily quotes whole passages learned by heart, although we cannot be sure how conscious Edgar is of this assimilation himself.

Double Perspective

Originally conceived as a film script, and later revised for the stage, Plenzdorf's *Die neuen Leiden des jungen W.* has retained some features of the dramatic genre. At the same time, like Goethe's *Die Leiden des jungen Werther*, the novel also operates on four different narrative levels: documentary evidence of the newspaper advertisements, dialogue, monologue, and quotation. *Die neuen Leiden des jungen W.* opens up with a number of public notices, taken from various newspapers, announcing the accidental death of Edgar Wibeau. The advertisements, specifying a date and the name of the papers, lend authenticity to the following narrative in the same way that the fictional editor's framework does in *Die Leiden des jungen Werther*. There is no further comment. On the next page we find ourselves in the middle of a dialogue between Edgar's parents. Edgar's father is trying to reconstruct the life of a dead son whom he had not seen since he was five years old. In the course of the narrative he speaks to all those people who might know something about Edgar's life during his last few months. These conversations, which follow the pattern of a detective story, are given in dialogues that are interspersed throughout the narrative. The initial dialogue between Edgar's parents is soon interrupted by Edgar's own commentary, speaking from "jenseits des Jordan" (*PL,* 16). In ever-lengthening monologues Edgar recounts the events that led to his death from his own point of view. In his inquiry into Edgar's life, the father finds out very little. All the physical evidence left is a series of tape recordings that Edgar had sent to his friend Willi. These recordings are all quotes from Goethe's *Die Leiden des jungen Werther* and, stripped of their original context, they remain garbled nonsense as far as the protagonists of the novel are concerned. The reader, on the other hand, recognizes the source of the tape recordings, and is challenged to interpret their intrinsic meaning. The quotes, which so alienate Edgar's friends, become a kind of insider code between Edgar and the reader, who becomes Edgar's only confidant and to whom Edgar appeals in the postmortem contemplation on his life. The *Werther* quotes mark Edgar's growing identification with Werther by giving us an insight into Edgar's thought patterns and, of course, they serve to emphasize the parallel fates of the two protagonists beyond the level of the plot.

Thus, in Plenzdorf's novel we also find four narrative levels, each using a distinct linguistic register: (1) a preamble, consisting of various newspaper notices, lends the work authenticity and uses an appropriate register of factual language; (2) an inner frame, consisting of various interviews conducted by Edgar's father, rendered in dialogue form using colloquial speech (visually distinct from frequent interruptions by Edgar commenting on his life from beyond the grave); (3) Edgar's monologues, which occupy the largest part of the novel and are delivered in teenage jargon; thus, he provides a critical commentary on the events of his own life and on the perceptions others have of him; and (4) quotations from Goethe's *Die Leiden des jungen Werther,* partly recorded on cassette and partly quoted by Edgar as he relates his story.[18]

While there are no direct equivalents between Goethe's and Plenzdorf's narrative structures, these four differing perspectives are nevertheless related to one another: (1) the appeal for sympathetic understanding by the editor in Goethe's novel is contrasted by the impersonal announcements of the newspaper telling us the outcome of the story; (2) Werther's letters to Wilhelm find their equivalent in Edgar's tapes to Willi in form, and to Edgar's monologue in content; (3) the last few days of Werther's life, in which the narrative perspective changes from the first person to the third person, is mirrored by the dialogues in *Die neuen Leiden des jungen W.,* but in reverse order: whereas Werther ceases to speak for himself, Edgar has the last word and the dialogues lose prominence during the narrative; and (4) in both narratives other works of literature are quoted and move the plot: *The Poems of Ossian* in *Die Leiden des jungen Werther,* and Goethe's *Die Leiden des jungen Werther* in *Die neuen Leiden des jungen W.*

Edgar's monologues, which make up by far the largest part of the novel, are related in a spontaneous and nonsentimental teenager jargon. Edgar tells us of his feelings and opinions in a subjective but totally uninhibited way. In contrast, when still alive Edgar seems hardly to have communicated with his environment at all. He never really speaks with his mother, he sends messages to his friend, knowing that Willi will not be able to understand them, and, after finally finding his father, he visits him incognito and feels unable to make himself known to him (*PL,* 108). Two phrases come up time and again during the narrative: various forms of "Ich weiß nicht, ob mich einer versteht, Leute,"[19] and "Ich Idiot."[20] These signify that Edgar has undergone a maturing process after his death, which is the perspective of his narrative. The artificially constructed distance to the events of his life has caused Edgar to be critical of almost all of his attitudes and actions when still alive, to the effect that his inability to integrate, and become a productive and responsible comrade in socialist society is seen merely as a sign of juvenile immaturity. Thus, Plenzdorf constructs a double perspective: on the one hand, the novel tells the story of tongue-tied and impulsive adolescent, and on the other, it offers the perspective of the more mature young man who reflects on his actions, and who distances himself from many of his earlier sentiments.

The first episode in which this double perspective becomes apparent is at the same time the trigger for the whole of the narrative. The prospect of having to openly repent for his bad behavior towards his foreman is too humiliating and causes Edgar to run away from Mittenberg to Berlin (*PL,* 15). During life he could not face the practice of public self-criticism, which was so much part of socialist life. However, after his death Edgar modifies almost all of his earlier opinions. In that sense he becomes a positive hero in socialist terms — but he has to die in the process. By using this device, Plenzdorf avoids the heavy hand of the censor. The most fundamental social criticism is contained in the fact that while still alive Edgar is unable to communicate with his surroundings and craves for creative and meaningful work and the satisfaction that comes from working outside the collective. In other words, here we come across a young person (and a role model to his readership) who lives in almost complete isolation and feels utterly alienated from the prevailing values of a society that prides itself on providing care from cradle to grave. This biting criticism, aimed at the very core of socialist ideology, is revised and modified by Edgar himself, and can therefore remain part of the narrative.

Edgar finds access to the classical work only after having stripped it of its literary context, the title page, and the editorial notes at the back of the book. Had he known the novel was written by Goethe, Edgar might never have touched the book. In spite of the widely discussed attempt of integrating Germany's literary heritage into the socialist culture of the GDR (*Erbaneignungsdiskussion*), Edgar did not recognize the Goethe text, and thus his reception of the novel was immediate and innocent of the idea that the novel was a probable contender for the school syllabus. At least initially, Edgar's approach to the novel is purely naive. He rejects *Die Leiden des jungen Werther* utterly, both on account of the plot and of the language. Had he not been compelled by the lack of any other reading material to return to the little paperback time and again, to the point that he could recite passages from it by heart, it is unlikely that he would have achieved this strong identification with Werther. But gradually he does identify with the eighteenth-century protagonist and, as a result of the intensive study of the classic, Edgar gains an increased understanding of himself and the society he lives in. At the same time he becomes ever more alienated from the values of the socialist state. This, according to Franz Peter Waiblinger, is one of the terrible ironies of Plenzdorf's novel: the protagonist absorbs and learns from Germany's literary heritage, but this maturing process does not lead the individual back into socialist society.[21]

Quotation as a Means of Social Criticism

The relationship between the Goethe's *Die Leiden des jungen Werther* and the modern reworking clearly operates by way of the parallels found in the plot and the character constellation. At a deeper level, both texts have complicated narrative structures, which likewise have a number of comparable features and devices. In addition to the features already cited, the carefully selected use of quotation from Goethe's *Die Leiden des jungen Werther* ties the two works even more closely together. On his search to get a picture of the son he never knew, Edgar's father comes across a set of tapes Edgar had sent to Willi. Before any parallels with Goethe's *Die Leiden des jungen Werther* become apparent, the text of seven recorded messages, all passages from *Die Leiden des jungen Werther,* are listed without any context (*PL,* 17–18). With one exception, these taped quotes are repeated later in the text as part of Edgar's ongoing narrative. Whereas the reader has been alerted to the probable source of these quotes by Plenzdorf's choice of title, the protagonists can make nothing of it. Even Edgar himself apparently never got to know the title of the book that influenced him so profoundly (*PL,* 19).

Altogether there are sixteen *Werther* quotes which occur in the course of Plenzdorf's novel. Seven are recorded messages sent to Willi back home in Mittenberg. The others are either utterances, which Edgar uses to impress the people around him, or reflections on the part of Edgar as he analyzes his own situation. The quotes can be grouped according to four different functions identified in the text. A number signify the different stages of the love affair. A further few serve as evidence of the degree to which Edgar has internalized Goethe's *Die Leiden des jungen Werther*. If these two categories are rather inward looking, the next two are directed at the world outside. Edgar attacks others by citing passages from *Die Leiden des jungen Werther,* a means of self-defense he himself calls his "*Werther* pistol." Finally, Goethe's words are used to deliver a sharp social criticism of the GDR society in a manner that is secure from the heavy hand of the censor.

The first five quotes of the recordings sent to Willi mark out the development of the love affair between Edgar and Charlie.[22] Edgar constantly emphasizes the similarity of the two unfolding love stories — between Werther and Lotte, and between himself and Charlie respectively. It all started as a joke. Having read the titleless paperback, and initially dismissing it as irrelevant, Edgar is suddenly able to make a connection, for the simple reason that his own friend bears the same name as Werther's friend, and because he has met a girl he fancies whose name, incidentally, is *not* Charlotte ("Wieso Charlotte? Ich heiß doch nicht Charlotte!" *PL,* 44).

> Kurz und gut, Wilhelm, ich habe eine Bekanntschaft gemacht, die mein Herz näher angeht . . . Einen Engel . . . Und doch bin ich nicht imstande, dir zu sagen, wie sie vollkommen ist, warum sie vollkommen ist, genug, sie hat allen meinen Sinn gefangengenommen. Ende. (*PL,* 51)

Not all quotations are reproduced exactly as they appear in Goethe's *Die Leiden des jungen Werther*. When Edgar records a message onto tape, we can assume that he does not need to recite from memory, but is able to assemble the messages deliberately with the Goethe text at hand. In several instances some of Goethe's text has been omitted, and occasionally a quote is put together from two different letters. The full text from which the above quote is taken is as follows:

Werther: Kurz und gut, [Wilhelm] ich habe eine Bekanntschaft gemacht, die mein Herz näher angeht. *Ich habe — ich weiß nicht. Dir in der Ordnung zu erzählen, wie's zugegangen ist, daß ich eins der liebenswürdigsten Geschöpfe habe kennen lernen, wird schwer halten. Ich bin vergnügt und glücklich, und also kein guter Historienschreiber.* Einen Engel! — *Pfui! das sagt jeder von der Seinigen, nicht wahr?* Und doch bin ich nicht imstande, dir zu sagen, wie sie vollkommen ist, warum sie vollkommen ist; genug, sie hat allen meinen Sinn gefangengenommen. (*GW*, 19)²³	*Edgar:* Kurz und gut, Wilhelm, ich habe eine Bekanntschaft gemacht, die mein Herz näher angeht ... Einen Engel ... Und doch bin ich nicht imstande, dir zu sagen, wie sie vollkommen ist, warum sie vollkommen ist, genug, sie hat allen meinen Sinn gefangengenommen. Ende. (*PL*, 51)

In contrast to Werther, who reflects on his own situation and sees himself in an ironic light, Edgar merely relates facts as they appear to fit his own situation. During the next stage of their acquaintance Edgar thinks he can detect a response to his feelings from Charlie and, referring to Werther, he sends the following message to Willi. "Nein, ich betrüge mich nicht! Ich lese in ihren schwarzen Augen wahre Teilnehmung an mir und meinem Schicksal. Sie ist mir heilig. Alle Begier schweigt in ihrer Gegenwart. Ende" (*PL*, 58; *GW*, 38, 39). Edgar and Werther both know that their respective girls are already engaged to other men. Reality brings them back to earth with the arrival of the fiancé and Edgar records: "Genug, Wilhelm, der Bräutigam ist da! ... Glücklicherweise war ich nicht beim Empfange! Das hätte mir das Herz zerrissen. Ende" (*PL*, 72; *GW*, 42). In both works alike, the protagonists seem to settle down to an uneasy triangular relationship, in which the respective women carry the advantage. Edgar sends this analysis of his situation to Willi: "Er will mir wohl, und ich vermute, das ist Lottens Werk ..., denn darin sind die Weiber fein und haben recht; wenn sie zwei Verehrer in gutem Vernehmen miteinander erhalten können, ist der Vorteil immer ihr, so selten es auch angeht. Ende" (*PL*, 78; *GW*, 42).

Eventually, both Werther and Edgar come to the point when they realize that the status quo cannot continue. They begin to look for work as a way to free themselves from their relationships, and to give their lives another focus. The trigger, which introduces the turning point in their lives, comes in the form of pressure from outside, namely their respective mothers. Edgar receives the message from his mother in which she pleads: "Hauptsache, du arbeitest und gammelst nicht" (*PL,* 84). On the surface Edgar's answer to the appeal to return to work appears to be totally irrelevant:

> Ich hörte mir das an. Ich wußte sofort was von Old Werther darauf paßte:
>
> Das war eine Nacht! nun überstehe ich alles. Ich werde sie nicht wiedersehen!... Hier sitz ich und schnappe nach Luft, suche mich zu beruhigen, erwarte den Morgen, und mit Sonnenaufgang sind die Pferde ... (*PL,* 84)

And the tape breaks off. This quote is taken from the last letter of Book I of *Die Leiden des jungen Werther* (*GW,* 56), and in some ways it describes the high point of Werther's career: acknowledging his undying love for Lotte, Werther leaves her of his own free will, and attempts to give his life a new direction. But, as it turns out, rather than gaining a sense of purpose and independence, from that time onwards Werther is increasingly subject to emotions and moods that he is unable to control. For Edgar, on the other hand, the boast of a night that never happened hides a growing despair. In spite of his newly found independence, he has not found fulfillment, and he decides to return to work, to look for it there. "Ich analysierte mich kurz und begriff, daß die ganze Kolchose und das nicht mehr popte. Ich dachte nicht daran, zurück nach Mittenberg zu gehen, das nicht. Aber es popte einfach nicht mehr" (*PL,* 84). By this stage Edgar has identified with Werther to such a degree that although the quote is not an appropriate response to his mother's strictures, he quotes from the equivalent moment in Werther's life. If the five taped quotes are indeed a summary of Edgar's relationship with Charlie, as suggested by Jürgen Thomaneck, the reader has to regard Edgar's last recording as wishful thinking, rather than a description of an actual event.

Further parallels between Werther's and Edgar's lives begin when Edgar recites lines from *Die Leiden des jungen Werther* to himself in an internal dialogue. His first reading of the novel leaves him repulsed by the flowery language. With the idea of using quotation in his communication, or rather noncommunication, with Willi, he begins to appreciate Werther's attitude to the society around him more and more. As his feelings for Charlie grow and become more complex, he also begins to comprehend Werther's actions. At the first reading of the novel, Edgar does not understand why Werther does not try harder to seduce Lotte and win her for himself (*PL,* 36). But, when he visits Dieter and Charlie after their wedding, he has to admit to himself that he had never thought he would be able to understand Werther on this point (*PL,* 124). Edgar writes a note to Charlie borrowing from Werther's letter to Lotte: "Wenn Sie mich sähen, meine Beste, in dem Schwall von Zerstreuung! Wie ausgetrocknet meine Sinne werden; . . . nicht eine selige Stunde! nichts! nichts!" (*PL,* 116; *GW,* 65). But this letter is never sent off, because Edgar realizes that he cannot communicate with Charlie in that manner, though neither can he express himself using his own words. "Mir wurde klar, daß ich mit Werther schon keine Chancen mehr bei ihr hatte. Damit konnte ich ihr nicht mehr kommen. Bloß, mir fiel nichts anderes ein" (*PL,* 116).

On two other occasions Edgar puts his own feelings regarding Charlie and Dieter into Werther's words. He is relieved at never having to witness any tenderness between Dieter and Charlie, and he thinks to himself: "Auch ist er so ehrlich und hat Lotten in meiner Gegenwart noch nicht ein einzigmal geküßt. Das lohn ihm Gott. — Ich begriff zwar nicht, was das mit ehrlich zu tun hatte, aber alles andere begriff ich" (*PL,* 124; *GW,* 42). At the same time he resents Dieter's apparent neglect of Charlie and says to himself: "Zieht ihn nicht jedes elende Geschäft mehr an als die teure köstliche Frau? . . . Sattigkeit ist's und Gleichgültigkeit!" (*PL,* 129; *GW,* 94). These last two quotes show once more how limited Edgar's understanding of Goethe's language is. He delights in the appealing phrases, but his access to the text is on the emotional level only. He takes the words literally: "Nun war ja Dieter kein Geschäftsmann und Charlie alles anders als eine teure Frau. Und Sattigkeit war's bei Dieter auch nicht. Klar, daß er von wegen der Armee ein hohes Stipendium hatte. Aber unsereins verdiente garantiert dreimal soviel mit der Pinselei" (*PL,* 129). But gradually, by way of coming to understand Werther, Edgar learns more about himself. With Werther's help he grows up. The Goethe novel clarifies his situation and allows him to speak in a private code, which no one understands except himself and the reader. He begins to ponder on the universal experiences of love, fulfillment in life, and, eventually, on the question of death.

After the initial idea of sending these incomprehensible messages on tape to his friend Willi, Edgar also uses *Werther* quotations in face-to-face communications with his acquaintances. Edgar even constructs situations simply in order to "fire off" one of his quotes. Playing up to impress Charlie, he tears out a lettuce from the vegetable garden next to the nursery, eats it there and then, and "shoots."

> Der Sand knirschte, aber ich wollte nur folgendes loswerden:
>
> Wie wohl ist mir's, daß mein Herz die simple harmlose Wonne des Menschen fühlen kann, der ein Krauthaupt auf seinen Tisch bringt, das er selbst gezogen. . . . Ich glaube, ich hatte an dem Tag soviel Charme wie nie. (*PL,* 69–70; *GW,* 29–30)

This behavior is, of course, merely a gag, but the borrowed identity builds up Edgar's own self-confidence. Just as Edgar's situation increasingly resembles Werther's life, Edgar himself begins to comprehend and to empathize with the fictional Werther. The language of Goethe's novel, which initially formed a barrier between Edgar and Werther, increasingly becomes a means of self-expression.

At first Edgar uses the *Werther* quotes to bewilder and confuse his surroundings. Later, when Edgar feels he has to protect himself, he goes on the attack, and the quotations take on a more aggressive nature. The borrowed language, which Willi tries to decipher as a code, becomes for Edgar a weapon that he uses to defend himself against the world at large. When he feels himself in a corner, he draws his "Werther Pistole" (*PL,* 100), which has become his "schärfste Waffe" (*PL,* 75, 82), and which lends him a bravado he does not otherwise possess. Thus, he confounds Dieter who is trying to make sense of his rather "abstract" paintings by quoting Goethe:

> Man kann zum Vorteile der Regeln viel sagen, ungefähr was man zum Wohle der bürgerlichen Gesellschaft sagen kann. Ein Mensch, der sich nach ihnen bildet, wird nie etwas Abgeschmacktes und Schlechtes hervorbringen, wie einer, der sich durch Gesetze und Wohlstand modeln läßt, nie ein unerträglicher Nachbar, nie ein merkwürdiger Bösewicht werden kann; dagegen wird aber auch alle Regel, man rede was man wolle, das wahre Gefühl von Natur und den wahren Ausdruck derselben zerstören! (*PL,* 75–76; *GW,* 15)

Any attempt on Dieter's part to approach Edgar is effectively silenced by this mode of conversation. When Edgar plays the clown and fools around with Dieter's real gun and Dieter wants to stop him, Edgar again lets go the first words that come into his mind:

> Mein Freund . . ., der Mensch ist Mensch, und das bißchen Verstand, das einer haben mag, kommt wenig oder nicht in Anschlag, wenn Leidenschaft wütet und die Grenzen der Menschheit einen drängen. Vielmehr — ein andermal davon.

> Die Grenzen der Menschheit, unter dem machte es Old Werther nicht. Aber ich hatte Dieter voll getroffen. Er machte den Fehler, darüber nachzudenken. (*PL*, 82; *GW*, 50)

Edgar's naive reception of *Die Leiden des jungen Werther* does not enable him to understand that in the quoted passage "die Grenzen" refers to the key factor of Werther's suffering, the *Begrenzung* or *Einschränkung*, the boundaries and limitations of human existence. And yet, the quote is appropriate. Just like Werther before him, Edgar rebels passionately against the soulless, rational world around him, which constantly denies the need of the individual to develop independent thought and gain personal freedom.

The repeated reading of *Die Leiden des jungen Werther* opens up Edgar's perception of the world, just as it helps him to articulate what he perceives there. He uses *Die Leiden des jungen Werther* to characterize those around him, such as when he mocks Addi, the leader of the *Brigade*:

> Er ist der pünktlichste Narr, den es nur geben kann; Schritt vor Schritt und umständlich wie eine Base, ein Mensch, der nie mit sich selbst zufrieden ist und dem es daher niemand zu Danke machen kann." (*PL*, 99; *GW*, 61)

Yet paradoxically, it is primarily to Addi that he wants to prove his own ability, and to justify his original invention (*PL*, 139). These attacks on Dieter and Addi are funny because of their ingenuity, and because, unlike the other protagonists, the reader can see the quotes in context. On the other hand, both Addi, the leader of a successful *Brigade*, and Dieter, a former soldier preparing to take an entry examination for university in order to study German literature, are exemplary representatives of the socialist society and therefore not to be taken too lightly. Edgar's bitter mockery is directed not only against these two individuals, but also against the values and mediocrity of the society they stand for. On that level of understanding, the *Werther* quotes lend the adolescent a means by which he is able to express his deep instincts about the weaknesses of his society.

Finally, Edgar uses *Die Leiden des jungen Werther* to put his feelings about the world around him into words, and thus communicates directly with the reader. Edgar's attacks leave the other protagonists speechless (*PL*, 56, 76). The reader, however, is called upon to examine further the nature of the critique. Two quotes stand out in the text, the first because Edgar uses it twice, once addressing Charlie and once in an attack on Addi. The second quote is significant because it appears only on the tape and Edgar's narrative does not reveal the circumstances as to where and how it fits into the events of his life. When Charlie criticizes Edgar for not working, he lashes out: "Es ist ein einförmiges Ding um das Menschengeschlecht. Die meisten verarbeiten den größten Teil der Zeit, um zu leben, und das bißchen, das ihnen von Freiheit übrigbleibt, ängstigt sie so, daß sie alle Mittel aufsuchen, um es loszuwerden" (*PL,* 56, 100; *GW,* 11).

Edgar also mocks Addi with the same words after yet another attempt to construct the spraygun has failed. This quote, the first and the last shot from Edgar's *Werther* pistol, hits particularly hard because it is aimed at one of the core values of socialist society, the significance of work as the true purpose of human existence. Edgar's critique becomes even more biting if we look at the original context. In his letter to Wilhelm of May 17, 1771, Werther describes the new society he finds himself in. The above quote is preceded by the ominous sentence: "Wenn du fragst, wie die Leute hier sind, muß ich dir sagen: wie überall" (*GW,* 11). Werther continues to complain about the superficiality of life, as he perceives it. Life is well-ordered and pleasant, and yet — "nur muß mir nicht einfallen, daß noch so viele andere Kräfte in mir ruhen, die alle ungenutzt vermodern und die ich sorgfältig verbergen muß. Ach das engt das ganze Herz so ein" (*GW,* 11–12).

One of the most essential values upon which the socialist society is built is questioned here: the realization of personal freedom and human dignity through work. In socialism work is of intrinsic value. According to Engels, "Arbeit . . . ist die erste Grundbedingung alles menschlichen Lebens, und zwar in einem solchen Grade, daß wir in gewissem Sinn sagen müssen: Sie hat den Menschen selbst geschaffen."[24] According to this view, workers in a capitalist society are forced to prostitute their capacity to work and sell it in the marketplace. It constitutes a form of alienation by which the worker becomes a mere commodity. In contrast, in a socialist state, in which workers work for themselves, work is an expression of human dignity, and an end in itself. Work should ideally be the ultimate form of self-expression, providing the highest degree of individual fulfillment. But after more than thirty years of socialism in the GDR, Edgar feels that his experience of the workplace stifles his development as an individual, and suppresses all creativity. He rebels against the traditional and boring training methods in the factory at Mittenberg, and he criticizes the attitude of his foreman Flemming as old-fashioned and feudal (*PL,* 13). In protest Edgar retires to his private world for any expression of his individuality, and secretly begins to paint. After his flight to Berlin, he initially opts out of employment altogether, thus attempting to express his individuality not in work but in his newly found independence.

The second quote, which stands out because it appears only on the initial list of tape recordings, must have been sent to Willi at the time when Edgar was working as a member of the painting *Brigade*. It reads as follows:

> o meine Freunde / warum der strom des genies so selten ausbricht / so selten in hohen fluten hereinbraust und eure staunende seele erschüttert — liebe freunde / da wohnen die gelassenen herren auf beiden seiten des ufers / denen ihre gartenhäuschen / tulpenbeete und krautfelder zugrunde gehen würden / die daher in zeiten mit dämmen und ableiten der künftig drohenden gefahr abzuwenden wissen — das alles / wilhelm / macht mich stumm — ich kehre in mich selbst zurück und find eine welt — ende. (*PL*, 18–19)

The first part is taken from Werther's letter of May 26, 1771, the same letter that contains the passage fired at Dieter ("Man kann zum Vorteil der Regeln viel sagen . . ." *GW*, 15), in which Edgar rebels against a life that is ordered and restricted by countless rules that curb all spontaneity and creativity. The final sentiment ("das alles macht mich stumm . . .") comes from the preceding letter of May 22, 1771. Again, the original context adds a significant dimension. Where Edgar chooses to be silent, Werther speaks out.

> Wenn ich die Einschränkung ansehe, in welcher die tätigen und forschenden Kräfte des Menschen eingesperrt sind; wenn ich sehe, wie alle Wirksamkeit dahinaus läuft, sich die Befriedigung von Bedürfnissen zu verschaffen, die wieder keinen Zweck haben, als unsere arme Existenz zu verlängern, und dann, daß alle Beruhigung über gewisse Punkte des Nachforschens nur eine träumende Resignation ist, da man sich die Wände, zwischen denen man gefangen sitzt, mit bunten Gestalten und lichten Aussichten bemalt — Das alles, Wilhelm, macht mich stumm. Ich kehre in mich selbst zurück und finde eine Welt! (*GW*, 13)

This key passage describes Werther's (and Edgar's) suffering: both suffer from the limitations of human existence they constantly experience, namely the discrepancy between their own nameless desires and the dullness of society which places certain demands on them. This leads them to rebellion against the restrictive life on the one hand, and resignation and a withdrawal into the private sphere on the other.[25]

In the light of such a fundamental critique of the socialist society, the last remaining quote on the tape also takes on a new significance. Edgar is fired by the *Brigade* for ridiculing its failed efforts to build a new type of paint spraygun, and he records a message for Willi: "Und daran seid ihr alle schuld, die ihr mich in das Joch geschwatzt und mir soviel von Aktivität vorgesungen habt. Aktivität! ... Ich habe meine Entlassung ... verlangt! ... Bringe das meiner Mutter in einem Säftchen bei. Ende" (*PL*, 101; *GW*, 62). The quote is once more assembled from two different letters of Goethe's *Die Leiden des jungen Werther*. The first part is from December 24, 1771, exactly one year before Werther's death. Again, if we return to *Die Leiden des jungen Werther*, the surrounding text assumes a startling significance in the context of GDR society. The words speak for themselves:

> Und das glänzende Elend, die Langeweile unter dem garstigen Volke, das sich hier neben einander sieht! die [*sic*] Rangsucht unter ihnen, wie sie nur wachen und aufpassen einander ein Schrittchen abzugewinnen; die elendesten, erbärmlichsten Leidenschaften, ganz ohne Röckchen. (*GW*, 62–63)

The second part of the recording comes from a short letter from March 24, 1772 in which Werther asks Wilhelm to pass on the news of his resignation from work to his mother. The passage just preceding this letter shows Werther's present preoccupation with suicide:

> Ach, ich hab' hundertmal ein Messer ergriffen, um diesem gedrängten Herzen Luft zu machen. Man erzählt von einer edlen Art Pferde, die, wenn sie schrecklich erhitzt und aufgejagt sind, sich selbst aus Instinkt eine Ader aufbeißen, um sich zum Atem zu helfen. So ist mir's oft, ich möchte mir eine Ader öffnen, die mir die ewige Freiheit schaffte. (*GW*, 70–71)

Werther leaves his post of his own accord; Edgar is temporarily suspended from work. The recording that delivers Edgar's apparent revolt against work in the collective also underscores his inability to communicate with his mother directly, thus demonstrating that two of the ideals of socialist society, the intrinsic value of work and a strong and supportive social network, have failed him. The preoccupation with death, which forms the content of the *Werther* letters from which these quotes are taken, suggests a deeper level of despair and resignation on Edgar's part than is immediately apparent from the text itself. Indeed, the reader who feels inspired enough to return to Goethe after the reading of *Die neuen Leiden des jungen W*. will find that in the light of Goethe's novel the whole narrative can be read as a social critique in an encoded form. Additionally, the quotations, citing the words of Germany's classical past, have proved an effective way around official censorship of the state.

Thus, we can summarize three functions of the Goethe quotes in the *Die neuen Leiden des jungen W.*: (1) Edgar reads *Die Leiden des jungen Werther* and internalizes the classic without knowing that he is doing so. The use of quotation forms an enticing narrative device by which the author engages the reader's interest not only in his own work, but also, again, in Goethe's classic, which is particularly relevant in the context of the *Erbaneignungsdiskussion* of the GDR; (2) Edgar uses passages from the text to alienate and confuse his contemporaries. At the same time Werther's fictional world helps to clarify Edgar's own experiences. A great deal of the humor contained in Plenzdorf's novel comes from the clash between these two worlds; (3) some of the *Werther* quotes can be interpreted as a fundamental criticism of the socialist society of the 1970s. In a country where state censorship has the final say, and where Plenzdorf himself would have to be silent, Goethe is allowed to speak.

The Effect of the Reworking

Plenzdorf's work would almost certainly not have attained the high political profile it achieved had it not been for its relationship with Goethe's *Werther*. Still, *Die neuen Leiden des jungen W.* achieved its popular success, both as a stage play and as a novel, largely because it went to the heart of the problems that most occupied young people in both Germanys: communication with the adult world, the first experiences of love, and adapting to the working environment.[26] *Die neuen Leiden des jungen W.* triggered a lively debate among the younger readership, which was not concerned with the legitimacy of borrowing so freely from Goethe's classic. The key to Plenzdorf's success lay in the highly accessible language and in the issues it raised by the example of Edgar's life and death.

Yet, the answer to one of the most central questions of the novel, namely what caused Edgar's death, seemed to depend almost entirely on the geographical location of the critics.[27] Is Edgar a positive or a negative hero? Did he die in spite of or because of real existing socialism? Was Edgar's death a sheer accident, akin to suicide, or just a literary necessity? Did Edgar overcome his inability to communicate with his environment, or did he perish because he had severed all ties with his friends and his family? Would his invention have worked, or was it a gigantic failure? None of these questions are answered in the text. On the whole, critics from the GDR tended to interpret the novel positively. Edgar has problems with his environment, but he learns to overcome his alienation, is about to be fully reintegrated into society, and is on the verge of making an important invention, when death suddenly strikes him down — an ironic accident! This view is confirmed by Edgar's resolution to get on with his life: "Ich wollte die Spritze fertigmachen, sie Addi auf den Tisch knallen und dann abdampfen nach Mittenberg und von mir aus die Lehre zu Ende machen. So weit war ich" (*PL,* 139). According to this view, the novel describes a society that is evolving in the right direction and even outsiders and difficult cases will eventually find their own place within that society. Again Edgar's own words support this interpretation: "Ich hatte auch nichts gegen den Kommunismus und das, die Abschaffung der Ausbeutung auf der ganzen Welt.... Kein einigermaßen intelligenter Mensch kann heute etwas gegen den Kommunismus haben" (*PL,* 80–81).

Critics from West Germany paint a very different picture. According to that view, Edgar's fate shows that he lives in a society that does not allow for individual growth and freedom of choice. He receives one setback after another, his apprenticeship is highly unsatisfactory, he is rejected from art school, he will not integrate into the *Brigade,* and finally he fails to build the spraygun. The invention was a fake and Edgar's death is the inevitable conclusion to his isolation and despair. Members of the GDR society, so the argument goes, are suffering from an almost complete breakdown of communication, which is demonstrated by the fact that no one knows anything about Edgar when his father makes inquiries. Creativity can flourish only in the outsider, and in complete secrecy.

And what about the author himself, what is Plenzdorf's reaction to the speculations made by the critics? Is Edgar a representative figure of (East) German youth, or not? Is his death the necessary conclusion to his growing alienation from society, or a terrible accident shortly before he would have been fully reintegrated into society? Plenzdorf will not commit himself to any answers, but simply states: "Im Moment [1973] bin ich einfach in der Situation, dazusitzen und zu sammeln und glücklicherweise auch Dinge interpretiert zu hören, von denen ich nicht dachte, daß sie drinstehen.... Der Text ist bewußt auf Auslegbarkeit geschrieben."[28] The wide spectrum of opposing interpretations of *Die neuen Leiden des jungen W.* arises from the fact that Edgar's own comments are not always reliable. He has already revised some of his attitudes in the light of his afterlife. However that might be, the possibility of his complete reintegration into society, the importance of the invention of the spraygun, and the underlying causes of Edgar's death are all left open to a wide range of different readings. And it is possible that finding a definitive answer to any of the above questions is less important than raising them in the first place. Just as the success of *Die Leiden des jungen Werther* was due to the fact that the young people of the 1770s felt that their emotions and frustrations were given a voice, the appeal of *Die neuen Leiden des jungen W.* lies to a large extent in acknowledging the existence of the feelings and struggles of adolescents in the 1970s, and finding an appropriate language in which to do so.

Edgar tells us that before he found *Die Leiden des jungen Werther*, he was fascinated by two other literary works: *The Catcher in the Rye*, by J. D. Salinger (1951), and *The Life and Strange Surprising Adventures of Robinson Crusoe*, by Daniel Defoe (1719). There are several parallels to be drawn between *Die neuen Leiden des jungen W.* and these two classics. *The Catcher in the Rye* is an account of the adventures of a runaway schoolboy in New York. The story is told in retrospect at a time when the first person narrator, Holden Caulfield, is presumably in some institution after a nervous breakdown. Edgar might well have dreamed of similar adventures in Berlin when he decided to leave for the big city. Edgar's passion for dance seems to come straight from Salinger's novel, as does the intimacy of the teenage jargon, which is directed at the reader to the exclusion of everyone else. Like his reception of *Die Leiden des jungen Werther*, Edgar's approach to Salinger's novel is immediate and nonreflective. He does not even distinguish between Salinger, the author, and Holden Caulfield, the character:

> Dieser Salinger ist ein edler Kerl. Wie er da in diesem nassen New York rumkraucht und nicht nach Hause kann, weil er von dieser Schule abgehauen ist, wo sie ihn sowieso exen wollten, das ging mir immer ungeheuer an die Nieren. Wenn ich seine Adresse gewußt hätte, hätte ich ihm geschrieben, er soll zu uns rüberkommen. (*PL,* 33)

As is the case with Werther, Edgar empathizes with the fictional character as if he were a friend. The great contrast between *The Catcher in the Rye* and *Die neuen Leiden des jungen W.* is that the former is permeated by a deep sense of melancholy and desolation from the very beginning. Holden Caulfield *exists* without being able to *live* in a mental state not unlike that of Büchner's Lenz after his confinement in Strasbourg. A key passage in *The Catcher in the Rye* has a friend and former teacher describe Holden's situation in life:

> This fall I think you are riding for — it's a special kind of fall, a horrible kind. The man falling isn't permitted to feel or hear himself hit the bottom. He just keeps falling and falling. The whole arrange-

ment's designed for men who, at some time or other in their lives, were looking for something their own environment couldn't supply them with. Or they thought their own environment couldn't supply them with. So they gave up looking. They gave it up, before they ever really got started.[29]

As was the case with Schneider's *Lenz* narrative, the deliberate allusions to *The Catcher in the Rye* in Plenzdorf's novel suggest a much darker, more troubled side of Edgar's soul than is immediately apparent from the text alone. In addition, Thomaneck[30] has drawn attention to a number of parallels between Edgar and Defoe's *Robinson Crusoe*: both are of foreign descent (Edgar prides himself on his Huguenot name), and are nearly of the same age, Edgar being seventeen and Robinson eighteen years old; both leave a way of life which would have led to a secure career and fall into complete isolation; neither can endure this state, and both make attempts to break out of their solitude. Again, the moral value of work is an important theme in Defoe's text. Robinson complains about the status quo, using almost the same words as Werther in his letter of May 17, 1771 (*GW*, 11) cited above: "I saw the world busy around me; one part laboring for bread, another part squandering in vile excesses or empty pleasures equally miserable . . ."[31] And yet there is an essential difference between Robinson Crusoe, who is intensely practical in his outlook and lives by the dictates of his reason, and Werther, who is solely guided by his emotions, and eventually falls victim to despair. Thus, Edgar has chosen three very different fictional young men as role models, who are all vastly removed from him in time and space: the highly educated Werther, who views the world with his heart and displays an excess of feeling; Robinson Crusoe, the self-made young man who strives to control his environment by virtue of his discipline and reason; and Holden Caulfield, the dreamer, who expresses himself in teenage jargon and views the world from an outsider perspective. The evoked presence of these three literary texts, which influence Edgar so strongly, complete the picture of Edgar's suffering. They imply a tale, which may not be told in any other way.

In the light of the close links between *Die Leiden des jungen Werther* and *Die neuen Leiden des jungen W.*, we should not underestimate the depth of despair reached by Edgar. Edgar's resemblance to Werther in this respect is easily overlooked because of the seemingly careless language. Edgar is telling his story in retrospect, from the viewpoint of eternity as it were. Nevertheless, judging by the importance of those incidents he chooses *not* to disclose to us, there is a side to Edgar's emotional life the reader can only guess at. We learn nothing of his feelings at the rejection from art school, which must have come as a hard and unexpected blow to him; the episode of his anonymous visit to his father is merely described on a factual level, but Edgar shares neither the hatching of the plan, nor his disappointment after the meeting; and he hides the strength of his passion for Charlie, only admitting casually: "Kann auch sein, daß meine Nerven nicht die besten waren zu der Zeit, wegen der Sache mit Charlie. Es ging mir doch mehr an die Nieren, als ich gedacht hatte" (*PL*, 88). Pain, failure, and death are difficult topics to raise in our successful age. The modern reader might even hesitate to witness the dimensions of suffering that are suggested. This shyness certainly applies to Karin, the central character, in Volker Braun's *Unvollendete Geschichte,* a narrative that bears a strong affinity to Büchner's *Lenz*. Karin has read both Goethe's and Plenzdorf's novels and compares the two *Werther* figures. She draws the conclusion that a book that would accurately describe Edgar's and with it the depth of her own suffering, would be too much to bear.

> Nur war ihr, als sie nachdachte, der *junge W.,* zu jung, zwei Jahre wenigstens: sie verstand ihn, aber verstand sich davon nicht besser. Er sprach sich mal herrlich aus — aber der Werther, den er immer zitierte, hing noch anders mit der Welt zusammen. . . . Der stieß sich an ihrem Kern. W. stieß sich an allem Äußeren, das war lustig, und ging per Zufall über den Jordan. Das Ungeheure in dem *Werther* war, daß da ein Riß durch die Welt ging, und durch ihn selbst. Das war eine alte Zeit. Und doch war auch in all dem Äußeren ein *Inneres,* W. drang nur nicht hinein, ein tieferer Widerspruch — den man finden müßte! Wie würde ein Buch sein — und auf sie wirken, in dem heute einer an den Riß kam . . . in den er stürzen mußte. Sie würde das Buch vielleicht hassen.[32]

Boredom and Revolutions

The 1770s in Germany — the Age of Subjectivity — was a time of relative political stability. The focus returned to the private world of the individual: feelings, relationships with others, the nature of intuition and motivation were under scrutiny. At the same time a deep sense of the monotony of life, of boredom and world-weariness, permeated the age. In *Dichtung und Wahrheit* Goethe characterizes his time thus:

> Von unbefriedigten Leidenschaften gepeinigt, von außen zu bedeutenden Handlungen keineswegs angeregt, in der einzigen Aussicht, uns in einem schleppenden, geistlosen, bürgerlichen Leben hinhalten zu müssen, befreundete man sich, in unmutigem Übermut, mit dem

Gedanken, das Leben, wenn es einem nicht mehr anstehe, nach eigenem Belieben allenfalls verlassen zu können, und half sich damit über die Unbilden und Langeweile der Tage notdürftig genug hin. Diese Gesinnung war so allgemein, daß eben *Werther* deswegen die große Wirkung tat, weil er überall anschlug und das Innere eines kranken jugendlichen Wahns öffentlich und faßlich darstellte.[33]

Werther has no sense of purpose in his life. He does not seem to be under pressure to achieve anything in particular, his livelihood is secure, he has no attainable ideals to strive for. When he eventually finds employment, he resents the boredom and the routine of his working day, and he takes offense at the idea of becoming a replaceable part in a functioning organism larger than himself. He suffers from the fact that his creativity and his freedom to please himself at all times are severely curbed. After having left his employment, Werther drifts through life, thinking lofty thoughts and giving himself over to his emotions. His goals are not anchored firmly in the reality of this world. This makes him crave for the liberty to enter the next. Arrogant pride and the stunted development of his individuality contribute to his death as much as the suffering caused by a love affair without prospects. Dissatisfaction with the world and the frustration of his desires, a lethal mixture, are not merely Werther's personal weaknesses, but also identify him as a product of his age.

If the Enlightenment laid the foundation for the rise of the middle classes in society, it also contained the seeds of the popular revolutions of the late eighteenth and early nineteenth century in central Europe. In Germany these revolutions were preceded by a long phase of impatience and frustration. Peter Wapnewski argues that Werther is a typical representative of the restless generation of young men of the pre-revolutionary period, whose subjectivity knew no bounds. In this, these young men were out of touch with the spirit of the times, which favored the rapid establishment of the industrious and increasingly prosperous middle classes. Thus, their sensibility was directed towards the private sphere, and from time to time this excess of emotions had fatal consequences.[34] History goes in cycles. In the 1970s Edgar suffers from the same disease as Werther did two hundred years before him. He, too, cannot find satisfaction in the workplace, he is frustrated in love, he sets himself unrealistic goals and persists in a state of a heightened sense of self — he wants to go it alone. But at the same time, Edgar is also a child of his own time. The early 1970s was a period of idealistic aspirations and a great if somewhat naïve faith in the possibility of real social change in the spirit of a New Enlightenment (*Neue Aufklärung*). However, by the middle of the decade that idealism was proved to be unfounded, and much of the burning desire for improvement turned initially into impatience and later into a deep sense of disillusionment, particularly on the part of the younger generation.[35]

The parallels Wapnewski draws between the 1770s and the 1970s proved to be prophetic. The second half of the eighteenth century was a period of apparent middle-class complacency and economic stability. At the same time it was characterized by a sense of boredom and frustration for the younger generation. This period of quiet before the storm was followed by the upheavals of the French Revolution. East Germany of the early 1970s witnessed a similar complacency and was permeated by a deep sense of having arrived. In a speech of 1973 Wilhelm Girnus is able to proclaim in direct reference to Goethe: "Stellen Sie sich vor, hochverehrte Gouvernanten, der Sozialismus ist für unsere Jugend bereits ein *Erbe*. Ein Erbe eben, daß es zu *erwerben* gilt."[36] Writing in 1975, Wapnewski could not have known that almost two hundred years after the French Revolution, the complacent 1970s in East Germany would once more be followed by political and economic upheaval, or that the GDR would collapse from a complete loss of faith in the system, bringing in turn the peaceful revolution of 1989.

Plenzdorf's treatment of Goethe's *Die Leiden des jungen Werther* is one of the most faithful reworkings of a model. The transference of the *Werther* motifs into the 1970s is both creative and successful insofar as it captures the spirit of the times. Although numerous minor incidents and characters from the Goethe model have been omitted, and new ones created, Plenzdorf retains the constellation of the central protagonists, and the direction of Goethe's plot. Central features of the narrative structure of *Die Leiden des jungen Werther* reappear in a different guise. Quotation becomes the primary means by which the reader learns what cannot otherwise be said about Edgar's inner state of alienation. At the same time Plenzdorf uses Goethe's words as a vehicle for his most biting social and political criticism. Last but not least, Edgar's application of Werther's language might confuse his fictional contemporaries, but it furnishes the novel with abundant humor.

6: Constellation of Character: Goethe's *Die Wahlverwandtschaften*; Hugo von Hofmannsthal's *The Chandos Letter*; and John Banville's *The Newton Letter*

> Certainly the whole story is not
> written here, but it is suggested.
> *Olive Schreiner*

An Irish Reworking

IN ONE WAY JOHN BANVILLE'S NOVEL *The Newton Letter*[1] (1982) begins to transgress the limits of this study, because it is written in English and is thus addressed to a readership who might not be expected to recognize the features of the reworking. Whereas most reworkings already draw attention to their connection with a literary model by means of the title, Banville's *The Newton Letter* gives no obvious indication that this novel is intimately connected to not only one but two models from German literature. But the reader who is familiar with *Die Wahlverwandtschaften*[2] (1809) will very quickly recognize the references to Goethe's novel, and in a note Banville himself draws attention to the fact that his novel owes essential sentiments to Hugo von Hofmannsthal's *Ein Brief* (or *Chandos Letter* [1902]).[3] Once it has been recognized that *The Newton Letter* constitutes a reworking of both Goethe's *Die Wahlverwandtschaften* and Hofmannsthal's *Chandos Letter*, Banville's short novel suddenly shows a complexity and depth that is otherwise barely discernible. Thus, *The Newton Letter* must rank among the most subtle and creative reworkings of the selection introduced in this volume. On the one hand, it is vastly enriched by its links with its models; on the other, it re-evaluates the models by making quite clear how much they — particularly *Die Wahlverwandtschaften* — are products of their respective age. The nature of the subject — an investigation into the relationship between the human being and the realm of natural laws — invites the reader to go beyond the arts as a basis for understanding human nature, and to engage with fundamental questions of philosophy of science concerning the effect of scientific paradigm changes that have fashioned the worldview of the twentieth and twenty-first century.

Published in 1982, *The Newton Letter* is a short novel by the Irish writer John Banville. It forms the third novel of a tetralogy[4] on scientists whose ideas have fundamentally changed the way we perceive the universe. The first two novels, *Dr Copernicus* (1976) and *Kepler* (1981), are both fictional biographies, and are set at the historical time and place of the respective central protagonists. *The Newton Letter*, on the other hand, seems at first glance to be almost exclusively about the experiences of a twentieth-century historian engaged in writing a biography of Isaac Newton, and is set at the present time in Ireland. The last novel of the series, *Mefisto* (1986), is even more removed from the actual lives of the great mathematicians of the twentieth century, such as Kurt Gödel[5] or Albert Einstein, who inspired it, but once more the title suggests another possible link to Goethe's work.

The primary aim of the natural sciences is to order the world according to different categories, and to discover its underlying laws. This is done initially by observation of natural phenomena and subsequently by constructing a scientific model. The use of a theoretical model by the scientist is akin to the practice of the writer to express thoughts in metaphors. Thus, even though no one has ever seen electricity, when scientists use terms like "flow" and "current" in connection with electricity, the original model is one of water. Scientific models are not "real," and are in need of constant revision and modification. For example, three mutually exclusive models, the particle, the wave, and the ray, are used to describe different behavior of light, which demonstrates that science has not yet found a comprehensive model to represent the essence of light. Before the whole truth can be known, the scientist applies these models in order to manipulate nature, even if it is clear that the model is inadequate to capture the whole phenomenon. Niels Bohr, the physicist who "discovered" the current model of the atom, even went so far as to say: "The task of science is both, to extend the range of our experience and *to reduce it to order*."[6] The resulting order aims to deliver models on which one can build a cohesive picture of the natural world. But all models that are arrived at by this method have to be constantly evaluated as our understanding of the natural world increases and changes. When a model has to be discarded altogether and is replaced by an alternative one, such as the exchange of a geocentric to a heliocentric model of the universe, scientists talk about a paradigm shift.

What the model is to the scientist, the narrative form is to the novelist. Just like nature herself, a story may remain essentially the same throughout the ages, but the form in which it is told will belong to a certain period and a certain culture. In the context of writing fiction based on the lives and discoveries of significant scientists, scientific concepts may well be used as appropriate models for the narrative structure. And, as we shall see, the narrative structure of *The Newton Letter* accurately reflects an image of our current fragmented understanding of the natural world, just as the composition of Goethe's *Die Wahlverwandtschaften* mirrors the cohesive and unified order of the mechanistic Newtonian universe.

Content as an Aspect of Form

John Banville's prime concern has always been form before content, and in an interview of 1981 he states categorically: "If we employ, instead of the word story, the term content, then I would say that I consider form far more important. Content, I would maintain, is an aspect of form, no more."[7] Banville insists that it is not *what* is being said, but *how* it is said, that matters in the realm of aesthetics. Thus, Banville's method of constructing the world of his novel emulates that of a theoretical scientist. However, in the attempt to impose a theoretical concept of science on the structure of a novel, Banville makes one essential distinction, namely, that the subject matter of the novel must always be a living and acting entity, and not an abstract idea. Or, in his own words: "Fiction cannot dispense with people, or, if it does, it relinquishes its rights and powers and becomes something else."[8]

Banville experiments with and seeks new forms for the novel, forms appropriate to the present concept of reality, which at the same time serve as a means to illuminate the content matter of his story. In *Die Wahlverwandtschaften* he has found a perfect example for what he wants to achieve. Goethe's novel is a literary work in which content and form have reached complete agreement, and in which the aesthetic form is an expression of the current scientific worldview. But Goethe's novel is not the only literary predecessor that has left its mark on *The Newton Letter*. Rüdiger Imhof has identified numerous other literary links and connections that reach well beyond the particular range of this study.[9] Merely to hint at the complexities of the work must suffice. Francis Molloy has described the work of Banville using the metaphor of an iceberg:

> The tip of the iceberg is what happens on the surface of the novel — the actions of characters and so forth. Beneath the surface is a com-

plex web of references to works of literature and to genres of literature which gives an ironic perspective to the surface events and, as Banville claims, "gives the work resonance."[10]

From the above it becomes clear that Banville entertains some very ambitious notions in the inception of *The Newton Letter*. His novel, set in the twentieth century, comments on the importance of the Newtonian revolution; it aims to overcome the traditional divide between art and science by adopting a scientific concept as a model for a fictional narrative; it seeks to establish a link between German and Irish culture by referring to two German literary models in a novel written in English.

In order to investigate how these ideas are realized in *The Newton Letter*, it will be necessary to widen the term *form* to include not just the narrative style, the language, symbolism, and recurring themes, but also the character constellation and the setting. As we will see, both the setting and the choice of names for the protagonists add meaning to the whole, and introduce new dimensions not otherwise present. This intimate connection between form and content can be demonstrated by a simple test.

The Newton Letter is the story of a nameless first-person narrator, a historian working on a Newton biography, who sums up the events of the novel himself: "I spent a summer in the country, I slept with one woman and thought I was in love with another; I dreamed up a horrid drama, and failed to see the commonplace tragedy that was playing itself out in real life" (*NL*, 79). This brief summary of the events of the summer does tell us crudely what actually happens in the course of the novel, but it gives no inkling of a possible comment on Newton's work, something we would expect of a "book on Newton." That only comes about if we take a closer look at the significance added to the narrative by the constellation of the characters, and direct and indirect references to other literary and scientific works.

Before we explore the deeper regions of the iceberg, let us take a closer look at what we see on the surface of *The Newton Letter*. The place is Ireland, and the story is set in an isolated, crumbling country house called Ferns with a large, rambling garden. Ferns is occupied by four people: a married couple, a child, and a young woman, the niece of the wife. The narrator moves into the lodge in order to finish his Newton biography in the peace and quiet of the country. Increasingly he gets involved with the inhabitants of the big house. He has an affair with the niece, while discovering that he is really in love with the wife. He has a mental breakdown, which prevents him finishing his book.

At the end of the summer he finds himself unable to stay. He flees from the house, not back into his previous employment, but to a short-term teaching post somewhere in Lapland. Yet his crisis is caused not by his romantic entanglement with the two women, but by a deep sense of alienation from the world around him. His work has become meaningless, while his contact with other people and his relationship to his environment seem to have become unintelligible. The narrator states at the very beginning:

> No I'm not sick, I have not had a breakdown. I am, you might say, in retirement from life. Temporarily. I have abandoned my book. . . . How can I make you understand that such a project is now for me impossible, when I don't really understand it myself? Shall I say I've lost my faith in the primacy of text? Real people keep getting in the way now, objects, landscapes even. (*NL*, 1)

Only two details of Newton's life are mentioned in the course of the narrative: a fire in his library that destroyed much of his scientific work (*NL*, 22–21), and two letters that he allegedly sent to John Locke (*NL*, 5, 50).

Francis Molloy's image of the iceberg invites the reader to move to a deeper level and examine how two central themes are held together — first, seventeenth-century scientific and philosophical thought, as represented by Newton's life and his correspondence with John Locke, and second, the relevance thereof to the twentieth-century narrator and the circumstances he finds himself in. The first clue that leads beyond the immediate events on the surface of *The Newton Letter* lies in the names of the inhabitants of Ferns, the country house.

Die Wahlverwandtschaften — Scientific Model of Human Experience

The husband and wife of *The Newton Letter* are called Edward and Charlotte, which may be familiar enough to the English reader, but the niece bears the unusual name of Ottilie. There is another well-known literary constellation of Eduard married to a Charlotte, and a niece called Ottilie: in Goethe's novel *Die Wahlverwandtschaften*. In an advertisement for his novel, published in 1809, Goethe clearly states his intention of using a scientific concept as a basis for his investigation into human concerns:

> Es scheint, daß den Verfasser seine fortgesetzten physikalischen Arbeiten zu diesem seltsamen Titel veranlaßten . . . und so hat er auch wohl *in einem sittlichen Falle eine chemische Gleichnisrede* zu ihrem

geistigen Ursprung zurückführen mögen, um so mehr, als doch
überall nur *eine* Natur ist.[11]

And Goethe draws particular attention to the complexity of the novel
when he writes to Johann Friedrich Cotta: "Es ist manches hineinge-
legt, das, wie ich hoffe, den Leser zu wiederholter Betrachtung auf-
fordern wird."[12] Starting from his holistic view of the world, of there
being only *one* nature at work in the whole of creation, Goethe justifies his attempt to apply a law from the natural sciences, the phenomenon of the so-called *elective affinities*, to the human realm. To
this day *Die Wahlverwandtschaften* is subject to continuous scholarly
research and heated discussion, and no attempt is made here to do
justice to the intricacies of the novel. This chapter will concentrate
only on those aspects of *Die Wahlverwandtschaften* and of Goethe's
scientific method that have any impact on *The Newton Letter*.

At the heart of *Die Wahlverwandtschaften* lies the conversation on
chemistry about the elective affinities of inorganic substances. Various
experiments with calcium have proven that affinities between certain
substances are stronger than those between others, that in fact the introduction of a new substance to a chemical compound will cause an
existing chemical bond to be broken and a new composite to be
formed. Goethe takes this observation about chemical substances, and
applies it to a number of carefully selected people in a great variety of
circumstances and combinations. The novel then traces the effects of
this ever-changing pattern on individuals, showing which affinities
crystallize out as the strongest.

Eduard and Charlotte have invited the Hauptmann (the captain)
to stay with them, despite some misgivings on the part of Charlotte,
who is reluctant to include a third party so early into their new marriage. One evening, soon after the arrival of the Hauptmann, Eduard
reads aloud from a book on chemical experiments and there follows an
important conversation. The Hauptmann describes the chemical process in such a way that Charlotte immediately applies the natural phenomena to human relationships:

> [Hauptmann:] "Hier ist eine Trennung, eine neue Zusammenset-
> zung entstanden, und man glaubt sich nunmehr berechtigt, sogar
> das Wort Wahlverwandtschaft anzuwenden, weil es wirklich aussieht,
> als wenn ein Verhältnis dem anderen vorgezogen, eins vor dem an-
> deren erwählt würde."
>
> "Verzeihen Sie mir," sagte Charlotte, "wie ich dem Naturforscher
> verzeihe; aber ich würde hier niemals eine Wahl, eher eine Natur-
> notwendigkeit erblicken, und diese kaum; denn es ist am Ende viel-

leicht gar nur eine Sache der Gelegenheit. Gelegenheit macht Verhältnisse, wie sie Diebe macht; und wenn von Ihren Naturkörpern die Rede ist, so scheint mir die Wahl bloß in den Händen des Chemikers zu liegen, der diese Wesen zusammenbringt. Sind sie aber einmal zusammen, dann gnade ihnen Gott!" (*WV*, 274)

Where the Hauptmann is so willing to see choice, Charlotte sees necessity. Who is right? In the realm of natural science there is no choice: calcium does as it must. Is human behavior likewise determined by laws that govern the fate of individuals and to which there no alternative but death? In the case of the attraction between Eduard and Ottilie, the answer is suggested in the penultimate chapter of *Die Wahlverwandtschaften:*

Und so blieb er, wie er wollte, wie er mußte.... auch sie konnte sich dieser seligen Notwendigkeit nicht entziehen. Nach wie vor übten sie eine unbeschreibliche, fast magische Anziehungskraft gegeneinander aus.... Das Leben war ihnen ein Rätsel, dessen Auflösung sie nur miteinander fanden. (*WV*, 478)

By contrast, Charlotte and the Hauptmann seem to be able to control their mutual passion and eventually lead separate lives. But a number of questions remain. How binding is this force of the elective affinities? And why do the protagonists not submit to their feelings and enter new alliances, which would result in the mutual happiness for all involved? What is the force that works against the natural attraction between the lovers, and that will not allow the elective affinities to work to their logical conclusion? The narrator of *Die Wahlverwandtschaften* does not answer these questions. He merely arranges the comings and goings of the subjects and describes the events. Within the context of the novel the protagonists are subject to absolute forces, and when the laws of elective affinity clash with those of moral choices, the battle inevitably leads to a tragic outcome.

Constellations

Although different in length and structure from *Die Wahlverwandtschaften*, *The Newton Letter* borrows extensively from Goethe's novel. First, there is the constellation of the main characters. Eduard/Edward is married to Charlotte; the Hauptmann/the first-person narrator comes as an outsider to the house; and Ottilie is Charlotte's niece. Just as the baby Otto seems to bear a strong resemblance not to his parents but to Ottilie and the Hauptmann, in *The Newton Letter* there is a child, Michael, whose parentage greatly puzzles the narrator. Even the minor character of Mittler appears (married, with two children) in *The Newton Letter* at crucial moments, but he fulfills a different role.

Both works are set in an isolated country estate where the "experiment" can run its course without any interference from the outside. The plane trees, which have such an important symbolic meaning in *Die Wahlverwandtschaften*, reappear as sycamores and line the drive that leads up to Ferns.[13] Ottilie's greenhouse in *Die Wahlverwandtschaften* becomes Charlotte's place of work, and the summer house of *Die Wahlverwandtschaften* reappears as the lodge into which the narrator moves and where his love affair takes place. The glasses with the monograph of E and O, which to Eduard seem to justify his alliance with Ottilie as preordained, re-appear in *The Newton Letter* as two cups with identical cracks (*NL*, 27). We have music in the house, but in *The Newton Letter* it is Edward who plays the piano rather than one of the women. The narrator always associates Ottilie with the oboe, Eduard's instrument in *Die Wahlverwandtschaften* (*NL*, 40, 42).

The *tableaux vivants*, which illuminate the contrasts between the characters of Ottilie and Luciane in *Die Wahlverwandtschaften*, appear in Banville's work, but only in the imagination of the narrator. He has a fleeting vision of Edward, Ottilie, and Michael as if they were grouped in a painting of the Holy Family (*NL*, 40). However, although this image might foreshadow Ottilie in the role of a mother, it conveys no meaning to anyone else at that moment. In *Die Wahlverwandtschaften*, Charlotte's baby, Otto, is the symbolic link between all four protagonists. In *The Newton Letter* the child, Michael, turns into a symbolic figure only for the narrator. He sees Michael first as Cupid (*NL*, 42) who, after falling out of a tree, brings him and Ottilie together for the first time, and later as the Archangel Michael, casting him out of Ferns with a flaming sword (*NL*, 76).

Banville's choice of names form the explicit link to Goethe's novel, and the significance of names and naming constitutes an integral part of both narratives. In *Die Wahlverwandtschaften* the main characters are bound together by a common name. Eduard and the Hauptmann, Charlotte, Ottilie and the child, all echo the name "Otto" in various forms.[14] Both Eduard and the Hauptmann were christened Otto, but Eduard renounced the name as a child. What Eduard gave up by choice, the Hauptmann has been forced to forego. Neither the narrator nor any of the protagonists ever call the Hauptmann by his name. He is only known by his rank and even that is not fixed. In the first part of the novel he is "der Hauptmann" a captain of the army, and in the second part he returns as "der Major."

He shares this apparent anonymity with the narrator of *The Newton Letter*, whose name is never disclosed. Most other characters of *Die Wahlverwandtschaften* are given no names at all, but are simply known by their function: the assistant, the architect, the English Lord, the count and the baroness, and "Mittler" which appears to be more an ironic title than a proper name.

Although the symbolic significance of the names, which in *Die Wahlverwandtschaften* forges a link between the central protagonists, is not exploited in Banville's novel, the names he uses are still descriptive. The family in *The Newton Letter* is called Lawless, except for the narrator, who remains nameless. The name Lawless suggests a group of people who live, or appear to live, beyond the law. At the same time the name reflects the postmodern absence of binding absolutes both in the sciences and in social and moral matters. In an age in which relativism is the predominant principle in all realms of life, laws apply only in a specific context. (Incidentally, the choice of name points to another literary predecessor of *The Newton Letter:* in Banville's own earlier novel *Birchwood*, the family who originally occupied the big house is also called Lawless.[15])

At first glance the characters in *The Newton Letter* appear to share many qualities with their namesakes. Eduard's lack of self-restraint becomes Edward's immoderate, apparently uncontrolled temper, "like a man with a hangover, trying to remember last night's crimes" (*NL*, 7). Charlotte's rationalism returns in the form of her well-bred, slightly distant attitude, and Ottilie's wish to please everybody is described as "inviolable innocence" (*NL*, 8), a quality she shares with Goethe's heroine. But gradually we realize that these impressions exist only in the mind of the narrator, who constantly misinterprets what he sees. In fact, the parallels between *The Newton Letter* and *Die Wahlverwandtschaften* that go beyond the names of the characters and the physical arrangement of the setting are almost exclusively the product of the narrator's imaginings: Edward's moodiness is caused not by his self-indulgence, as in *Die Wahlverwandtschaften*, but by his state of health: he is dying of stomach cancer. Charlotte's aloofness has nothing to do with her breeding but is rather the result of her being constantly "doped to the gills" with Valium (*NL*, 65). The narrator is unwilling to acknowledge Ottilie's real affection for him, making himself believe that she is merely satisfying her sexual desires in the same way as he is doing. He constantly speculates on the parentage of the child, Michael, who he thinks cannot be Charlotte's son and therefore must be Ottilie's (*NL*, 20). At a later stage he imagines him to be fathered by Edward (*NL,* 59). Eventually, it is revealed that Michael is wholly unconnected to the family, and had been adopted by the Lawlesses (*NL,* 67). Other illusions the narrator cherishes about the inhabitants of Ferns have to do with their social status. He judges them to be prosperous Protestants, but they turn out to be Catholics and on the brink of bankruptcy. In contrast to Goethe's Eduard, who is a rich baron and intent on improving his parklands purely for pleasure, Charlotte and Edward Lawless run a commercial nursery. Far from improving the property by controlling and manipulating nature as Eduard and Charlotte attempt to do, the owners of Ferns do not manage to keep the estate in order: the house is falling into disrepair, and the garden is returning into a state of wilderness.

On closer examination, in fact, the parallels with *Die Wahlverwandtschaften* become less and less tangible. Yes, we do have a married couple and a love affair, but the attraction is not between Edward and Ottilie, but between the narrator and Charlotte, whom he desires, and between the narrator and Ottilie, with whom he has an affair. The narrator's obsession with Charlotte, who is not aware of his feelings and certainly does not reciprocate his desire, is founded on his false interpretation of her character and of the state of her marriage. His infatuation ends with a "vast soft crash" (*NL,* 75) when he hears the truth about her Valium habit. Ottilie retains her warm, passionate nature in the reworking, but not her virginity; indeed, if we can believe the narrator, she seems to be the driving force behind their affair. Whereas the Hauptmann is the most restrained and least prominent figure of the four central protagonists of *Die Wahlverwandtschaften,* his successor, the narrator, has become the pivotal figure of the reworking, has lost the self-discipline of his predecessor, and is no longer reliable.

The important scene of the "spiritual adultery" in *Die Wahlverwandtschaften* is in fact no adultery at all in the reworking, as any love scenes take place only between the narrator and Ottilie, both of whom, as far as we know, are unmarried. Whereas Ottilie is apparently very much in love with the narrator, the narrator has visions of Charlotte joining them in bed for what he calls "these bouts of ghostly troilism" (*NL,* 53). This takes place not only once, but on many occasions. Charlotte and Ottilie, whom the narrator had mixed up from their very first appearance, merge into one and become "Charlottilie" (*NL,* 48) in the narrator's mind. At the same time his image of Charlotte has many features of the delicate Ottilie of *Die Wahlverwandt-*

schaften, whereas the *Newton Letter* Ottilie shares some of the pragmatism and robustness of Goethe's Charlotte.

The Narrator as Image of Scientific Paradigm

The titles of Banville's and Goethe's novels give us the first clues about the respective narrative forms. Both works reflect the scientific paradigm of their time. "Wahlverwandtschaften" is a term borrowed from eighteenth-century chemistry and alludes to the scientific framework of the novel. Scientific practice of the eighteenth and nineteenth century favored the unemotional and orderly setting of an experiment in which the scientist remained in charge and developed an objective, slightly distant attitude to the proceedings. In *Die Wahlverwandtschaften* this distance is achieved by a certain measure of irony. Irony is not only a stylistic device Goethe used in his literary work, but also one of these faculties he considered necessary to the scientist. In the *Vorwort zur Farbenlehre* (1808), Goethe stresses the importance for the scientific observer of developing inner qualities, which we normally regard as belonging to the domain of the artist.

> Jedes Ansehen geht über in ein Betrachten, jedes Betrachten in ein Sinnen, jedes Sinnen in ein Verknüpfen, und so kann man sagen, daß wir schon bei jedem aufmerksamen Blick in die Welt theoretisieren. Dieses aber mit Bewußtsein, mit Selbstkenntnis, mit Freiheit und, um uns eines gewagten Wortes zu bedienen, mit Ironie zu tun und vorzunehmen, eine solche Gewandtheit ist nötig, wenn die Abstraktion, vor der wir uns fürchten, unschädlich und das Erfahrungsresultat, das wir hoffen, recht lebendig und nützlich werden soll.[16]

The first four requirements, the ability to see, to observe, to reflect, and to make connections are necessary in the quest for knowledge of the natural world and are commonly regarded as essential in the scientific process. The focus of the observer is directed outwards, from the subject towards the object. However, Goethe adds four matching requirements that traditionally belong to the realm of the artist. Consciousness, self-knowledge, freedom, and irony are directed not outward towards the object, but inward towards the self, the observer. This combination of two movements, one outwards from observer to object, one returning inwards from object to the observer's mind, creates the unity between subject and object that Goethe seeks. Such scientific observation can be conducted only by using essentially human capacities: the senses and language, the very faculties Newtonian science has aimed to exclude altogether.

Goethe's quarrel with Newtonian science is well known. In the twentieth century, however, the apparent contradiction of Goethe's and Newton's color theories is viewed in a different light and prominent physicists such as Werner Heisenberg have suggested that a scientific method involving the holistic approach as outlined by Goethe might still have something to contribute in the future.[17] Despite its phenomenal success over the last two centuries, the traditional objective and detached approach by the scientist aiming to understand the world by reducing it to mathematical formulas and abstract models can no longer be maintained in the twentieth century. Science, according to Banville, "is no longer able to make definite statements about the universe. The scientist is now like the artist; he must employ his imagination in conducting research, not just his reason."[18] This is a position Goethe had taken all along.

For all their differences, Goethe, like Newton, believed in an ordered universe of absolute truths and certainties that can be discovered by observation and scientific method. At first glance the narrator of *Die Wahlverwandtschaften,* like the traditional scientist of the eighteenth century, merely observes the phenomena he is interested in, and remains outside the lives of the protagonists. His role is to follow and report the events as the narrative unfolds.[19] At the same time, even with his opening sentence the narrator asserts his authority, he "imposes order" by naming his creatures: "Eduard — *so nennen wir* einen reichen Baron" (*WV,* 242, my emphasis). And as the plot develops, it becomes clear that the characters themselves are taking part in some grand experiment. This is expressed in the metaphorical language[20] and also in the very construction of the novel.[21]

The narrator emphasizes the nature of the novel as an experiment by the words he puts into Eduard's and Charlotte's mouths. After the decision had been taken to invite the Major and Ottilie, Eduard says with a great deal of pathos: "in Gottes Namen, sei *der Versuch* gemacht!" (*WV,* 252, my emphasis). Likewise, Charlotte agrees to the visit of the Hauptmann with the ominous words: "Solche neue Verhältnisse können fruchtbar sein an Glück und an Unglück, ohne daß wir uns dabei Verdienst oder Schuld sonderlich zurechnen dürfen.... Laß uns *den Versuch* machen!" (*WV,* 256, my emphasis). Just as Goethe requires of the scientist in his essay *Der Versuch als Vermittler zwischen Objekt und Subjekt* (1792),[22] the narrator proceeds to set up related experiments to describe a wider field of the chosen phenomenon. He exposes the central protagonists to a range of other individuals or couples, and then observes mutual or one-sided attraction and repulsion as they arise according to the laws of the elective affinities, until finally a stable situation is reached. The first variable in this chemical equation occurs when the union between Charlotte and Eduard is supplanted by the working relationship between Eduard and the Hauptmann. Soon after, Ottilie is invited to join the group, and the two women reside in one half of the house, while the men stay in the other. Even after the final combination, Eduard and Ottilie, and Charlotte and the Hauptmann, has been formed, the narrator continues, by Eduard's absence, to experiment with the attraction Ottilie holds for other, new characters such as the architect, the assistant, and Nanny. Thus, it is not surprising that the same expressions are chosen to describe the natural phenomenon of the elective affinities and first passionate embrace between Eduard and Ottilie.

Elective affinities: A wird sich zu D, C zu B werfen, ohne daß man sagen kann, wer das andere zuerst verlassen, wer sich mit dem andern zuerst wieder verbunden habe.
(*WV,* 276)

Eduard and Ottilie: 'Du liebst mich!' rief er aus [...] Wer das andere zuerst ergriffen, wäre nicht zu unterscheiden gewesen. (*WV,* 324)[23]

However, as we get to know him better, we discover that Goethe's narrator is by no means wholly objective. The language is cold and unromantic for what could be an intensely romantic story. Little emphasis is placed on feelings. All we learn about the characters' emotions and motives is what the narrator chooses to tell us, and that is far from all there is to tell. Why did Charlotte try to make a match between Eduard and Ottilie before she married him herself? Why did the forces of elective affinities not affect the four characters when they all met several years previously? The narrator glosses over many important scenes by reporting them in indirect speech, and he regularly uses the impersonal and neutralizing *man,* particularly at exciting junctures. For example, how did Eduard die? After having described Ottilie's death and funeral in such great detail, it is strange that the narrator tells us next to nothing of the circumstances and the cause of Eduard's death: "Was sollen wir bei diesem hoffnungslosen Zustande der ehegattlichen, freundschaftlichen, ärztlichen Bemühungen gedenken, in welchen sich Eduards Angehörige eine zeitlang hin und her wogten? *Endlich fand man ihn tot*" (*WV,* 490, my emphasis).

Not only is the narrator selective in what he chooses to tell the reader, he is also not as much in charge of his subjects as he pretends to be. It is a curious phenomenon that, in spite of the disciplined, symmetrical appearance of the two parts of *Die Wahlverwandtschaften,* a subversive, noncontrolled element enters particularly the second book, belying the authoritative stance of the narrator. The strong symmetry, according to which the novel is constructed, creates the impression that the characters can be directed like puppets, without a will of their own or the possibility of taking control of their own lives. The two books of the novel have eighteen chapters each; Mittler appears at the beginning, the middle, and the end of both the first and second books; events and objects, which seem to be incidental when they are first described, receive a special significance and symbolic meaning as they come up time and again, and these repetitions reveal a very consciously structured narrative in which nothing proves to be superfluous. As in a classical tragedy, where the outcome seems inevitable, the characters appear at first to follow a predestined pattern of behavior and remain unable to break away from their predetermined course. But in spite of this tightly controlled structure, the protagonists gain some independence from the ordered framework of the experiment, and it looks as though the narrator is overwhelmed by unforeseen circumstances and by the decisions taken by his characters. Especially Ottilie rises beyond the tight framework of the narrative and acquires the status almost of a saint.

In this experiment, focusing on the power of the natural forces that underlie human action, Goethe explores the realm of free will. To what degree are our lives determined by natural laws, and how can their force be broken? Goethe did not blindly apply the forces that operate in the inorganic sphere to the human level. Necessity — to which all human beings are subject — does not free the protagonists of taking responsibility for their actions, nor are they denied the chance to gain inner freedom. The central characters move between the poles of free will and determinism, between *Wahl* and *Verwandtschaft,* and rise above the natural laws to varying degrees. But, as is demonstrated by Ottilie's fate, moral resolution still does not deliver her from the all-powerful attraction to Eduard, and, while her moral strength wins in the last instance, this very victory destroys her.

The characters of *Die Wahlverwandtschaften* live in a world of absolutes, which will have been undermined from two sides by the time we get to *The Newton Letter.* First, the twentieth-century scientist has finally lost his objective, detached stance, and is forced to become part of his experiment — this is also the experience of the narrator of *The Newton Letter;* and second, the clash of irreconcilable demands no longer leads to death as was the case in the literature of previous centuries, but to an alienation from the world that may manifest itself in symptoms akin to mental illness.

The title of Banville's novel embraces the notion of the development from a science of absolute claims to the uncertainties of modern relativity. The name of *Newton* evokes the dawn of a great scientific era: the discovery of gravity and the mechanistic view of a clockwork universe. A *letter,* on the other hand, is a personal document, something written by an individual from an individual angle. On the surface, Newton and his age only make a relatively minor appearance in the pages of *The Newton Letter*. But in fact, the contrast between the absolute certainties of a Newtonian universe and the uncertainties and paradoxes of the Age of Relativity provides the starting point for Banville's novel. The narrator finds himself in a world devoid of all absolutes. This manifests itself even in the uncertainty with which he confronts everyday objects and events. Thus, he never overcomes his subjective frame of references, nor is he ever sure whether his experiences stem from reality or illusion.

One of the great changes in twentieth-century science is the realization that subject and object, the observer and the observed, can no longer be kept separate. The presence of the observer will always influence the outcome of the experiment, a view that Goethe maintained consistently. Accordingly, the narrator of *The Newton Letter* is central to the plot. In fact, without him there would be no story to tell. Far from being in control of the situation, the narrator experiences the world in unrelated fragments. He fails in his work and in his human relationships, and he has lost all sense of direction or meaning. Once more the opening words of the novel are symptomatic of the whole. "Words fail me" (*NL,* 1) is hardly a promising start for a book, a letter, a confession by a man who professionally deals in words.

Banville's *The Newton Letter* is a personal document, written by an individual from an individual angle. By choosing the structure of the quasi-epistolary novel, the language and the division into chapters can naturally be irregular and subject to mood changes. The narrator is selective in what he chooses to tell us, but, unlike the narrator of *Die Wahlverwandtschaften,* being a first person narrator without any claim to telling the truth, he is at least justified in making these omissions. Whereas we had to deduce the presence and the influence of the narrator of *Die Wahlverwandtschaften* gradually and carefully, we are immediately drawn into the entirely subjective world of the narrator of *The Newton Letter*. The fact that, despite his careful observations, the narrator constantly mistakes appearance and reality prevents the reader from identifying closely with him. At the same time, there is a sense of unreality and confusion about the whole experience of that summer that the reader is forced to share with the narrator. Occasionally, the narrator himself warns us not to believe everything he says. He interrupts the flow of the narrative and comments directly on his statements, emphasizing his own untrustworthiness. For example, he sees something move in the grass and gives his imagination free rein, only to take it all back in the next instance: "I thought it was the blackbirds. . . . But it was a rat. In fact it wasn't a rat. In fact all my time at Ferns I never saw a sign of a rat. It was only the idea" (*NL,* 8). On one occasion at least, the narrative voice breaks through the fictional framework and satirizes the whole of the narrative experiment, while at the same time drawing attention to the reworking aspect of the novel. When in distress, Goethe's Ottilie characteristically clasps her hands to her bosom. One afternoon, as Banville's narrator and Ottilie spend some time in the garden, he comments self-consciously: "We must have looked like an illustration from a Victorian novelette, marching forward across the swallow-swept lawn: had Ottilie her hands clasped to her breast?" (*NL,* 24–25). We will never learn whether his Ottilie *actually* shares that habit with her literary predecessor, but the narrator lets us know that he is conscious of the links he has constructed to Goethe's novel, thinly disguised as a "Victorian novelette" (24).

In his current state of mental crisis, which manifests itself in self-deception, and in a growing mistrust in the ability of language to communicate anything, the narrator constantly links apparently disconnected sense-impressions, hunches, and feelings. The reader, on the other hand, has to piece together the story from fragments of facts and reflections, and has to decide at all times which parts of the narration can be taken at face value, and which are merely products of the narrator's delusions. This is something the narrator himself is conscious of when he states: "Perhaps this sense of displacement will account for the oddest phenomenon of all, and the hardest to express. It was the notion of a time out of time, of this summer as a self-contained unit separate from the time of the ordinary world" (*NL,* 49).

By the connection to Goethe's *Die Wahlverwandtschaften,* which is established clearly and unambiguously through the names and constellation of central characters of *The Newton Letter,* the central theme of Banville's novel is suddenly expanded to include a discussion of the scientific paradigm of our age, which is primarily characterized by its uncertainties. Where Goethe himself explicitly draws the reader's attention to the fact that his novel is modeled on a scientific phenomenon, in the case of *The Newton Letter,* the reader has to deduce this from the novel's reference to Newton and the inherent relationship to Goethe's *Die Wahlverwandtschaften*. Thus, in this modest and short novel Banville uses the device of literary reworkings to suggest a discussion of no less than the workings of the universe ranging from Newton's mechanistic model to Einstein's paradoxical and mutually exclusive ideas on relativity and quantum physics, which leave the human object in a state of confusion and uncertainty, not unlike that of the narrator.

The Chandos Letter — the Relationship between Language and Reality

As the narrator withdraws into his disturbed and tortuous inner world during his stay at Ferns, he comes across Newton's correspondence with Locke. There he detects in the life of Newton that same doubt in the validity of knowledge and learning that had caused him to leave his job and seek the isolation of life at Ferns. At the end of the novel we find a "note" by the author pointing out that the second letter Newton reputedly sent to Locke is fictitious, and that some of the text was taken from Hugo von Hofmannsthal's *Ein Brief* or *Chandos Letter*.[24]

This note leads us yet deeper into the regions hidden under the events of the surface. Hofmannsthal's *Ein Brief* is an imaginary letter the young poet published in the Berlin newspaper *Der Tag* in October 1902. The fictional character Philip Chandos, younger son to the Earl of Bath, sends a letter, dated August 22, 1603, to Francis Bacon "um sich bei diesem Freunde wegen des gänzlichen Verzichtes auf literarische Betätigung zu entschuldigen" (*EB*, 45). Chandos goes on to explain to Bacon in great length and detail why he cannot write anymore. He describes how, as a young man, he was full of energy and had great plans for the future, outlining the great literary works he might have attempted. During this phase of his life Chandos had felt the great unity of the world and a strong affinity to all that was around him, a state already indicative of potential mental instability in the tradition of *Die Leiden des jungen Werther* and Büchner's *Lenz*. "Mir erschien damals . . . das ganze Dasein als eine große Einheit: geistige und körperliche Welt schien mir keinen Gegensatz zu bilden . . .; in allem fühlte ich Natur . . .; und in aller Natur fühlte ich mich selber" (*EB*, 47). As must be, he falls from this state of mystical union with nature, and his world shatters into fragments: "Mein Fall ist, in Kürze, dieser: Es ist mir völlig die Fähigkeit abhanden gekommen, über irgend etwas zusammenhängend zu denken oder zu sprechen" (*EB*, 48). Chandos feels like a fragment of some greater whole that has been lost, and is now utterly disconnected from the outside world, but at other times the natural world, in the form of random sense impressions, flows right into him, and he cannot put up any resistance to keep the world outside his innermost self. Thus, he appears a helpless victim of his feelings and imaginings, which he cannot direct or hold at bay any more. Added to this comes the inability to express himself in words: language has apparently ceased to be a meaningful way of communication. Chandos describes how words have become detached from their meaning and he has not only lost his ability to speak and to think coherently but also his ability to form judgements: "Es zerfiel mir alles in Teile, die Teile wieder in Teile, und nichts mehr ließ sich mit einem Begriff umspannen" (*EB*, 49). Like Büchner's Lenz, Chandos experiences moments of utter loneliness and isolation from his surroundings, but then again, these are contrasted by the sudden mysterious significance of random objects, something we encountered in Schneider's *Lenz*. The sight of a watering can, a garden rake, or a dog lying in the sun, suddenly triggers a rush of complex emotions Chandos is unable to control (*EB*, 50).

This is also what happens to the narrator of Banville's *The Newton Letter*. At the very beginning of his train ride to Ferns, ordinary objects suddenly move into focus, and seem to gain an unexpected importance and a hidden meaning. Items such as drainpipes, a broken fanlight, a straggling garden take on an overwhelming significance during his stay at Ferns, and on his return journey he is still unable to keep these sense impressions from affecting him: "There it all was, the backs of the houses, the drainpipes, a cloud out on the bay, just like the first time, only in reverse order" (*NL*, 77). The symmetry of the journey to and from Ferns betrays an overall narrative order beneath the apparently random structure of the personal letters that make up *The Newton Letter*. Chandos gives us a graphic description of an experience how, after he had laid some rat poison, the agony of the dying creatures suddenly appeared in his mind, and how he had to share with them the struggle and the pain, without being able to shut these images from his vision. Banville's narrator has the same experience after having watched two rat men passing by: "All at once I was assailed by an image of catastrophe, stricken things scurrying in circles, the riven pelts, the convulsions, the agonized eyes gazing into the empty sky or through the sky into endlessness" (*NL*, 8).

Within the context of *The Newton Letter* these experiences of the narrator appear merely strange, and from his own words, it is difficult to appreciate the severity of the crisis the narrator actually goes through. Only the repeated references to Hofmannsthal's *Chandos Letter* give an idea of how close to a total breakdown the narrator actually is and how deep his sense of alienation from his surroundings goes. Banville's and Chandos's narrators have both lost the boundaries of their own identity, a mental state which Hermann Broch has described as the most severe form of panic.[25] Banville uses the same technique we have encountered to a certain degree in the reworking of Kroetz, but more explicitly in those of Plenzdorf and Schneider. In comparison to Goethe and Büchner, but also to Hofmannsthal and Salinger, the author of a reworking shies back from describing the depth of despair or the seriousness of the mental breakdown of his characters. Instead he refers the reader to a literary predecessor in order to fully comprehend the extent of the crisis the protagonist endures.[26]

Banville's Newton

The acknowledged quotation from Hofmannsthal's *Chandos Letter*, allegedly written by Newton in a letter to John Locke, raises the problem of language itself.

Chandos to Bacon: nämlich weil die Sprache, in welcher nicht nur zu schreiben, sondern auch zu denken mir vielleicht gegeben wäre, weder die lateinische, noch die englische . . . ist, sondern eine Sprache, von deren Worten mir auch nicht eines bekannt ist, eine Sprache, in welcher die stummen Dinge zu mir sprechen, und in welcher ich vielleicht einst im Grabe vor einem unbekannten Richter mich verantworten werde. (*EB*, 54)	*Newton to Locke:* My dear Doctor, expect no more philosophy from my pen. The language in which I might be able not only to write but to think is neither Latin nor English, but a language none of whose words is known to me; a language in which commonplace things speak to me; and wherein I may one day have to justify myself before an unknown judge. (*NL*, 51)

On the surface the *Chandos Letter* seems to speak of the loss of ability to write on the part of a promising young talent. But at a deeper level the text is about the problem of language. What is the relationship of language to reality? How can we put reality, as we perceive it, into words? Indeed, is it possible at all?

Banville borrowed not just the acknowledged quote from Hofmannsthal's *Chandos Letter,* but a whole series of other qualities as well. First there is the title, both texts being written as fictional letters. Second, we have the apparent paradox in both cases that the ailment, the alienation from the world, caused by a breakdown of a relationship to the word, to language, is communicated in a superbly eloquent piece of written text. And then the mental crisis, his gradual coming to pieces, his inability to make sense of the persons and things around him, his failure to continue his work, even an involuntary vision of dying rats, are all experiences the narrator of *The Newton Letter* has in common with Philip Chandos. Hofmannsthal's fictional Chandos wrote his letter in 1603, suffering from what has been described as the malaise of the modern writer. Is this breakdown really a symptom only of the modern writer?

The historical Newton and the fictional narrator of Goethe's *Die Wahlverwandtschaften* operate on the same assumption, that the world can be observed objectively, that an experiment can be controlled. As an academic, the narrator of *The Newton Letter* probably shared these assumptions until he is so shaken by the summer spent at Ferns. During the course of *The Newton Letter* the narrator tells us of two events in Newton's life that might have thrown doubt on this certainty. Puzzling over the eternal question of "what is truth?" the narrator begins to wonder about the faithfulness of his own account of Newton's life:

> Oh yes, you can see, can't you [Clio], the outline of what my book would have been, a celebration of action, of the scientist as hero, a gleeful acceptance of Pandora's fearful disclosures, wishy-washy medievalism kicked out and the age of reason restored. . . . Not that I think any of it untrue, in the sense that it is fact. It's just that another kind of truth has come to seem to me more urgent, although, for the mind, it is nothing compared to the lofty verities of science. (*NL,* 22)

The narrator illustrates that other kind of truth with an occurrence in Newton's life. In 1693, he tells us, Newton had a fire in his library that destroyed many of his scientific papers. Understandably, Newton went almost out of his mind with the loss of his work. Suddenly, in the light of his own experiences, the narrator sees these events differently:

> The joke is, it's not the loss of the precious papers that will drive him temporarily crazy, but the simple fact that *it does not matter*. It might be his life's work gone, the *Principia* itself, the *Opticks,* the whole bang lot, and it still wouldn't mean a thing.... Someone else asks what has been lost. Newton's mouth opens and a word like a stone falls out: *Nothing.* (*NL*, 22–23)

Both the fire of the library and Newton's crisis in the autumn of 1693 have been well documented.[27] Newton suffered a mental breakdown, which he admits to in his correspondence with Locke.[28] Afterwards he turned his attention away from scientific research to the study of alchemy and of the Bible. The fire, although not fiction, as the narrator would have us believe later (*NL*, 22), probably happened as early as 1678, that is fifteen years before the dramatic reorientation of Newton's work. The inner processes of Newton's mind in the face of that loss cannot be known to us, but we can follow the interpretation of the narrator. The phenomenon of Newton turning away from science and moving towards more spiritual, alchemist topics for research can indeed be understood as a dissatisfaction with the nature of scientific research in the quest for truth. Was there a breakdown in Newton's relationship to the language of science? Banville's narrator seems to see it like this when he describes Newton's state of mind after the fire:

> It had needed no candle flame, it was already ashes. Why else had he turned to deciphering Genesis and dabbling in alchemy? Why else did he insist again and again that science had cost him too dearly, that given his life to live over, he would have nothing to do with physics?... The fire, or whatever the real conflagration was, had shown him something terrible and lovely, like flame itself. *Nothing.* . . . For the nothing automatically signifies the everything. He does not know what to do, what to think. He no longer knows how to live. (*NL*, 23)

Not only Chandos and the narrator go through this crisis of finding themselves in a world which does not speak to them any more, and to which they can no longer relate: Banville's Newton comes to the same point. The four figures — the historical Newton, Hofmannsthal, the fictional narrator, and Chandos — become closely entangled and in some way they assume a common identity through the experiences they share. In our imagination they begin to merge into one, the work of one throwing momentary glimpses of light onto our understanding of the others. Fictional and historical figures mingle in an extraordinary way.[29]

The Effect of the Reworking

As we have seen, the unacknowledged link with *Die Wahlverwandtschaften* has opened up new themes surrounding the nature of the relationship between the narrator and his story as an image of the relationship between the scientist and his experiment. Equally, the inclusion of Banville's acknowledged source, the *Chandos Letter,* introduced the problematic nature of the relationship between language and reality and raised the question whether language can ever represent anything other than itself. The form of a fictional letter, the central experience of the main protagonists, the link between the twentieth and the seventeenth century, provide the first set of parallels between the two works. The integration of Hofmannsthal's *Chandos Letter* into *The Newton Letter* illuminates and explains the experiences of the narrator, and forges a closer link to the figure of Newton as seen by the narrator. In this light *The Newton Letter* can be regarded as a novel about the nature of scientific progress and the scientific endeavor for truth.

The Newton Letter and *Die Wahlverwandtschaften* both deal with scientific themes within a social fictional context. In *Die Wahlverwandtschaften* Goethe applies the scientific concept of elective affinities to human relationships. He shows that even in the human context we can observe, and are apparently subject to, the natural forces of attraction and repulsion. Yet other, moral laws also influence the outcome of such constellations. In *The Newton Letter* the scientific idea that dictates the fate of the characters is not so obvious. Rather than talking *about* the experiment, as the narrator of *Die Wahlverwandtschaften* does, the narrator of *The Newton Letter* is himself the subject of the experiment.

Subject and Object of the Experiment

The "shattering" experiences suffered by the narrator during the course of the novel remind us of the modern, segmented world, which cannot bring into a single framework mutually exclusive concepts such as the theory of relativity and that of quantum physics. Of the work of Copernicus, the main protagonist of Banville's first novel in the series on scientists, Goethe said:

> Doch unter allen Entdeckungen und Überzeugungen möchte nichts eine größere Wirkung auf den menschlichen Geist hervorgebracht haben, als die Lehre des Kopernikus. Kaum war die Welt als rund anerkannt und in sich selbst abgeschlossen, so sollte sie auch auf das ungeheure Vorrecht Verzicht tun, der Mittelpunkt des Weltalls zu

sein. Vielleicht ist noch nie eine größere Forderung an die Menschheit geschehen: denn was ging nicht alles durch diese Anerkennung in Dunst und Rauch auf: ein zweites Paradies, eine Welt der Unschuld, Dichtkunst und Frömmigkeit, das Zeugnis der Sinne, die Überzeugung eines poetisch-religiösen Glaubens; kein Wunder, daß man dies alles nicht wollte fahren lassen, daß man sich auf alle Weise einer solchen Lehre entgegensetzte, die denjenigen, der sie annahm, zu einer bisher unbekannten, ja ungeahnten Denkfreiheit und Großheit der Gesinnung berechtigte und aufforderte.[30]

The impact Goethe attributes to Copernicus's theorem can be equally applied to Newton's work. With his theory of gravitation, Newton's radical achievement was to bring previously unconnected and apparently mutually exclusive theories under one amazingly simple, unifying law. At the same time, a mechanistic universe in which the movements of the planets are determined by the forces of gravity rather than by divine decree removes man yet one step further from the cherished place at the center of the universe. Is this new picture of the universe the whole truth? Will the earth keep moving without the finger of God? Undoubtedly it will at the level of mere facts. Yet Newton, and with him Chandos and our narrator, still search for that other kind of truth.

In his book *The Sleepwalkers,* Arthur Koestler describes Newton's singular achievement thus:

> What he achieved was rather like an explosion in reverse. When a projectile blows up, its shiny, smooth, symmetrical body is shattered into jagged, irregular fragments. Newton found fragments and made them fly together into a simple, seamless, compact body, so simple that it appears as self-evident, so compact that any grammar-schoolboy can handle it.[31]

But this state of affairs was not to last. After the "dream of unity"[32] of the old, Newtonian cosmos, the modern world has lost this sense of certainty once more.

Insofar as the history of scientific development is also the evolution of human consciousness, the natural sciences and the human sciences, including literature and the arts, reflect the same underlying view of the world in any given culture. In our multicultural society the "principle of relativity" rules supreme, not only in our understanding of space and time, but also in our aesthetic and moral judgments. We have moved into a world that differs fundamentally from the ordered construct of reason of a previous age. Yet, according to Mikhail Bakhtin, this very disintegration offers new opportunities and reveals a new order with a different underlying unity. "Einstein's world possesses a far deeper and more complex unity than Newton's; it is a higher level unity, of a qualitatively different order."[33]

Beyond the Mechanistic Universe

Banville's *The Newton Letter* is not a "book on Newton," nor does it reflect on Newton's ideas or achievements. The literary device of reworking opens a new dimension in the contemporary work. *The Newton Letter* shares the plot with its literary predecessors, but it uses the given framework to treat modern themes: the isolation of the individual within society, the loss of a coherent view of the world. The message might have changed, the reworking might be an updated version of the original, or, indeed an anti-work. But the conscious inclusion of the classical works of Goethe and Hofmannsthal, like the constant presence of a shadowy *Doppelgänger*, not only adds depth to the reworking, but might also rekindle an interest in our own (literary) past and become a key to a renewed understanding. The reference to Goethe's *Die Wahlverwandtschaften* and Hofmannsthal's *Chandos Letter* in *The Newton Letter* serves as an example of the deeper, more complex unity underlying the modern world in which the boundaries between different languages, between art and science, and between mind and matter are ever diminishing. As a work of fiction, *The Newton Letter* is about human concerns: the relationship of language to reality — a question of consciousness, and the extent to which the human being is subject to natural forces — a question of moral freedom.

Conclusion

> Es ist nicht wunderbar, aber es erregt doch Verwunderung, wenn man bei Betrachtung einer Literatur, besonders der deutschen, beobachtet, wie eine ganze Nation von einem einmal gegebenem und in einer gewissen Form mit Glück behandelten Gegenstand nicht wieder loskommen kann, sondern ihn auf alle Weise wiederholt haben will.
> *Goethe*

The Effect of Reworkings

THIS INVESTIGATION INTO THE phenomenon of reworkings in the context of German literature took as its starting point Gottfried Keller's general claim (made at the opening of his own rendering of the Romeo and Juliet story — *Romeo und Julia auf dem Dorfe*) that all great works of literature are, by their very nature, essentially reworkings. Keller holds that only a limited number of universal character constellations and plots exist, and that these are endlessly reworked throughout the ages. This premise of inherent relationships found throughout all literature gave rise, in this study, to the concept and analysis of a much more specific type of reworking, defined as "literary reworking." Examples of literary reworkings are produced in all genres, and the foregoing analysis and interpretation of two works each, chosen from drama, novella, and novel respectively, form the basis of the following observations as to the nature and the full scope of reworkings. The results of any particular investigation into how the link between model and reworking is constructed, and to what effect the device has been put, can be found in the section entitled "The effect of the reworking" in each of the previous chapters. This concluding chapter will provide a summary of a more general nature of the relationship between model and reworking, illustrating the diversity of narrative devices applied in the field. After a brief summary of the different intentions behind each reworking in turn, we can reach some tentative conclusions as to what commentary is made by reworkings on the literary trends of the present age.

Brecht's *Die heilige Johanna der Schlachthöfe* and Kroetz's *Maria Magdalena*, the two examples taken from drama, show how slight the textual link between model and reworking can be constructed or, alternatively, how faithfully a playwright can reproduce the character constellation and the plot of his model and still create a contemporary and original work. Brecht's *Die heilige Johanna der Schlachthöfe* alludes to the Schiller model by drawing a number of striking parallels, and by parodying the verse form of the classical model, but the twentieth-century American setting tells an essentially modern story. If we did not pay specific attention to the title of Brecht's drama, *Die heilige Johanna der Schlachthöfe* would hardly be recognizable as belonging to the Joan of Arc tradition at all. That link is primarily established by alluding to particular features of Schiller's *Die Jungfrau von Orleans*. But even given these tentative parallels, the two dramas are paradoxically bound together by the ideological contrasts that gave rise to their inception. Brecht attacks what he regards as Schiller's outdated idealism, namely the notion that the moral improvement of the individual will bring about a better world. According to Brecht, this better world can be achieved only by imposing radical changes upon the economic structure on which society is founded. On the other hand, in their passionate belief in the importance of the theater, Schiller and Brecht have a great deal in common when it comes to the *means* by which a better world might come about.

The essential role of economic realities as a fundamental principle directing human actions also plays a part in the relationship between Hebbel's and Kroetz's respective dramas. Kroetz tells us the same story as Hebbel, but has transferred it to a different historical context. The suffocating narrowness of the moral and social code of the nineteenth century, which results in Meister Anton being solely concerned with his reputation, has been replaced by a society that lives, first and foremost, according to economic priorities. Compared to the loose correspondence between Schiller's and Brecht's variations on the Joan of Arc theme, Kroetz's reworking of Hebbel's *Maria Magdalena* operates on the opposite principle, namely reconstruction. Kroetz's "comedy" introduces the same characters, follows the model scene by scene, and even uses the same figures of speech at times. Ironically, at the point where the plot of the reworking departs from its model, namely at the expected comic ending, the situation of the title figure actually approaches the tragic. In this way, even the inherent difference anticipated when a tragedy is rewritten as a comedy is eliminated. Where Brecht emphasizes the difference between his age and that of Schiller's, Kroetz seems to show that over a similar period history might have moved on, but the situation in which Hebbel's heroine and his own find themselves has not changed in any fundamental way.

If the above examples of reworkings of drama have focused on social and historical perspectives of the last two hundred years, the following two reworkings of two novellas shift their emphasis to psychological conditions — Freud, rather than Marx. In a pattern similar to Brecht's treatment of Schiller, Koeppen rejects the philosophical foundation of *Der Tod in Venedig*, and sets out deliberately to unmask the idealized world that is projected in the model. The shifting narrative perspective of *Der Tod in Rom* and the representation of Aschenbach in the form of several different characters draw attention to the fundamentally different outlooks on life on which the two works are built. In *Der Tod in Rom* Koeppen draws a picture of the human condition that is deeply pessimistic. Aschenbach's apparently easy identification with the aesthetic ideals of the classical world proves to be an illusion. What remains is the shattered individual, utterly alone in the world. Read separately, both Mann's *Der Tod in Venedig*, and Koeppen's *Der Tod in Rom* take up extreme positions. Where one describes an existence of living in a world of illusion and of being wrapped up in the pursuit of aesthetic ideals at the danger of ignoring the ambiguity of everyday existence, the other outlines a state of melancholy disillusion with the reality of existence without offering any redeeming features, or any vision of a better world. However, when they are read in conjunction, the one-sidedness of each text is dissolved: we are reminded that Aschenbach's flight of fancy into the realm of classical values must be transposed into a social context, and the disabling sense of hopelessness that permeates Koeppen's *Der Tod in Rom* is lifted into a realm in which beauty and the striving of the individual might still make a difference. This modification of both texts is achieved by the persistent allusions to the model made in the reworking on a textual level, and the fragmented narrative technique on a structural level.

Whereas Koeppen rejects the ideology of the model, Schneider's *Lenz* draws heavily on Büchner's novella, importing certain narrative features and a number of near-quotes to the effect that the suffering of the new Lenz, suggested in the reworking, resonates with that endured by Büchner's Lenz. This integration of the atmosphere of the model is achieved not by using Kroetz's device of closely following the plot and constructing the same character constellation, but by applying a technique similar to the one used by Brecht in *Die heilige Johanna der Schlachthöfe*. Schneider alludes to and imitates the characteristic linguistic styles of the model, and adorns his own protagonist with some of the attributes of the literary predecessor. Schneider's *Lenz* is thus given considerably more depth on a psychological as well as on a historical level. In turn, the reworking highlights the economic factors, which contributed to the mental instability not only of his own, but also of Büchner's *Lenz* figure. The recognition that the inherent contradictions of Protestant-capitalist ethics had such a destabilizing effect on Lenz's psyche is already implied in Büchner's novella, but this is easily overlooked, since Büchner's *Lenz* is traditionally read as a psychological study, focusing on the gradual breakdown of the individual.

An underlying theme that unites the two reworkings of Goethe's novels *Die Leiden des jungen Werther* and *Die Wahlverwandtschaften* can be found in the realm of language and the problem of overcoming speechlessness. In his reworking, *Die neuen Leiden des jungen W.*, Plenzdorf is much more direct than Schneider. He freely quotes long passages from Goethe's novel. The central protagonist Edgar openly acknowledges, and learns to appreciate, the borrowed language. Writing in the GDR at the height of the Cold War, Plenzdorf also makes full use of the Goethe model to express biting social criticism that could not easily have been published in any other way in a totalitarian state subject to extensive censorship. As in Schneider's *Lenz,* the link with Goethe's *Die Leiden des jungen Werther* suggests a greater depth of suffering on the part of Edgar than is immediately apparent from the text. Like Koeppen, Plenzdorf also engages with the model on the level of the narrative structure, but in contrast to Koeppen, who deliberately rejects and breaks up the underlying unity of Thomas Mann's *Der Tod in Venedig*, Plenzdorf retains the complex narrative structure of the model, modifying it only to suit his own specific narrative purposes.

If Edgar gradually learns to empathize with his literary predecessor from the past, the process is reversed in the case of the characters in Banville's *The Newton Letter*. In this instance the four central protagonists of Goethe's *Wahlverwandtschaften* have been catapulted into the present, and the reworking can be regarded as a sort of continuation of the *Wahlverwandtschaften* plot. As was the case in Goethe's "experiment" the characters of *The Newton Letter* appear to be still subject to natural forces, except that the current scientific paradigm has changed. The experiment is no longer concerned with the *actual* effect of elective affinities, but rather with the nature of observation. This results in an account of *perceived* effects taken from a subjective point of view. Added to this is the discussion about the relationship between language and the natural world, introduced by incorporating a second model into the reworking, namely Hofmannsthal's *Chandos Letter*.

The Intention Behind Reworkings

From the above it becomes clear that the concept of "literary reworkings" includes a great diversity of literary devices used to create the connection between model and reworking. In addition, the intention with which a reworking is written can also vary greatly, ranging from an endorsement of the ideals according to which the model is constructed to a complete subversion of these. Whereas Brecht and Koeppen reject the aesthetics of their models, wanting to show how much the world has changed, Kroetz and Schneider integrate their respective models, emphasizing how little society has altered. Brecht's *Die heilige Johanna der Schlachthöfe* and Koeppen's *Der Tod in Rom* are both anti-works, in the sense that the reworking aims to lay bare the ineffectuality of the *Weltanschauung* of the respective models. Brecht uses allusion as the overriding principle on which his work establishes a connection to its literary model, and Koeppen's reworking has fragmented the unified narrative form of *Der Tod in Venedig*. Kroetz's *Maria Magdalena* is so obviously based on its model that the term "reproduction" has been used to describe the principal literary device on which the play is constructed. Similarly, it can be said of Schneider's *Lenz* that the reworking has so thoroughly integrated essential features of the model that the two protagonists, though separated by two hundred years of political and industrial transformation, still fall victim to the same dilemma. The unbridgeable gap between idealism and the social realities of the day initially contributed to the mental illness of the historical eighteenth-century J. M. R. Lenz. In the nineteenth century, the same plight moved Büchner into writing one of the most memorable fictional accounts of the onslaught of insanity, which triggered a whole tradition of literary successors in the twentieth century. Of these, Schneider's reworking found a huge echo among the young people who had taken part in the student protests all over Germany, and itself influenced a whole generation.

Plenzdorf and Banville both acknowledge the passage of time, albeit in different ways. Thus, in their dialogue, reworking and model retain a definite autonomy, which is less apparent in the earlier examples. Plenzdorf has made quotation the overriding principle linking the reworking to its model. In terms of Edgar's inner development the borrowed words are gradually internalized until Edgar understands Werther to such a degree that he can almost completely identify with him. Banville also establishes the link to the Hofmannsthal model by quotation, drawing attention to his source in an endnote. But the explicit link to Goethe's *Wahlverwandtschaften* is created by the names and the constellation of the central protagonists. If the reader is willing to engage with the text as a reworking of the two German models, and is ready to understand the term constellation in its widest sense, the whole of the history of science from Newton via Goethe to Einstein resonates in *The Newton Letter*.

Literary techniques applied by authors of reworkings vary greatly. At the same time, the apparent intention of the author can range from a decided rejection of the model, as is the case with Brecht's *Die heilige Johanna der Schlachthöfe* and Koeppen's *Der Tod in Rom*, to different forms of imitation, as we have encountered in Kroetz's *Maria Magdalena* and Schneider's *Lenz*. Plenzdorf, on the other hand, creates such a strong correlation between Goethe's *Die Leiden des jungen Werther* and his own *Die neuen Leiden des jungen W.* that model and reworking may be read as almost evolving side by side. Likewise, Banville's *The Newton Letter* emerges as an independent entity that freely draws on other literary works without either criticizing or endorsing the respective models.

Characteristics of Twentieth-Century Literary Reworkings

As a literary technique the practice of reworking has not always been given its due, as can be seen in Marcel Reich-Ranicki's criticism of Plenzdorf's *Die neuen Leiden des jungen W.*, in which he dismisses the connection between reworking and model, between Edgar and Werther, merely as "amüsanter Trick, frappierender Gag."[1]

Common to all reworkings is the fact that, by means of the reference to a literary predecessor, they gain an added dimension of historical depth, and resound with values and conventions from the past. All literature can be read as an interpretation of the cultural environment and the age in which it was written, and commentary on the present is, of course, by no means limited to reworkings alone. However, certain observations are thrown into relief much more clearly here than by other contemporary fiction, because the reworking deliberately invites the reader to compare and contrast the narrative set in the present with that of the time when the respective model was written. Without fail, this effect enhances the contemporary text. Likewise, particular aspects of the literary model can be illuminated by the contemporary work, so that we can say that as a result of reading model and reworking, one in the light of the other, an extra dimension can be detected. This third narrative, which arises solely as a consequence of allowing the reworking and the model to enter into a dialogue with each other, can be understood as directly commenting on the present by highlighting either certain political and socio-economic developments that have brought about change over the last century or two or, alternatively, the lack of progress over that same period. In the attempt to interpret the nature of our present historical situation we are encouraged by Götz Grossklaus, who insists: "Daß mit diesem historischen Verfahren über eine dialektische Reihe von Entsprechungen und Nichtentsprechungen eine durchaus exakt zu nennende Bestimmung der Gegenwart gelingt, will zum Beispiel einem Marcel Reich-Ranicki nicht in den Kopf."[2]

The following reflections must necessarily remain tentative if we remember the cautionary warning uttered by Walter Benjamin, that in an analysis of contemporary literature we can only discern its material content, *Sachgehalt*, whereas the truth content, *Wahrheitsgehalt*, of literature will only emerge over time: "jede zeitgenössische Kritik [umfaßt . . .] mehr die bewegende als die ruhende Wahrheit, mehr das zeitliche Wirken als das ewige Sein."[3] Although the selection of texts discussed in this study has been made on the basis of the range of different literary *devices* employed, nevertheless a significant number of the chosen works are also held together by a common *thematic* link that stretches in a long line of protagonists from Goethe's Werther via Büchner's Lenz and Hofmannsthal's Chandos, to Plenzdorf's Edgar, Schneider's Lenz, and Banville's narrator in *The Newton Letter*. A strong correlation already exists between Goethe's *Die Leiden des jungen Werther* and Büchner's *Lenz*. Not only are both texts written in a narrative style that allows for an exceptionally intimate relationship between protagonist and reader, but both protagonists find themselves in a very similar situation, namely, that they suffer from an ever-increasing sense of marginalization and alienation, leading to suicide in one case and madness in the other. Both works were, in turn, reworked in 1973, by Ulrich Plenzdorf and Peter Schneider respectively. Once more, the protagonists of the reworkings establish a close bond with the reader, and both Edgar and Lenz quickly became figures with whom a whole generation of East and West Germany identified. If we add Hofmannsthal's Chandos, and thus also the narrator of Banville's *The Newton Letter* to the line of fictional characters who suffered and sometimes even died as a result of their inability to communicate with the world around them, we must conclude that Werther's "Krankheit zum Tode" (*GW*, 48) was not merely a malaise of his particular age, but an ailment recurring century after century.

There are, however, some significant developments in the theme that have taken place during the time since *Die Leiden des jungen Werther* was written almost 230 years ago. In Goethe's novel the emphasis is on Werther's personal life. Although Werther's failure to find a meaningful occupation contributes significantly to his lack of purpose in life, the novel has always been regarded as a love story, and Werther's end is closely associated with his failure to win Lotte's heart and hand. It is quite otherwise in *Die neuen Leiden des jungen W.* Essentially Edgar suffers from his inability to find an outlet for his youthful creativity and energy. The love affair with Charlie is secondary to his frustration at not finding the type of work that would lead to an inner fulfillment and let him express his individuality. In other words, the reworking seems to suggest a thematic shift in emphasis from love to work, from the dilemma of a private individual to that of a member of society. Plenzdorf's reworking draws renewed attention to the fact that the issue of the lack of gainful employment was already present in Goethe's text, but in the twentieth-century reworking this has become a central theme.

If we look at Büchner's and Schneider's *Lenz* from the same point of view, we can detect a similar development. Whereas we meet Büchner's Lenz as a suffering individual, not inclined to occupy a functional place in society, Schneider's Lenz has his individual problems but withdraws into the private sphere only temporarily, and his increasing public engagement is seen as a measure of regaining his mental balance. Once again, a shift in emphasis from the private to the public realm can be observed. The reworking draws attention to the fact that certain socio-economic conditions have a direct effect on the mental state of individuals with certain sensibilities, an idea already present in the model. But whereas Büchner raises these issues only in passing, focusing much more intensely on the inner development of Lenz's mental condition, in the reworking the discussion of political matters, of Lenz as a person who seeks fulfillment in his society, and has an influence on it, has taken center stage. We know nothing of Chandos's eventual fate, but the narrator of *The Newton Letter* also re-enters regular employment after the crisis that befell him that summer at Ferns. In an outcome not dissimilar to the eventual recovery of Schneider's Lenz, it is suggested that, after suffering a mental breakdown, the narrator is able to return to work and to construct a life that bears, at least, a semblance of normality.

From this it becomes apparent that the above protagonists, covering a development of well over two hundred years, all suffer from a mental condition caused by a dilemma brought about by the inherent contradictions between an individual striving for fulfillment and the socio-economic restrictions imposed by the society of their respective ages. For Werther and Edgar this leads to death, for Büchner's Lenz to a state of chilling limbo, and for Schneider's Lenz and Banville's narrator to eventual recovery. Over this period we may also observe a change of emphasis in the narrative focus, which can be described as essentially a transfer from love to work, from the private to the public realm. This change was already anticipated in the transition from the concept of individual freedom, upon which Schiller's *Die Jungfrau von Orleans* is built, to the call for liberty, made in Brecht's *Die heilige Johanna der Schlachthöfe*.

If we add *The Newton Letter* into the equation, we are faced with the paradox that over that same period that, in literature, saw the shift from the private to the public role of an individual, from subject to object, the dominant scientific paradigm underwent a change from an objective model of the natural world to a subjective, relativistic model. The emergence of modern science in the seventeenth century was built upon the certainty that ultimate truth exists, and that the natural world is governed by absolute laws. Today, we have to accept that our perception of the world is necessarily subjective, and that there are contradictions in our understanding of the natural world that cannot be resolved. If the scientists of previous centuries could confidently claim "the world is," today we can only say, "the world is what we perceive." This development is a reflection of the change in the scientific paradigm, which likewise saw a shift from the idea of an objective world that can be explained from the outside, to the recognition that the distance between object and subject can no longer be maintained. The transition from an objective point of view to one that is wholly subjective can also be found in the difference between the narrative voice found in certain models compared to their reworking. The third-person-narrator of *Die Wahlverwandtschaften* claims the position of the objective observer who simply tells the story, apparently unaffected by the fate of his protagonists. In contrast, the first-person-narrator of *The Newton Letter* has become the helpless subject of the novel himself. A similar picture emerges from the comparison between *Der Tod in Venedig* and *Der Tod in Rom*. Both works deal with a certain rejection of the world, which the protagonists ultimately have to pay for. But, whereas there emerges a continually growing distance between the narrator of *Der Tod in Venedig* and Aschenbach that leads to a judgmental narrator letting Aschenbach perish in the end, the multiple narrative voices in *Der Tod in Rom,* particularly that of Siegfried, themselves constitute a rejection of the reality he finds himself in.

A further development can be observed by comparing the setting and the time scale of models and their respective reworkings. In all but two cases, the setting has moved from a rural environment into an industrial, urban one: Brecht's Johanna lives and dies in Chicago, the new Lenz no longer walks though the mountains, but moves in the urban centers of Berlin, Rome, and Trento, and the new Werther exchanges Wahlheim for East Berlin as a place of refuge. In the two cases in which the rural or provincial location has not been significantly changed, the environment of the reworking is one of decline: in Kroetz's *Maria Magdalena* Meister Anton, an independent local tradesman in a pre-industrial provincial town, has been transformed into a mere salesman, no longer manufacturing but selling goods in a struggling economy. Likewise, rather than being improved, as is ostensibly the case with Eduard's country estate in *Die Wahlverwandtschaften,* the estate in *The Newton Letter,* now a commercial nursery, is falling into a state of disrepair. The one significant instance in which this shift from the country to the city does not take place is with Koeppen's *Der Tod in Rom* where the model, itself published in the twentieth century, is already set in the city. The conscious choice of moving the plot from a rural setting in the model to an urban setting, preferred by the writers of twentieth-century reworkings, enforces the general observation that the Romantic involvement with nature of nineteenth-century German literature has been truly laid to rest.

The time span of the narratives tends to be shorter in the reworkings compared to that of the models. Unlike *Der Tod in Venedig,* in which we trace Aschenbach's passion as it grows over several weeks, *Der Tod in Rom* covers the events of only two days. In Schneider's *Lenz,* the quality of a time out of time, so characteristic of Büchner's *Lenz,* has given way to a narrative with a beginning, a progression, and an end. In contrast to Werther's suffering, which stretches over about twenty months, Edgar dies within a few weeks of his arrival in East Berlin. Likewise, *Die Wahlverwandtschaften* covers a period of some two years, whereas the involvement of the narrator with the other characters of Banville's *The Newton Letter* lasts only one summer. If the narrow focus on rural society has expanded onto the wider, more complex environment of the urban landscape, the longer time span of the models has contracted to specific periods in the lives of the protagonists of the reworkings. The limitation imposed by the shortened time span is, to a certain degree, overcome again by the open endings of several of the reworkings. The sense of inevitability, which results in the death of so many characters in the literary models, is replaced by the uncertainties concerning the future of the protagonists of the modern works.

Final Matters

We live in an age in which the present and the future loom so much larger than a preoccupation with the past, yet the practice of reworking literary texts of previous ages continues to flourish. Reworkings are written to describe, to analyze, and to reflect on the present by drawing attention to relevant experiences from the past, which are then used to comment on the predicament of the literary successors. This technique allows the reader to appreciate the reworking in a threefold way. Initially, through an immediate, naive reception, the reader is free to read the text merely as a contemporary narrative. Next, the reworking may refer the reader back to the literary model, possibly to re-reading it. Finally, by way of the different associations and interpretations arising in addition to the conscious links created by the author in the construction of the reworking, a third narrative may emerge in the mind of the reader, composed from the internal dialogue between reworking and model.

Although not a frequent occurrence, new reworkings are published at regular and consistent intervals in the German literature of the late twentieth century. It is remarkable that not only the literary treatment, but also the *choice* of model is a reflection on what literary trends are emerging in any one decade. In the 1950s Koeppen related to the sense of unease in *Der Tod in Venedig* that foreshadowed the First World War, and amplified the effect in the period immediately following the Second World War. Not surprisingly, the 1970s, which themselves have been labeled *Neue Subjektivität*, saw a resurgence of an interest in models such as Goethe's *Die Leiden des jungen Werther* and Büchner's *Lenz*. The 1980s and 1990s, on the other hand, seem more preoccupied with formal matters and the non-emotional style of *Die Wahlverwandtschaften*.[4] What kind of society and which age will inspire the authors of the future to create reworkings of models perhaps chosen from the works of Franz Kafka, Günter Grass, or Max Frisch?

Works Cited

Banville, John. *The Newton Letter.* London: Minerva, 1992. First published in London: Warburg & Secker 1982. Cited as *NL*.

———. "Physics and Fiction: Order from Chaos." *The New York Times,* April 21, 1985. Book Review section.

Benjamin, Walter. "Goethes *Wahlverwandtschaften.*" In *Gesammelte Schriften,* by Walter Benjamin. Vol. 1, *Abhandlungen.* Frankfurt am Main: Suhrkamp, 1991. 123–201.

Berg, Jan. "Friedrich Hebbel: *Maria Magdalena* und die Bearbeitung von Franz Xaver Kroetz." In *Von Lessing bis Kroetz. Einführung in die Dramenanalyse. Kursmodelle und sozialgeschichtliche Materialien für den Unterict,* edited by Jan Berg et al. 3rd ed. Königstein/Ts: Scriptor, 1979. 43–67.

Bortoft, Henri. *Goethe's Scientific Consciousness.* Tunbridge Wells: Institute for Cultural Research, 1986.

Brandes, Ute. *Zitat und Montage in der neueren DDR-Prosa.* Frankfurt am Main: Peter Lang, 1984.

Braun, Volker. *Unvollendete Geschichte.* Frankfurt am Main: Suhrkamp, 1977.

Brecht, Bertolt. *Werke: große kommentierte Berliner und Frankfurter Ausgabe.* 30 vols. Berlin and Weimar: Aufbau, Frankfurt am Main: Suhrkamp, 1988–98. Cited as *BFA*.

Broch, Hermann. "Hugo von Hofmannsthals Prosaschriften." 1951. In *Hofmannsthal im Urteil seiner Kritiker,* edited by Gotthart Wunberg. Frankfurt am Main: Athenäum, 1972. 435–54.

Büchner, Georg. *Sämtliche Werke und Briefe: Historisch-kritische Ausgabe mit Kommentar.* 2 vols. Hamburg: Christian Wegner, 1967–71. Cited as *BW*.

Burgess, Gordon J. A. "Büchner, Schneider and Lenz: Two Authors in Search of a Character." In *Georg Büchner: Tradition and Innovation: Fourteen Essays,* edited by Ken Mills and Brian Keith-Smith. Bristol: U of Bristol P, 1990. 207–26.

Carl, Rolf-Peter. *Franz Xaver Kroetz. Autorenbücher.* Munich: Beck, 1987.

Celan, Paul. *Ausgewählte Gedichte. Zwei Reden.* 3rd ed. Frankfurt am Main: Suhrkamp, 1967.

Cohn, Dorrit. "The Second Author of *Death in Venice*." In *Thomas Mann: "Death in Venice": A New Translation: Backgrounds and Contexts: Criticisms*, edited and translated by Clayton Koelb. New York and London: Norton, 1994. 78–195.

Donnenberg, Joseph. "Schiller: *Die Jungfrau von Orleans* und Brecht: *Die heilige Johanna der Schlachthöfe*. Zur Interpretation und Rezeption." In *Festschrift für Adalbert Schmidt zum 70. Geburtstag*, edited by Gerlinde Weiss and G. D. Stein. Stuttgart: Heinz, 1976. 257–87.

Dürrenmatt, Friedrich. *Theater-Schriften und Reden*. Zurich: Arche, 1966.

Eliot, T. S. "Tradition and the Individual Talent." 1919. In *Selected Prose of T. S. Eliot*, edited by Frank Kermode. London: Faber and Faber, 1975, 37–44.

Erlach, Dietrich. *Wolfgang Koeppen als zeitkritischer Erzähler*. Upsala: Studia Germanistica upsaliensia, 1973.

Frenzel, Elisabeth. *Stoffe der Weltliteratur*. Stuttgart: Kröner, 1992.

Freud, Sigmund. "Der Dichter und das Phantasieren," 1907. In *Bildende Kunst und Literatur, Studienausgabe*, Sigmund Freud. Vol. 10. Frankfurt am Main: Fischer, 1969. 170–79.

Garland, Mary. *Hebbel's Prose Tragedies*. Cambridge: Cambridge UP, 1973.

Girnus, Wilhelm. "Lachen über Wibeau . . . aber wie?" In *Plenzdorfs "Neue Leiden des jungen W.,"* edited by Peter J. Brenner, Frankfurt am Main: Suhrkamp, 1982. 189–204.

Glenn, Jerry H. "The Title of Hebbel's *Maria Magdalena*." *Papers on Language and Literature* 3 (1967): 122–33.

Goethe, Johann Wolfgang. *Goethes Werke. Hamburger Ausgabe in 14 Bänden*. Hamburg: Christian Wegner, 1948–60. Cited as *HA*.

Grimm, Reinhold. *Love, Lust, and Rebellion: New Approaches to Georg Büchner*. Madison, Wisconsin: The U of Wisconsin P, 1985.

Grossklaus, Götz. "West-östliches Unbehagen. Literarische Gesellschaftskritik in Ulrich Plenzdorfs *Die neuen Leiden des jungen W.* und Peter Schneiders *Lenz*." *Basis, Jahrbuch für deutsche Gegenwartsliteratur* 5 (1975): 80–99.

Haffner, Herbert. *Dramenbearbeitungen*. Munich: Oldenbourg, 1980.

Hebbel, Friedrich. *Werke*. 5 vols. Munich: Carl Hanser, 1963–67. Cited as *HW*.

Heisenberg, Werner. "Die Goethesche und die Newtonsche Farbenlehre im Lichte der modernen Physik." 1941. In *Goethe im XX. Jahrhundert. Spiegelungen und Deutungen*, edited by Hans Mayer. Hamburg: Christian Wegner, 1967. 418–32.

Herwig, Oliver. "Wolfgang Koeppens Absage an den Ästhetizismus. Die Strategie der literarischen Auseinandersetzung mit Thomas Mann im Roman *Der Tod in Rom*." *Zeitschrift für Germanistik* 5:3 (1995): 544–53.

Hofmannsthal, Hugo von. *Sämtliche Werke.* Vol. 31. Frankfurt am Main: Fischer, 1991. Cited as *EB.*

Hölderlin, Friedrich. *Sämtliche Werke.* 8 vols. Stuttgart: Cottasche Buchhandlung, 1946–85.

Hollis, Andy. "Introduction." In *Volker Braun: "Unvollendete Geschichte."* Manchester: Manchester UP, 1988. 1–29.

Holquist, Michael. *Dialogism: Bakhtin and His World.* London: Routledge, 1990.

Hurst, Matthias. *Erzählsituationen in Literatur und Film.* Tubingen: Niemeyer, 1996.

Hutchinson, Peter. *Games Authors Play.* London: Methuen, 1983.

Imhof, Rüdiger. *John Banville: A Critical Introduction.* Dublin: Wolfhound, 1989.

———. "My Readers, That Small Band Deserve a Rest: An Interview with John Banville," *Irish University Review* 11 (1981): 5–12.

Jäger, Georg. *Die Leiden des alten und neuen Werther.* Munich: Carl Hanser, 1984.

Jauss, Hans Robert. "Klassik — wieder modern?" *Der Deutschunterricht* 30 (1978): 35–51.

Kafitz, Dieter. "Ästhetischer Radikalismus. Zur Kunstauffassung Wolfgang Koeppens." In *Wolfgang Koeppen,* edited by Eckart Oehlenschläger. *Materialien.* Frankfurt am Main: Suhrkamp, 1987. 75–88.

Kant, Immanuel. *Kants gesammelte Schriften.* Vol. 4. Berlin: Reimer, 1903.

Kaul, F. K. "Diskussion um Plenzdorf, *Die neuen Leiden des jungen W.*" In *Plenzdorfs "Neue Leiden des jungen W.,"* edited by Peter J. Brenner. Frankfurt am Main: Suhrkamp, 1982. 151–53.

Keitel, Eveline. "Recent literary trends. Verständigungstexte — Form, Funktion, Wirkung." *German Quarterly* 56:3 (1983): 431–55.

Keller, Gottfried. *Werke.* 6 vols. Zurich/Berlin: Atlantis, n.d.

Keuler, Dorothea. *Die wahre Geschichte der Effi B.* Zurich: Haffmans, 1998.

Knapp, Mona. "Moderner Ödipus oder blinder Anpasser? Anmerkungen zu *Homo faber* aus feministischer Sicht." In *Frischs "Homo faber,"* edited by Walter Schmitz. Frankfurt am Main: Suhrkamp, 1983. 188–207.

Knopf, Jan. *Grundlagen und Gedanken zum Verständnis des deutschen Dramas. Bertolt Brecht: "Die heilige Johanna der Schlachthöfe."* Frankfurt am Main: Diesterweg, 1985.

Koeppen, Wolfgang. *Die elenden Scribenten. Aufsätze,* edited by Marcel Reich-Ranicki. Frankfurt am Main: Suhrkamp, 1981.

———. *Der Tod in Rom*. 1954. 4th ed. Frankfurt am Main: Suhrkamp, 1982. Cited as *TR*.

Koestler, Arthur. *The Sleepwalkers: A History of Man's Changing Vision of the Universe*. 1959. Harmondsworth: Penguin, 1968.

Kraus, Karl. *Die Fackel*. Nov. 1900. Cited in Hugo von Hofmannsthal. *Sämtliche Werke*, vol. 28. Frankfurt am Main: Fischer, 1975.

Kroetz, Franz Xaver. *Ein Lesebuch*. 1976. Reinbek bei Hamburg: Rowohlt, 1982.

———. *Stücke II*. Frankfurt am Main: Suhrkamp, 1989. Cited as *KMM*.

Kurscheidt, Georg. "*Maria Magdalena* — Hebbels bürgerliches Trauerspiel in der Bearbeitung von Franz Xaver Kroetz." *Wirkendes Wort: Deutsche Sprache in Forschung und Lehre* 6 (1982): 405–18.

Laemmle, Peter. "Büchners Schatten. Kritische Überlegungen zur Rezeption von Peter Schneiders Erzählung *Lenz*." *Aspekte* 5 (1974): 467–78.

Leppla, Otmar, and Hartmut Fischer. *Stundenblätter Plenzdorf. Die neuen Leiden des jungen W*. Stuttgart: Klett/ Schulpraxis, 1985.

Lessing, Gotthold Ephraim. *Werke*. 4 vols. Munich: Carl Hanser, 1970–79.

Mann, Thomas. *"Death in Venice": A New Translation: Backgrounds and Contexts: Criticisms*, edited and translated by Clayton Koelb. New York: Norton, 1994.

———. *Gesammelte Werke*. Vol. 8. Frankfurt am Main: Fischer, 1974.

Marx, Karl and Friedrich Engels. *Ausgewählte Schriften in zwei Bänden*. Berlin: Dietz, 1951.

———. *Werke*. Vol. 1. Berlin: Dietz, 1958.

Mayer, Hans. *Bertolt Brecht und die Tradition*. Pfullingen: Neske, 1961.

———. "Johanna oder die Vernunft des Herzens." *Theater heute* 9 (1968): 22–27.

———. "Der Tod in Venedig. Ein Thema mit Variationen." In *Literaturwissenschaft und Geistesgeschichte. Festschrift für Richard Brinkmann*, edited by J. Brumnack et al. Tubingen: Niemeyer, 1981. 711–24.

McClelland, Denny. "The Discrepancy Between Kant and Schiller." In *Friedrich Schiller and the Drama of Human Existence*, edited by Alexej Ugrinsky. New York: Greenwood Press, 1988. 135–40.

Menke, Timm Reiner. *Lenz-Erzählungen in der deutschen Literatur*. Hildesheim: Olms, 1984.

Meyer, Herman. *Das Zitat in der Erzählkunst*. Stuttgart: Metzlersche Verlagsbuchhandlung, 1961.

Miller, R. D. *Schiller and the Ideal of Freedom*. 1959. Oxford: Clarendon Press, 1970.

Molloy, Francis C. "The Search for Truth: The Fiction of John Banville." *Irish University Review* 11 (1981): 29–51.

Morawski, Stefan. "The Basic Functions of Quotation." In *Sign, Language, Culture*, edited by A. J. Greimas et al. The Hague: Mouton, 1970. 690–705.

Morris, Leslie. "Aesthetic, Political or Anti-Idyll? 'Das Italienerlebnis' in Works by Christine Wolter, Birgit Pausch and Peter Schneider." *Neue Germanistik* 4:2 (1986): 13–23.

Müller, Gerd. *Das Volksstück von Raimund bis Kroetz. Die Gattung in Einzelanalysen*. Munich: Oldenbourg, 1979.

Müller-Waldeck, Gunnar and Michael Gratz. *Wolfgang Koeppen — Mein Ziel war die Ziellosigkeit*. Hamburg: Europäische Verlagsanstalt, 1998.

Murphy, Harriet. *The Rhetoric of the Spoken Word in "Die Wahlverwandtschaften."* Frankfurt am Main: Peter Lang, 1990.

Niedermeier, Michael. *Das Ende der Idylle. Symbolik, Zeitbezug, "Gartenrevolution" in Goethes Roman "Die Wahlverwandtschaften."* Berlin: Peter Lang, 1992.

Panzner, Evalouise. *Franz Xaver Kroetz und seine Rezeption. Die Intention eines Stückeschreibers und seine Aufnahme durch die Kritik*. Stuttgart: Klett, 1976.

———. "Weiterungen im Theater des Franz Xaver Kroetz." In *Text und Kritik: Franz Xaver Kroetz*, edited by Ludwig Arnold. 57 Munich: edition text + kritik, 1978. 20–28.

Pascal, Roy. *The Dual Voice*. Manchester: Manchester UP, 1977.

Pender, Malcolm. "Historical Awareness and Peter Schneider's *Lenz*." *German Life and Letters* 37:2 (1984): 150–60.

Pizer, John. "From a *Death in Venice* to a *Death in Rome*: On Wolfgang Koeppen's Critical Ironization of Thomas Mann." *The Germanic Review* 68:3 (1993): 98–107.

Plenzdorf, Ulrich. "Diskussion." In *Plenzdorfs "Neue Leiden des jungen W.,"* edited by Peter J. Brenner. Frankfurt am Main: Suhrkamp, 1982. 173–88.

———. *Die neuen Leiden des jungen W*. Frankfurt am Main: Suhrkamp, 1976. First published in *Sinn und Form*, 1973. Cited as *PL*.

Pörnbacher, Karl. *Erläuterungen und Dokumente. Friedrich Hebbel: "Maria Magdalena."* Stuttgart: Reclam, 1970. New extended ed., 1980.

Reddick, John. *Georg Büchner: The Shattered Whole*. Oxford: Clarendon Press, 1994.

Reed, T. J. *Thomas Mann: "Der Tod in Venedig." Text, Materialien, Kommentar*. Munich: Carl Hanser, 1983.

Reich-Ranicki, Marcel. "Der Fänger im DDR-Roggen. Ulrich Plenzdorfs jedenfalls wichtiger *Werther*-Roman." In *Plenzdorfs "Neue Leiden des jungen W.,"* edited by Peter J. Brenner. Frankfurt am Main: Suhrkamp, 1982. 262–69.

———. "Der Fall Wolfgang Koeppen." In *Literarisches Leben in Deutschland*, by Marcel Reich-Ranicki. Munich: Piper and Co. 1965. 26–31.

Reis, Ilse H. *Ulrich Plenzdorfs Gegen-Entwurf zu Goethes Werther.* Bern: Franke, 1977.

Richner, Thomas. *Der Tod in Rom. Eine existential-psychologische Analyse von Wolfgang Koeppens Roman.* Zurich and Munich: Artemis, 1982.

Riewoldt, Otto, ed. *Franz Xaver Kroetz.* Frankfurt am Main: Suhrkamp, 1985.

Riordan, Colin. "Peter Schneider: A Biographical Sketch." In *Peter Schneider*, edited by Colin Riordan. Cardiff: U of Wales P, 1995. 13–23.

Rothmann, Kurt. *Erläuterungen und Dokumente, J. W. Goethe, Die Leiden des jungen Werther.* Stuttgart: Reclam, 1971.

Rülicke-Weiler, Käthe. "Bertolt Brecht: *Die heilige Johanna der Schlachthöfe* — Notizen zum Bau der Fabel." In *Das deutsche Drama vom Expressionismus bis zur Gegenwart*, edited by Manfred Brauneck. Bamberg: Buchner, 1977. 144–54.

Ryan, Judith. "Views From the Summerhouse: Goethe's *Wahlverwandtschaften* and its Literary Successors." In *Goethe's Narrative Fiction: The Irvine Symposium*, edited by W. J. Lillyman. Berlin: Gruyter, 1983. 145–60.

Salinger, J. D. *The Catcher in the Rye.* London: Penguin Books, 1951.

Schiller, Friedrich. *Schillers Werke. Nationalausgabe.* 42 vols. Weimar: Hermann Böhlhaus Nachfolger, 1943–2000. Cited as *NA*.

Schlaffer, Heinz. "Nachwort." In *Die Wahlverwandtschaften*, by Johann Wolfgang Goethe. 2nd ed. Munich: Goldmann, 1988. 245–68.

Schneider, Peter. *Lenz. Eine Erzählung.* Berlin: Rotbuch, 1973. Cited as *SL*.

Schueler, H. J. *The Old Retold.* New York: Peter Lang, 1996.

Schulz, Gudrun. *Die Schillerbearbeitungen Bertolt Brechts. Eine Untersuchung literarhistorischer Bezüge im Hinblick auf Brechts Traditionsbegriff.* Tubingen: Niemeyer, 1972.

Seaman, A. T. "Celtic Myth as Perceived in Eighteenth- and Nineteenth-Century Literature in English." In *Celtic Languages and Celtic People*, edited by C. J. Byrne, M. Harry, and P. Ó Siadhail. Halifax, NS: Saint Mary's University, 1992. 443–60.

Shaw, Bernard. *Saint Joan: A Chronicle Play in Six Scenes and an Epilogue.* 1924. Harmondsworth: Penguin, 1965.

Sudau, Ralf. *Werkbearbeitung, Dichterfiguren. Traditionsaneignung am Beispiel der deutschen Gegenwartsliteratur.* Tubingen: Niemeyer, 1985.

Tate, Dennis. *The East German Novel: Identity, Community, Continuity.* Bath: Bath UP, 1984.

Thomaneck, Jürgen. *Ulrich Plenzdorf: "Die neuen Leiden des jungen W."* 2nd ed. Glasgow: University of Glasgow French and German Publications, 1992.

Thomas, N. L. "Werther in a new Guise: Ulrich Plenzdorf's *Die neuen Leiden des jungen W.*" *Modern Languages: Journal of the Modern Language Association* 57 (1976): 178–82.

Todorov, Tzvetan. *Mikhail Bakhtin: The Dialogical Principle.* Manchester: Manchester UP, 1984.

Turnbull, H. W., ed. *The Correspondence of Isaak Newton, 1688–1694.* Vol. 3. Cambridge: Cambridge UP, 1961.

Wagner, Peter. "Bertolt Brechts *Die heilige Johanna der Schlachthöfe*. Ideologische Aspekte und ästhetische Strukturen." *Jahrbuch der deutschen Schillergesellschaft* 12 (1968): 493–519.

Waiblinger, Franz Peter. "Zitierte Kritik. Zu den Werther-Zitaten in Ulrich Plenzdorfs *Die neuen Leiden des jungen W.*" *Poetica* 8 (1976): 71–88.

Walsøe-Engel, Ingrid. *Fathers and Daughters: Patterns of Seduction in Tragedies by Gryphius, Lessing, Hebbel and Kroetz.* Columbia, SC: Camden House, 1993.

Wapnewski, Peter. "Zweihundert Jahre Werthers Leiden, oder: Dem war nicht zu helfen." In *Plenzdorfs "Neue Leiden des jungen W.,"* edited by Peter J. Brenner. Frankfurt am Main: Suhrkamp, 1982. 324–44.

Weber, Max. *The Protestant Ethic and the Spirit of Capitalism.* 1905. Translated by Talcott Parsons. London: George Allen and Unwin Ltd., 1930.

Weimann, Robert. "Goethe in der Figurenperspektive." *Sinn und Form* 25 (1973): 222–38.

Westfall, Richard. *Never at Rest: A Biography of Isaac Newton* Cambridge: Cambridge UP, 1980.

Widdig, Bernd. "Melancholie und Moderne: Wolfgang Koeppens *Der Tod in Rom.*" *The Germanic Review* 66:4 (1991): 161–68.

Williams, Rhys W. "'Ein gewisses Maß subjektiver Verzweiflung . . .': Peter Schneider's *Lenz.*" In *Peter Schneider,* edited by Colin Riordan. Cardiff: U of Wales P, 1995. 50–67.

Wolf, Christa. "Lesen und Schreiben." In *Lesen und Schreiben. Aufsätze und Prosastücke,* by Christa Wolf. Darmstadt: Luchterhand, 1972. 181–220.

Zmegac, Victor. "Zu einem Thema Goethes und Thomas Manns: Wege der Erotik in der modernen Gesellschaft." *Goethe Jahrbuch* 103 (1986): 152–66.

Notes

Notes to Introduction

[1] Gottfried Keller, *Romeo und Julia auf dem Dorfe*, in Gottfried Keller, *Werke*, vol. 4 (Zurich and Berlin: Atlantis, n.d.), 70, my emphasis.

[2] See for example, Mona Knapp, "Moderner Ödipus oder blinder Anpasser? Anmerkungen zu *Homo faber* aus feministischer Sicht," in Walter Schmitz, ed., *Frischs "Homo faber"* (Frankfurt am Main: Suhrkamp, 1983).

[3] Throughout this study, the term "reworking" refers to "literary reworking" as defined in this chapter.

[4] Hans Mayer, "Der Tod in Venedig. Ein Thema mit Variationen," in J. Brumnack et al., *Literaturwissenschaft und Geistesgeschichte. Festschrift für Richard Brinkmann* (Tubingen: Niemeyer, 1981), 712.

[5] See Hans-Robert Jauss, "Klassik — wieder modern?" *Der Deutschunterricht* 30 (1978): 35–51. "Als dialektische Vermittlung zwischen Vergangenheit und Gegenwart hebt die verjüngende Rezeption den Mangel der Einseitigkeit einer nur traditionsgebundenen Wiedergabe oder einer nur formalistischen Erneuerung klassischer Werke auf" (39).

[6] See also Gordon J. A. Burgess, "Büchner, Schneider and Lenz: Two Authors in Search of a Character," in Ken Mills and Brian Keith-Smith, eds., *Georg Büchner: Tradition and Innovation: Fourteen Essays* (Bristol: U of Bristol P, 1990), 207–26. "Three main features of this phenomenon are as follows: one, a modern literary work is based, quite consciously and quite openly, upon an earlier literary work; two, both works are in the vernacular; and three, the earlier text is either reasonably well known or is by an author well known to the educated native reader. This last point is particularly important, since the mechanism of the literary reworking depends, to some extent, on knowledge shared by author and reader, on one level a sort of 'in-joke' which loses its point if the reader fails to see the connection" (207).

[7] Götz Grossklaus, "West-östliches Unbehagen. Literarische Gesellschaftskritik in Ulrich Plenzdorfs *Die neuen Leiden des jungen W.* und Peter Schneiders *Lenz*," *Basis, Jahrbuch für deutsche Gegenwartsliteratur* 5 (1975): 80–99.

[8] Herman Meyer, *Das Zitat in der Erzählkunst* (Stuttgart: Metzlersche Verlagsbuchhandlung, 1961), 15.

[9] Herbert Haffner, *Dramenbearbeitungen* (Munich: Oldenbourg, 1980).

[10] Ralf Sudau, *Werkbearbeitung, Dichterfiguren* (Tubingen: Niemeyer, 1985).

[11] H. J. Schueler, *The Old Retold* (New York: Peter Lang, 1996), 1.

[12] Eveline Keitel, "Recent Literary Trends: Verständigungstexte — Form, Funktion, Wirkung," in *German Quarterly* 56:3 (1983): 431–55. "Ein Grund für das Fehlen einer theoretischen Aufarbeitung jener neuen Kommunikations- und Wirkungsweisen mag darin liegen, daß die Verständigungstexte zunächst als höchst heterogen und divergent erscheinen. Generalisierende Aussagen über ein derart uneinheitliches Untersuchungsfeld gestalten sich problematisch" (432).

[13] Michael Buselmeier, *Deutsche Volkszeitung*, Dusseldorf, May 24, 1973, in Evalouise Panzner, *Franz Xaver Kroetz und seine Rezeption. Die Intention eines Stükkeschreibers und seine Aufnahme durch die Kritik* (Stuttgart: Klett, 1976), 110.

[14] Georg Hensel, *Darmstädter Echo*, May 8, 1973. In Panzner, *Franz Xaver Kroetz und seine Rezeption*, 107.

[15] Jauss, "Klassik — wieder modern?": "Darunter verstehe ich eine Aufarbeitung des Prozesses der Rezeption, der zwischen der Vergangenheit eines Werks und seinem gegenwärtigen Verständnis liegt — eine Aufarbeitung, *die notwendig wählend und verkürzend sein muß*, aus dieser Not aber die Tugend der Belebung und Verjüngung des Vergangenen gewinnt" (38). My emphasis.

[16] Volker Braun, *Unvollendete Geschichte* (Frankfurt am Main: Suhrkamp, 1989; orig. ed., 1977): "Karin gefiel die Geschichte [*Die neuen Lieden*], und es schien ein authentischer Fall zu sein . . . aber der Werther, den er [Edgar] immer zitierte, hing noch anders mit der Welt zusammen" (43–44).

[17] Karl Kraus, *Die Fackel*, Nov. 1900, cited in Hugo von Hofmannsthal *Sämtliche Werke*, vol. 28: *Erzählungen*, 1 (Frankfurt am Main: Fischer, 1975), 222–23.

[18] Ilse H. Reis, *Ulrich Plenzdorfs Gegen-Entwurf zu Goethes "Werther"* (Bern: Franke, 1977). "Die direkten Zitate sind Strukturelemente und haben Verweisungscharakter; sie lassen kryptische Zitate vermuten, die aufzuspüren wären. Der 'gebildete' Leser kann sich somit stärker am Spiel beteiligen" (8).

[19] Dorothea Keuler, *Die wahre Geschichte der Effi B.* (Zurich: Haffmans, 1998), 234.

[20] Karl Marx, "Der achtzehnte Brumaire des Louis Bonaparte," in Karl Marx and Friedrich Engels, *Ausgewählte Schriften* 1 (Berlin: Dietz, 1951), 226.

[21] Karl Marx, "Zur Kritik der Hegelschen Rechtsphilosophie. Einleitung," in Karl Marx and Friedrich Engels, *Werke*, vol. 1 (Berlin: Dietz, 1958), 382.

[22] Friedrich Dürrenmatt, "Theaterprobleme" (1954/55), in *Theater-Schriften und Reden* (Zurich: Arche, 1966), 122.

[23] See, for example, Hugo von Hofmannsthal, *Erlebnis des Marschalls von Bassompierre* (1900), based on an episode from Goethe's *Erzählungen deutscher Ausgewanderter;* Ludwig Thoma, *Magdalena — eine bayrische Emilia Galotti* (1912); Wolfgang Hildesheimer, *Mary Stuart — eine historische Szene* (1970); Peter Hacks, *Das Jahrmarktsfest zu Plundersweilen* (1975); Christa Wolf, *Neue Lebensansichten eines Katers* (1980); Sigrid Damm, *Ich bin nicht Ottilie* (1992); Christa Schmidt, *Die Wahlverwandten* (1992); Rolf Hochhuth, *Effis Nacht* (1996); Dorothea Keuler, *Die wahre Geschichte der Effi B.* (1998).

[24] See, for example, Ingrid Walsøe-Engel, *Fathers and Daughters: Patterns of Seduction in Tragedies by Gryphius, Lessing, Hebbel and Kroetz* (Columbia, SC: Camden House, 1993).

[25] See, for example, Timm Reiner Menke, *Lenz-Erzählungen in der deutschen Literatur* (Hildesheim: Olms, 1984).

[26] See, for example, Dennis Tate, *The East German Novel* (Bath: Bath UP, 1984).

[27] Peter Hutchinson, *Games Authors Play* (London: Methuen, 1983), 57.

[28] Andy Hollis, "Introduction," in *Volker Braun: "Unvollendete Geschichte"* (Manchester: Manchester UP, 1988), 23.

[29] Stefan Morawski, "The Basic Functions of Quotation," in A. J. Greimas et al., *Sign, Language, Culture* (The Hague: Mouton, 1970), 690.

Notes to Chapter 1

[1] Elisabeth Frenzel, *Stoffe der Weltliteratur* (Stuttgart: Kröner, 1992).

[2] Friedrich Schiller, *Die Jungfrau von Orleans*, vol. 9 in *Schillers Werke. Nationalausgabe* (Weimar: Hermann Böhlhaus Nachfolger, 1948). All references to Schiller's works are taken from this edition using the abbreviation *NA*. Subsequent references to *Die Jungfrau von Orleans* (*NA*, 9) are cited in the text using the abbreviation *JO* and line reference.

[3] Schiller to Wieland, Oct 17, 1801, *NA*, 3:65.

[4] Bertolt Brecht, *Die heilige Johanna der Schlachthöfe*, in *Bertolt Brecht. Berliner und Frankfurter Ausgabe* (Berlin and Weimar: Aufbau, Frankfurt am Main: Suhrkamp, 1988). All references to Brecht's works are from this edition using the abbreviation *BFA*. Subsequent references to *Die heilige Johanna der Schlachthöfe* (*BFA*, 3:127–234) are cited in the text using the abbreviation *HJ* and page number.

[5] For a discussion of the differences between Schiller and Kant see: Denny McClelland, "The Discrepancy Between Kant and Schiller," in Alexej Ugrinsky, ed., *Friedrich Schiller and the Drama of Human Existence* (New York: Greenwood Press, 1988), 135–40. "Kant considered one to be moral in one's action only when one's will is freely submitted to the moral law, by steadfastly rejecting inclinations. . . . For Kant, duty and inclination had to be separated so that morality would have significance. . . . Schiller recognized that the imperative nature of moral obligation — as prescribed by Kant's system — was so incompatible with inclinations that it restricted one's freedom of action in reaching a moral decision" (136).

[6] Schiller to Goethe, December 24, 1800, *NA*, 30:224.

[7] George Bernard Shaw, *Saint Joan: A Chronicle Play in Six Scenes and an Epilogue* (1924; reprint, Harmondsworth: Penguin, 1965), 21–22 (page citations are to reprint edition).

[8] Joseph Donnenberg, "Schiller *Die Jungfrau von Orleans* und Brecht *Die heilige Johanna der Schlachthöfe*. Zur Interpretation und Rezeption," in Gerlinde Weiss and G. D. Stein, eds., *Festschrift für Adalbert Schmidt zum 70. Geburtstag* (Stutt-

gart: Heinz, 1976), 257–87. "Sein Weg der Auseinandersetzung mit diesem Stoff ist aufschlußreich, nicht nur für Brechts sich wandelnde Beziehung zur Jeanne d'Arc-Thematik (nämlich von parodistischer Anspielung zu historischer Authentizität, von kämpferischer Parteilichkeit zur distanzierten Darstellung einer Widerstandskämpferin), sondern auch charakteristisch für die zeitgenössische Tendenz zum Dokumentarischen" (272).

[9] By taking up arms, Johanna is seen by her family as acting contrary to the natural order. See Thibaut's accusation: "Eine schwere Irrung der Natur" (*JO*, 62).

[10] See Donnenberg, "[Man] erkennt in der dramatischen Konstruktion das geschichts-philosophische Konzept des deutschen Idealismus, in dem der alte christliche Dreischritt: Paradies — Sündenfall — himmlische Erlösung wirksam ist" (266).

[11] See Hans Mayer, *Bertolt Brecht und die Tradition* (Pfullingen: Neske, 1961), 48–52.

[12] Full title: *Trutz Simplex Oder Ausführliche und wundersame Lebensbeschreibung Der Ertzbetrügerin und Landstörtzerin Courasche.*

[13] Brecht, "Kleiner Rat Dokumente anzufertigen," *BFA*, 21:164.

[14] Friedrich Hölderlin, "Hyperions Schicksaalslied," in *Sämtliche Werke*, 1.1 (Stuttgart: Cottasche Buchhandlung, 1946), 265.

[15] Schiller, stage instructions to *Die Jungfrau von Orleans*, *NA*, 9:315.

[16] Gudrun Schulz, *Die Schillerbearbeitungen Bertolt Brechts. Eine Untersuchung literarhistorischer Bezüge im Hinblick auf Brechts Traditionsbegriff* (Tubingen: Niemeyer, 1972). The terms *Urfassung* and *Originalfassung* are taken from this study.

[17] See Goethe, *Faust. Erster Teil* in *Goethes Werke. Hamburger Ausgabe in 14 Bänden* (Hamburg: Christian Wegner, 1948–60). All quotations from Goethe's works are taken from this edition cited as *HA*. "Du bist dir nur des einen Triebs bewußt; / O lerne nie den andern kennen! / Zwei Seelen wohnen, ach! in meiner Brust, / Die eine will sich von der andern trennen" (*Faust I*, *HA*, 3: lines 1110–13).

[18] Schulz, *Die Schillerbearbeitungen*, 136–37. Spelling as in Schulz.

[19] See Brecht, "Der 13. Versuch. *Die heilige Johanna der Schlachthöfe*," *BFA*, 3: "*Die heilige Johanna der Schlachthöfe* soll die heutige Entwicklungsstufe des faustischen Menschen zeigen" (128).

[20] Schulz, *Die Schillerbearbeitungen*: "Mauler [ist] ein Ensemble aller Königsfiguren bei Schiller und umfunktionierbar, je nach der literarisch vorgeprägten Situation, in die er gerät. Wie Wallenstein ist er ein großer Spieler, wie Philip von Spanien einsam, schlaflos, wie Maria Stuart plagen ihn Schuldgefühle und böse Ahnungen und wie Karl von Frankreich möchte er sein 'blutiges Geschäft' baldmöglichst aufgeben" (146).

[21] For more details, see Jan Knopf, *Grundlagen und Gedanken zum Verständnis des deutschen Dramas. Bertolt Brecht: "Die heilige Johanna der Schlachthöfe"* (Frankfurt am Main: Diesterweg, 1985), 9. Brecht himself draws attention to his debt to Hauptmann. Also, Brecht, "Der 13. Versuch. *Die heilige Johanna der Schlachthöfe*," *BFA*, 3: "Das Stück ist entstanden aus dem *Happy End* von Elisa-

beth Hauptmann. Es wurden außerdem einige klassische Vorbilder und Stilelemente verwendet: die Darstellung bestimmter Vorgänge erhielt die ihm historisch zugeordnete Form. So sollen nicht nur die Vorgänge, sondern auch die Art ihrer literarisch-theatralischen Bewältigung ausgestellt werden" (128).

[22] See Käthe Rülicke-Weiler, "Bertolt Brecht: *Die heilige Johanna der Schlachthöfe* — Notizen zum Bau der Fabel," in Manfred Brauneck, ed., *Das deutsche Drama vom Expressionismus bis zur Gegenwart* (Bamberg: Buchner, 1977), 144–54.

[23] Brecht, "Über die Verwendung von Musik für ein episches Theater," *BFA,* 22.1:158.

[24] Brecht, "Über die Darstellung von Geschäften im Drama," *BFA,* 21:376–77.

[25] Brecht, "Über die Klassiker," *BFA,* 22.1:483.

[26] Schiller, "Über den Gebrauch des Chors in der Tragödie," *NA,* 10:14.

[27] See Knopf, "Geschichte kann nicht nachträglich kritisch richtiggestellt werden.... In erster Linie ... gilt Brechts Parodie der Klassiker-Rezeption der Zeit. Obwohl die Entwicklungsstufe des faustischen Menschen in der kapitalistischen Realität solche Formen, wie sie das Drama zu ergründen sucht, angenommen hat, werden die Klassiker weiterhin als das Vorbild, ihr Idealismus als der wahre Inhalt der Kunst weitergereicht. Die hoffnungslose Überholtheit des klassischen Idealismus aufzudecken und zugleich die Widersprüche des klassischen Ideals sichtbar werden zu lassen, das vor allem leistet die Parodie im Hinblick auf die klassische Überlieferung" (74).

[28] Hans Mayer, "Johanna oder die Vernunft des Herzens," *Theater heute* 9 (1968): 24, my emphasis.

[29] R. D. Miller, *Schiller and the Ideal of Freedom* (Oxford: Clarendon Press, 1970, orig. published by Duchy, 1959), 64. Miller elaborates: "The idea of freedom is so fundamental in Schiller that all other ideas must be related to it, if they are to be properly understood. Freedom lies behind Schiller's conception of human reason.... Freedom explains human 'dignity'; it is also the hallmark of beauty and grace. It is the very principle of tragedy" (vii).

[30] Miller, *Schiller and the Ideal of Freedom:* "It is not moral conduct as such that the dramatist should portray, but only 'the possibility of absolute freedom of will' ... which possibility the hero demonstrates by showing that he can rise above natural necessity" (60).

[31] Immanuel Kant, "Grundlegung zur Methaphysik [*sic*] der Sitten" in *Kants gesammelte Schriften,* vol. 4 (Berlin: Reimer, 1903), 421.

[32] Kant, "Grundlegung": "Es ist überall nichts in der Welt, ja überhaupt auch außer derselben zu denken möglich, was ohne Einschränkung für gut könnte gehalten werden, als allein ein *guter Wille*" (393).

[33] See Peter Wagner, "Bertolt Brechts *Die heilige Johanna der Schlachthöfe.* Ideologische Aspekte und ästhetische Strukturen," *Jahrbuch der deutschen Schillergesellschaft* 12 (1968): 493–519. "Johannas menschliche Problematik besteht in dem Zwang zur Entscheidung zwischen individuellem Sendungsbewußtsein, das im Gewissen begründet ist, und der Unterordnung unter das Kollektiv, welche

der Verstand fordert. . . . Denn diese fordert nicht weniger als völlige Selbstaufgabe im Klassenkampf" (519).

[34] Schiller, "Was kann eine gute stehende Schaubühne eigentlich wirken?" (Better known as "Die Schaubühne als moralische Anstalt betrachtet," 1784) in *NA*, 20:100.

[35] Schiller, "Über die ästhetische Erziehung des Menschen. 7. Brief," 1795, *NA*, 20:328.

[36] Georg Büchner, *Woyzeck*, vol. 1 in *Sämtliche Werke und Briefe. Historisch-kritische Ausgabe mit Kommentar* (Hamburg: Christian Wegner, 1967), 172.

[37] Schiller, "Über die ästhetische Erziehung des Menschen. 9. Brief," *NA*, 20:332.

[38] Schiller, "Über die ästhetische": "Jetzt bin ich an dem Punkt angelangt, zu welchem alle meine bisherigen Betrachtungen hingestrebt haben. Dieses Werkzeug ist die schöne Kunst, diese Quellen öffnen sich in ihren unsterblichen Mustern" (333).

[39] Brecht, "Kleines Organon für das Theater" (1948/49), *BFA*, 23:79.

[40] Brecht, "'Katzgraben'-Notate. Episches Theater" (1953), *BFA*, 25:401.

Notes to Chapter 2

[1] Friedrich Hebbel, *Maria Magdalena. Ein bürgerliches Trauerspiel in drei Akten*, in *Werke*, vol. 1 (Munich: Carl Hanser, 1963), 301–82. Unless otherwise stated, all references to Hebbel's works are taken from this edition using the abbreviation *HW*. Subsequent references to *Maria Magdalena* are cited in the text using the abbreviation *HMM* and page number. There is some confusion as to whether Hebbel called his drama *Maria Magdalene* or *Maria Magdalena*, but the general consensus seems to be that the use of "Magdalene" arose from an early printing mistake, and the most commonly established form is "Magdalena." See, for example, Karl Pörnbacher, *Erläuterungen und Dokumente. Friedrich Hebbel. Maria Magdalena* (Stuttgart: Reclam, 1970, new extended ed. 1980), 12.

[2] Franz Xaver Kroetz, *Maria Magdalena* (1972), in *Stücke II* (Frankfurt am Main: Suhrkamp, 1989), 179–256. Subsequent references to this work are cited in the text using the abbreviation *KMM* and page number.

[3] Kroetz, "Liegt die Dummheit auf der Hand?" in Franz Xaver Kroetz, *Ein Lesebuch* (Reinbek bei Hamburg: Rowohlt, 1982; orig. published by Kiepenheuer, 1976), 558.

[4] Gotthold Ephraim Lessing, "Hamburgische Dramaturgie, 74. Stück," in *Werke*, vol. 4 (Munich: Carl Hanser, 1979), 574.

[5] Hebbel, "Vorwort zur *Maria Madgalene*" (1844), in *HW*, 1:326.

[6] Kroetz, "Ich säße lieber in Bonn im Bundestag," in *Ein Lesebuch*, 627–28.

[7] Bertolt Brecht, "Über die Möglichkeiten nichtaristotelischer Dramatiken. Kritik der *Poetik* des Aristoteles," *BFA*, 22.1:171.

[8] Brecht, "V-Effekte, Dreigespräch," *BFA*, 22.1:400.

[9] Brecht, "Kritik der *Poetik* des Aristoteles," *BFA*, 22.1:172.

¹⁰ Friedrich Dürrenmatt, "Theaterprobleme" (1954/55), in *Theater-Schriften und Reden* (Zurich: Arche, 1966), 120.

¹¹ Gerd Müller, *Das Volksstück von Raimund bis Kroetz. Die Gattung in Einzelanalysen* (Munich: Oldenbourg, 1979). "Ein Autor formuliert Einsichten, Erkenntnisse und Lehren im Hinblick auf eine Gruppe von Menschen, die er dieser sprachlichen Mitteilung für bedürftig hält. Er hat beobachtet, daß bestimmte Nachrichten diese Menschen überhaupt nicht oder nur verstümmelt erreichen, oder daß sie nicht die Wirkung zeigen, die von ihnen zu erwarten war. Er versucht nun seinerseits, seine Mitteilung möglichst präzise im Hinblick auf seine Zielgruppe zu formulieren" (144).

¹² Ingrid Walsøe-Engel, *Fathers and Daughters: Patterns of Seduction in Tragedies by Gryphius, Lessing, Hebbel and Kroetz* (Columbia, SC: Camden House, 1993), 143–44.

¹³ Georg Hensel, "Der unterwanderte Hebbel," *Theater heute* 14 (1973). Cited in Otto Riewoldt, ed., *Franz Xaver Kroetz* (Frankfurt am Main: Suhrkamp, 1985), 132.

¹⁴ Michael Buselmeier, "Vordergründig aktualisiert," *Deutsche Volkszeitung*, Dusseldorf, May 24, 1973. Cited in Riewoldt, *Franz Xaver Kroetz*, 132.

¹⁵ Rolf-Peter Carl, *Franz Xaver Kroetz. Autorenbücher* (Munich: Beck, 1987), 89.

¹⁶ Georg Kurscheidt, "*Maria Magdalena* — Hebbels bürgerliches Trauerspiel in der Bearbeitung von Franz Xaver Kroetz," *Wirkendes Wort: Deutsche Sprache in Forschung und Lehre*, 6 (1982): 405–18. "Bei Kroetz . . . hat der zum Proletarier bzw. 'Kleinbürger' degenerierte Bürger seine tragische Würde wieder verloren; sein Schicksal und das seiner Familie, deren Zustand (jedenfalls bei Kroetz) nunmehr unbeschönigt die *ökonomische* Krisenhaftigkeit einer modernen Konsum- und Warengesellschaft reflektiert, läßt sich nicht mehr mit dem wie immer verstandenen Begriffe des Tragischen erklären, es wird Anlaß zu bitterer Groteske und absurder Komik. Es scheint, als tue die gattungsgeschichtliche Entwicklung gleichsam einen Schritt zurück: Zurückverwiesen aus dem einst eroberten Bezirk des Tragischen bleibt dem Bürger die Rolle des Protagonisten in einer 'lächerlichen Tragödie'" (417).

¹⁷ Jan Berg, "Friedrich Hebbel: *Maria Magdalena* und die Bearbeitung von Franz Xaver Kroetz," in Jan Berg, et al., *Von Lessing bis Kroetz*, 3rd ed. (Königstein/Ts: Scriptor, 1979), 43–67. "Vor der Bearbeitung der Hebbelschen *Maria Magdalena* war Kroetz' Ruf als Protagonist der Sprachlosigkeit unbestritten. Sein Ruf gründete sich auf die These, daß mit der Sprachnot der Figuren ein qualifiziertes Darstellungsmittel der physischen und psychischen Verelendung des Menschen gefunden worden ist" (57).

¹⁸ See Berg, "Friedrich Hebbel": "Der Widerspruch, daß Sprachnot und Regression einmal thematisiert wird als das Characteristische des sozialen Elends, ein andermal als Karikierung des gleichen Elends, deutet . . . darauf, daß weder in der *Maria Magdalena* noch in anderen Stücken zuvor, Kroetz mit dem Konzept der Sprachnotbeschreibung in der Lage war, gesellschaftliche Widersprüche auf der Bühne zu entfalten" (58).

[19] Kroetz, "Über *Die Maßnahme* von Bertolt Brecht" (1975), in Kroetz, *Ein Lesebuch*, 606.

[20] The orthography reflects the adaptation of a southern German dialect, which Kroetz writes in; for example, "ist" is rendered as "is" and often the "e" is dropped at the end of verb forms such as in "dagewesn."

[21] Hebbel, "Tagebuch 2926," December 8, 1843, *HW*, 4:604–5.

[22] Hebbel, "Tagebuch 2910," December 4, 1843, *HW*, 4:602.

[23] See Jerry H. Glenn, "The Title of Hebbel's *Maria Magdalena*," *Papers on Language and Literature*, 3 (1967): 122–33.

[24] Auguste Stich-Crelinger to Hebbel, June 1, 1844. Cited in Pörnbacher, *Erläuterungen und Dokumente*, 59.

[25] This point has likewise been recognized by Kurscheidt, "*Maria Magdalena*": "In der klassischen Tragödie Schillers erleiden tragische Gestalten wie ... die Jungfrau von Orleans ihr Schicksal im vollen Bewußtsein der Sinnhaftigkeit ihres Untergangs, in der Überzeugung eines jenseitigen Triumphs; ihr irdisches Scheitern bedeutet in paradox scheinendem Sinne Selbstverwirklichung und Identitätsfindung, ihr Tod wird zur Apotheose. In Hebbels bürgerlichem Trauerspiel erfassen weder Anton noch Klara den Sinn dessen, was mit ihnen vorgeht; Klara stirbt ohne Hoffnung auf transzendente Rechtfertigung — es bleibt dem Zuschauer überlassen, jene Perspektive zu erkennen, die in der Figur des Sekretärs angedeutet, über das vordergründig ungerechtfertigt anmutende individuelle Schicksal hinausweist" (413).

[26] See, for example Pörnbacher, *Erläuterungen und Dokumente*, 12.

[27] Stage direction in *Maria Magdalena*, *KMM*, 198.

[28] Mary Garland, *Hebbel's Prose Tragedies* (Cambridge: Cambridge UP, 1973), 156.

[29] Kroetz's play concludes with the quote from Hebbel: "Mich selbst/ erschüttert / diese Klara / gewaltig / wie sie aus der Welt / herausgedrängt / wird" (*KMM*, 256).

[30] Hebbel, "Tagebuch 2926," December 8, 1843, *HW*, 4:605.

[31] Hebbel to Auguste Stich-Crelinger, December 11, 1843, *HW*, 5:585.

[32] See, for example, Evalouise Panzner, *Franz Xaver Kroetz und seine Rezeption. Die Intention eines Stückeschreibers und seine Aufnahme durch die Kritik* (Stuttgart: Ernst Klett, 1976). "Eigentliche Inhaltsangaben gibt es hier im Grunde nicht, weil man sofort den Vergleich zu Hebbels Stück zieht und dessen Thematik als bekannt voraussetzt" (48).

[33] Heinz Hilpert (no title), *Die Welt*, March 22, 1956. Cited in Pörnbacher, *Erläuterungen und Dokumente*, 79–80.

[34] Cited in Kroetz, "Ich säße lieber in Bonn im Bundestag," 628.

[35] Evalouise Panzner, "Weiterungen im Theater des Franz Xaver Kroetz," in Ludwig Arnold, ed., *Text und Kritik: Franz Xaver Kroetz* 57 (Munich: edition text + kritik, 1978), 22.

Notes to Chapter 3

[1] Walter Benjamin, "Goethes *Wahlverwandtschaften*," in *Gesammelte Schriften*, vol. 1 (Frankfurt am Main: Suhrkamp, 1991), 125.

[2] Thomas Mann, *Der Tod in Venedig*, in *Gesammelte Werke*, vol. 8 (Frankfurt am Main: Fischer, 1974), 444–525. Subsequent references to *Der Tod in Venedig* are cited in the text using the abbreviation *TV* and page number.

[3] Wolfgang Koeppen, *Der Tod in Rom*, 4th ed. (Frankfurt am Main: Suhrkamp, 1982). Subsequent references to *Der Tod in Rom* are cited in the text using the abbreviation *TR* and page number.

[4] Marcel Reich-Ranicki, "Der Fall Wolfgang Koeppen," in Marcel Reich-Ranicki, *Literarisches Leben in Deutschland* (Munich: Piper & Co., 1965), 31.

[5] Dietrich Erlach, *Wolfgang Koeppen als zeitkritischer Erzähler* (Upsala: Acta Universitatis Upsaliensis, Studia Germanistica upsaliensia, 1973), 205.

[6] Thomas Richner, *Der Tod in Rom. Eine existential-psychologische Analyse von Wolfgang Koeppens Roman* (Zurich and Munich: Artemis, 1982). The Swiss spelling of "ss" has been standardized to "ß" in all Richner quotations.

[7] See Oliver Herwig, "Wolfgang Koeppens Absage an den Ästhetizismus. Die Strategie der literarischen Auseinandersetzung mit Thomas Mann im Roman *Der Tod in Rom*," *Zeitschrift für Germanistik* 5:3 (1995): 544–53. "Im Licht der historischen Erfahrung zweier Weltkriege und des Nationalsozialismus vollzieht sich Koeppens radikale Absage an jeden Ästhetizismus. Seine forciert 'realistische' Gestaltungsweise verbindet sich mit einem Kulturpessimismus, der im Gegenzug die Historie als zyklische Wiederkehr von Machtmißbrauch und Schreckensherrschaft zeigt" (549).

[8] Viktor Zmegac, "Zu einem Thema Goethes und Thomas Manns: Wege der Erotik in der modernen Gesellschaft," *Goethe Jahrbuch* 103 (1986), 152–66, my emphasis. See also T. J. Reed, *Thomas Mann. "Der Tod in Venedig." Text, Materialien, Kommentar* (Munich: Hanser, 1983). "Man bewundert . . . Thomas Manns konzentriertestes Stilmuster, dessen souveräne Sprache und feierlicher Ton den fragwürdigen Stoff ins Hochliterarische rettet" (147).

[9] Bernd Widdig, "Melancholie und Moderne: Wolfgang Koeppens *Der Tod in Rom*," *The Germanic Review* 66:4 (1991): 161–68. "Aus geschichtlichen architektonischen und literarischen Bruchstücken zusammenmontiert, . . . gewinnt [Rom] eine eigenständige Dimension im Roman und überschattet die Gestaltung der Romanfiguren" (161).

[10] Herwig, "Wolfgang Koeppens Absage": "Die 'ewige Stadt' ist damit ebensosehr Verkörperung von Koeppens pessimistischer Geschichts- und Gesellschaftstheorie, wie Venedig den idealen, da ambigen Hintergrund für Thomas Manns Gestaltung der Künstlerproblematik abgab" (546–47).

[11] For an exhaustive analysis of the role of the narrator in *Der Tod in Venedig*, see Dorrit Cohn, "The Second Author of *Death in Venice*," in Clayton Koelb, trans. and ed. *Thomas Mann: "Death in Venice": A New Translation: Backgrounds and Contexts: Criticisms* (New York: Norton, 1994), 178–95.

¹² All English excerpts, and paraphrasing descriptions of *Death in Venice,* are taken from the translation by Clayton Koelb (New York: Norton & Company, 1994).

¹³ Reed, *Thomas Mann,* 143.

¹⁴ Matthias Hurst, *Erzählsituationen in Literatur und Film* (Tubingen: Niemeyer, 1996), 206. Hurst also numbers the ship officer who sells Aschenbach the ticket to Venice among these mysterious strangers.

¹⁵ Sigmund Freud, "Der Dichter und das Phantasieren" (1907), in Sigmund Freud, *Studienausgabe* 10 (Frankfurt am Main: Fischer, 1969), 177.

¹⁶ John Pizer, "From a *Death in Venice* to a *Death in Rome:* On Wolfgang Koeppen's Critical Ironization of Thomas Mann," *The Germanic Review* 68:3 (1993): 103. Pizer refers to the characters Johannes von Süde and his sister Emilie from Koeppen's novel *Die Mauer schwankt* (1935) who "share Aschenbach's rigidity, his principled asceticism and his latent passion" (104).

¹⁷ Richner, *Der Tod in Rom:* "Adolf [ist] in der Folge dieser Betrachtungen immer mehr vom alter ego der vermeintlichen Hauptgestalt des Romans, Siegfried, zur eigentlichen Hauptfigur des *Tod in Rom* geworden" (117).

¹⁸ Richner, *Der Tod in Rom,* describes "Adolf und sein[en] Vater als Partial-Ichs des Wolfgang Koeppen" (128).

¹⁹ Erlach, *Wolfgang Koeppen:* "Die entscheidende Abweichung vom literarischen Vorbild in der gesamten Thematik scheint mir aber darin zu liegen, daß Aschenbachs päderastische Verirrung als Zeichen für die abgründige Gefährdung des Künstlers eher als ein rein geistiges Problem dargestellt wird, während Siegfrieds Pädasterie auch von seinen soziopsychologischen Gründen her — der Erziehung in der Ordensburg — erhellt wird" (123–24).

²⁰ Koeppen, "Die Beschwörung der Liebe," first published in *Frankfurter Allgemeine Zeitung,* July 2, 1980. Cited in Wolfgang Koeppen, *Die elenden Scribenten. Aufsätze,* ed. Marcel Reich-Ranicki (Frankfurt am Main: Suhrkamp, 1981), 116.

²¹ Compare this advice with the terms of the devil in his pact with the composer Leverkühn in Thomas Mann's *Doktor Faustus:* "Liebe ist dir verboten, insofern sie wärmt. Dein Leben soll kalt sein, darum darfst du keinen Menschen lieben. . . . Eine Gesamterkältung deines Lebens und deines Verhältnisses liegt in der Natur der Dinge." Thomas Mann, *Gesammelte Werke,* vol. 6 (Frankfurt am Main: Fischer, 1974), 332.

²² Herwig, "Wolfgang Koeppens Absage": "Koeppens offene Darstellung der Homosexualität (unter bewußter Nichtbeachtung gesellschaftlicher Konventionen) [zeigt] das Elend der Pädasterie. Nicht mehr der nobilitierte Bürger und pflichtbewußte Familienvater verfällt einem schönen Knaben, sondern ein talentierter junger Mann, der sich als Spielstein einer zyklischen, auf Macht und Machtmißbrauch gegründeten Geschichte sieht und daraufhin jede auf Fortpflanzung gerichtete Beziehung ablehnt" (548).

²³ Siegfried also toys with the impulse of leaving Rome for Germany before receiving the prize that will firmly establish him as a composer. But on reflection he finds that the thought of Germany does not seriously tempt him (*TR* 173).

²⁴ Richner, *Der Tod in Rom:* "Auf den Tod deuten im Voraus das Intoxikationsmotiv und das Erschlaffungsmotiv hin: . . . Beide Motive sind Anspielungen auf den *Tod in Venedig*" (66).

²⁵ Pizer, "From a *Death in Venice* to a *Death in Rome*," 104.

²⁶ Herwig, "Wolfgang Koeppens Absage": "Durch das Attribut einer dunklen Sonnenbrille, die ihm 'ein geheimnisvolles, listiges, weithergereistes . . . Aussehen verlieh' [*TR*, 15], zu Aschenbachs erstem Todesboten in Beziehung gesetzt, zeigt sich an ihm mustergültig die 'Umwertung aller Motive'" (545).

²⁷ Richner, *Der Tod in Rom:* "Das Bild der Pfaffraths, diese bitter-böse Karikatur des Deutschtums, der Bürgerlichkeit und des Sippendenkens entlarvt die bürgerliche deutsche Familie als Keimzelle eines auch durch die Erfahrungen des tausendjährigen Reichs ungebrochenen, gefährlichen Nationalismus" (88).

²⁸ Dieter Kafitz, "Ästhetischer Radikalismus. Zur Kunstauffassung Wolfgang Koeppens," in Eckart Oehlenschläger, ed., *Wolfgang Koeppen. Materialien* (Frankfurt am Main: Suhrkamp, 1987), 84.

²⁹ See, for example, Gunnar Müller-Waldeck and Michael Gratz, *Wolfgang Koeppen — Mein Ziel war die Ziellosigkeit* (Hamburg: Europäische Verlagsanstalt, 1998), 9.

³⁰ Cited in Richner, *Der Tod in Rom*, 14.

³¹ Wolfgang Koeppen, "Die Beschwörung der schweren Stunde," first published in *Frankfurter Allgemeine Zeitung*, May 5, 1975. Cited in: Koeppen, *Die elenden Scribenten*, 107.

³² See, for example, T. J. Reed, "Einzelhinweise," 129, 136, 141, 144.

³³ Reich-Ranicki, *Literarisches Leben in Deutschland:* "Ein Teil der Presse ignorierte das Buch, der Rest sah in ihm lediglich einen gegen Faschismus, Neofaschismus und die Wirtschaftswunderwelt gerichteten politischen Zeitroman, dessen Aggressivität von manchen Rezensenten als höchst überflüssig empfunden wurde" (31).

³⁴ Kafitz, "Ästhetischer Radikalismus": "Sein Werk beschreibt nicht Wirklichkeit, sondern *ist* Wirklichkeit in all ihrer Zufälligkeit und all ihrem Chaos. Das bedeutet, daß die Sprache nicht als Ordnungsinstrument fungiert, sondern daß sich in ihr das Geräusch der Welt ausdrückt" (78).

³⁵ Richner, *Der Tod in Rom:* "Wir sehen den psychologisch analysierbaren Menschen und den dem Mythos entstammenden Totengott, den kleinen Gottlieb neben dem großen Hades, Psychoanalyse neben Mythos" (69).

Notes to Chapter 4

¹ Georg Büchner, *Lenz*, vol. 1 in Georg Büchner, *Sämtliche Werke und Briefe* (Hamburg: Christian Wegner, 1967), 77–101. Subsequent references to Büchner's *Lenz* are cited in the text using the abbreviation *BW*, and page number.

² Roy Pascal, *The Dual Voice* (Manchester: Manchester UP, 1977). "Through free indirect speech he [the narrator] repeatedly enriches his own account with Lenz's own perspective, and the mingling of the two perspectives is often so intimate that

we can speak of a dual voice. This is the most remarkable innovation of this *Novelle*. It does not affect actual speech, nor does is reproduce what would normally be considered to be thoughts" (62). The German term for Büchner's technique described here is "freie indirekte Rede."

[3] Dennis Tate, *The East German Novel* (Bath: Bath UP, 1984), 182–83. Tate lists Johannes Bobrowski, *Boehlendorf* (1965), Gerhard Wolf, *Der arme Hölderlin* (1972), Volker Braun, *Unvollendete Geschichte* (1977), Christa Wolf, *Kein Ort nirgends* (1979), and Erik Neutsch's *Forster in Paris* (1981).

[4] Timm Reiner Menke, *Lenz-Erzählungen in der deutschen Literatur* (Hildesheim: Olms, 1984). See also Reinhold Grimm, *Love Lust and Rebellion* (Madison, WI: The U of Wisconsin P, 1985), 206, note 35. Grimm lists a different selection of narratives influenced by Büchner's *Lenz:* Gerhart Hauptmann, *Bahnwärter Thiel* (1887), Alfred Döblin, *Die Ermordung der Butterblume* (1910), Georg Heym, *Der Irre* (1913).

[5] Christa Wolf, "Lesen und Schreiben," in Christa Wolf, *Lesen und Schreiben. Aufsätze und Prosastücke* (Darmstadt: Luchterhand, 1972), 204.

[6] Peter Schneider, *Lenz. Eine Erzählung* (Berlin: Rotbuch, 1973). Subsequent references to Schneider's *Lenz* are cited in the text using the abbreviation *SL* and page number.

[7] Menke, *Lenz-Erzählungen:* "Die Annahme, eine soziale Revolution aus den Reihen der Intelligenz in Bewegung setzen zu können, ist eine geschichtliche Illusion, der im 20. Jahrhundert wiederholt revolutionäre Bewegungen zum Opfer gefallen sind" (29–30).

[8] Karl Emil Franzos, 1878. Cited in *Metzlers Autoren Lexikon* (Stuttgart: Metzlersche Verlagsbuchhandlung, 1986), 91.

[9] John Reddick, *Georg Büchner: The Shattered Whole* (Oxford: Clarendon Press, 1994), 8.

[10] How closely the novella is modeled on the Oberlin diary can be seen in the section of Büchner's *Werke* in which the two texts are laid side by side, *BW*, 435–83.

[11] Whereas Büchner's original script does not mention the month, posthumously edited versions usually insert *Januar* or *Jänner,* relying on Oberlin's original diaries. (See, for example, *BW*, 79 and 437, or the Reclam edition.)

[12] See also Volker Braun, *Unvollendete Geschichte* (1977), who makes extensive use of this device.

[13] Colin Riordan, "Peter Schneider: A Biographical Sketch," in Colin Riordan, ed., *Peter Schneider* (Cardiff: U of Wales P, 1995), 17. See also Menke, *Lenz-Erzählungen:* "*Lenz* erschien 1973 und hat sich mit einer Auflage von 96.000 Exemplaren bis 1978 als ein Bestseller herausgestellt" (106).

[14] In Büchner's text this passage, which comes from the opening paragraph, is constituted from two sentences rather than one.

[15] Rhys W. Williams, "'Ein gewisses Maß subjektiver Verzweiflung . . .': Peter Schneider's *Lenz*," in Colin Riordan, ed., *Peter Schneider,* 52.

¹⁶ Paul Celan, "Der Meridian. Rede anläßlich der Verleihung des Georg Büchner Preises 1960," in *Ausgewählte Gedichte. Zwei Reden,* 3rd ed. (Frankfurt am Main: Suhrkamp, 1967), 141.

¹⁷ This also includes the historian/narrator in Banville's *The Newton Letter* (see chapter 6).

¹⁸ Williams, "'Ein gewisses Maß subjektiver Verzweiflung . . .,'" 52.

¹⁹ See Williams, "'Ein gewisses Maß subjektiver Verzweiflung . . .,'" 56.

²⁰ Williams, "'Ein gewisses Maß subjektiver Verzweiflung . . .,'" 55.

²¹ Max Weber, *The Protestant Ethic and the Spirit of Capitalism,* trans. Talcott Parsons (London: George Allen & Unwin Ltd., 1930), 157.

²² See Williams, "'Ein gewisses Maß subjektiver Verzweiflung . . .,'" 57. Other quotations from that same essay by Mao can be found in *SL,* 27–29.

²³ Peter Laemmle, "Büchners Schatten," *Aspekte* 5 (1974): 476.

²⁴ Malcolm Pender, "Historical Awareness and Peter Schneider's *Lenz,*" *German Life and Letters* 37:2 (1984): 156.

²⁵ Williams, "'Ein gewisses Maß subjektiver Verzweiflung . . .,'" 55.

²⁶ Leslie Morris, "Aesthetic, Political or Anti-Idyll? 'Das Italienerlebnis' in Works by Christine Wolter, Birgit Pausch and Peter Schneider," *Neue Germanistik* 4:2 (1986): 20.

²⁷ Gordon J. A. Burgess, "Büchner, Schneider and Lenz: Two Authors in Search of a Character," in Ken Mills and Brian Keith-Smith, eds., *Georg Büchner: Tradition and Innovation: Fourteen Essays* (Bristol: U of Bristol P, 1990), 222–23.

²⁸ T. S. Eliot, "Tradition and the Individual Talent" (1919), in Frank Kermode, ed., *Selected Prose of T. S. Eliot* (London: Faber & Faber, 1975), 38.

Notes to Chapter 5

¹ Goethe, *Die Leiden des jungen Werther* (1774), *HA,* 6:7–124. The revised edition, in the form we know today, appeared in 1787. Subsequent references to *Die Leiden des jungen Werther* are cited in the text using the abbreviation *GW* and page number.

² See, for example, Peter Wapnewski, "Zweihundert Jahre Werthers Leiden oder: Dem war nicht zu helfen" (1975), in Peter J. Brenner, ed., *Plenzdorfs "Neue Leiden des jungen W."* (Frankfurt am Main: Suhrkamp, 1982), 325.

³ See, for example, Kurth Rothmann, ed., *Erläuterungen und Dokumente, Johann Wolfgang Goethe, Die Leiden des jungen Werther* (Stuttgart: Reclam, 1971), 139–59. See also Georg Jäger, *Die Leiden des alten und neuen Werther, Kommentare, Abbildungen, Materialien* (Munich: Karl Hanser, 1984), 30–45.

⁴ Ulrich Plenzdorf, *Die neuen Leiden des jungen W.* (Frankfurt am Main: Suhrkamp, 1976; first published in *Sinn und Form,* 1973). Subsequent references to *Die neuen Leiden des jungen W.* are cited in the text using the abbreviation *PL* and page number.

⁵ Goethe, *Dichtung und Wahrheit, 13. Buch, HA,* 9:588.

⁶ See, for example, Franz Peter Waiblinger, "Zitierte Kritik. Zu den *Werther*-Zitaten in Ulrich Plenzdorfs *Die neuen Leiden des jungen W.*," *Poetica* 8 (1976): 71–88, or N. L. Thomas, "Werther in a New Guise: Ulrich Plenzdorf's *Die neuen Leiden des jungen W.*," *Modern Languages: Journal of the Modern Language Association* 57 (1976): 178–82.

⁷ Goethe, *Dichtung und Wahrheit, 13. Buch, HA,* 9:577–78, Goethe's emphasis.

⁸ See, for example, *GW,* 14, 22, 23, 33, 66, etc.

⁹ H. C. Robinson, "Bericht über ein Gespräch mit Goethe," in "Quellen und Daten zur Geschichte des *Werther*-Romans," *HA,* 6:536.

¹⁰ A. T. Seaman, "Celtic Myth as Perceived in Eighteenth- and Nineteenth-Century Literature in English," in C. J. Byrne, M. Harry and P. Ó Siadhail, eds., *Celtic Languages and Celtic People* (Halifax, NS: Saint Mary's University, 1992), 443.

¹¹ See Erich Trunz, "Anmerkungen," *HA,* 6: "Das aufgeschlagene Buch ist Hinweis, daß es Situationen gibt, die zum Tode führen müssen, nicht als Ausfluß sentimentaler Schwärmerei, sondern als Rettung sittlicher Freiheit. Aus Werthers Feder wäre ein solcher Hinweis denen, die seinen Tod sehen, belanglos, aus Lessings Feder müssen sie ihn anerkennen.... Werther weist darauf hin, daß man auch seinen Tod in solchem Lichte sehen solle.... Das erklärende Wort an die übrige Welt — ein sehr zurückhaltendes, taktvolles Wort, das ganz offen läßt, wieviel hier Zufall, wieviel Absicht sei — ist *Emilia Galotti*" (586).

¹² Erich Honecker, "Zu aktuellen Fragen bei der Verwirklichung der Beschlüsse unseres VIII. Parteitages. Aus dem Schlußwort des Ersten Sekretärs des ZK der SED, Genossen Erich Honecker," *Neues Deutschland,* December 18, 1971. Cited in Jürgen Thomaneck, *Ulrich Plenzdorf: Die neuen Leiden des jungen W.* (Glasgow: University of Glasgow, French and German Publications, 1988), 4.

¹³ Erich Honecker, "Rede vor dem 9. Plenum des ZK der SED im Mai 1973," in *Sonntag 23:* "Hier dem Neuen nachzuspüren, es aufzudecken und mitzugestalten, gelingt wohl nicht immer beim ersten Versuch und am wenigsten dadurch, daß versucht wird, *eigene Leiden* der Gesellschaft aufzuoktroyieren. Die in verschiedenen Theaterstücken und Filmen dargestellte Vereinsamung und Isolierung des Menschen von der Gesellschaft, ihre Anonymität in bezug auf die gesellschaftlichen Verhältnisse machen schon jetzt deutlich, daß die Grundhaltung solcher Werke dem Anspruch des Sozialismus an Kunst und Literatur entgegensteht" (cited in Thomaneck, *Ulrich Plenzdorf,* 4). Others used even stronger language in their criticism, dismissing the work out of hand. F. K. Kaul, a leading East German lawyer, writes in a letter to Wilhelm Girnus, editor of the literary journal *Sinn und Form,* in which *Die neuen Leiden des jungen W.* was first published: "Um mein Urteil knapp zu fassen: mich ekelt geradezu — um keinen anderen Ausdruck zu benutzen — die von einem unserer professionellen Theaterkritiker sogar noch 'mehr als ein hübscher Einfall' laudierte Inbezugsetzung eines verwahrlosten — der Fachmann würde sagen verhaltensgestörten — Jugendlichen mit der Goetheschen Romanfigur an; von dem Fäkalien-Vokabular, in dem des langen und breiten über die innige Funktionsverbindung von Niere und Darm der Plenzdorfschen Figur abgehandelt wird, ganz zu schweigen." F. K. Kaul, "Diskus-

sion um Plenzdorf, *Die neuen Leiden des jungen W.*" (1972), in Brenner, ed., *Plenzdorfs "Neue Leiden des jungen W.,"* 151.

[14] Robert Weimann, "Goethe in der Figurenperspektive," *Sinn und Form* 25 (1973): 222.

[15] Marcel Reich-Ranicki, "Der Fänger im DDR-Roggen. Ulrich Plenzdorfs jedenfalls wichtiger *Werther*-Roman" (1973), in Brenner, ed., *Plenzdorfs "Neue Leiden des jungen W.,"* 268.

[16] Ilse H. Reis, *Ulrich Plenzdorf's Gegen-Entwurf zu Goethes "Werther"* (Bern and Munich: Francke, 1977). "Es zeigen sich — außer einem Dreiecksverhältnis — wenig Gemeinsamkeiten. Da im Buch selbst niemand die Werther-Zitate erkennt, wäre zu überlegen, welcher Personenkreis Plenzdorf auf die Spur gekommen wäre, wenn er einen anderen Titel gewählt haben würde, und wenn er den Namen Werther nicht erwähnt hätte" (8).

[17] In the GDR, the workforce was organized into groups of five to twelve members under the leadership of the *Brigadeführer*. The *Brigade* worked together and competed with other brigades on the level of productivity. Ideally, the *Brigade* was also a social group who might spend time together after work, and members were encouraged to support each other privately.

[18] See also Ute Brandes, *Zitat und Montage in der neueren DDR-Prosa* (Frankfurt am Main: Lang, 1984), 101–2.

[19] *PL,* 32, 59, 72, 108, 109, 116, 123, 134, 139, etc.

[20] *PL,* 23, 24, 30, 31, 33, etc.

[21] Waiblinger, "Zitierte Kritik": "Hier steckt der politische Stachel des Werks: Vor dem durch die Aneignung des 'Erbes' mündig gewordenen Individuum versagt die gesellschaftliche Wirklichkeit; das Subjekt, das zu sich selbst gefunden hat, findet nicht zurück in die Gesellschaft" (85).

[22] See Thomaneck, *Ulrich Plenzdorf,* 46.

[23] Goethe's additional text is given in emphasis; "Wilhelm" is added by Edgar.

[24] Friedrich Engels, "Anteil der Arbeit an der Menschwerdung des Affen," in Karl Marx and Friedrich Engels, *Ausgewählte Schriften in zwei Bänden* 2 (Berlin: Dietz, 1952), 71.

[25] See also Erich Trunz, "Anmerkungen," *HA* 6. "Werther leidet ganz allgemein an der *Einschränkung* des Menschen, der das Unendliche ergreifen will und immer nur an seine Grenzen stößt" (564).

[26] See, for example, Otmar Leppla and Hartmut Fischer, *Stundenblätter. Plenzdorf. Die neuen Leiden des jungen W.* (Stuttgart: Klett, 1985) on the reception of *Die neuen Leiden des jungen W.* by young people in the GDR and GFR, 54–65.

[27] The editors Brenner, Jäger, Leppla, and Fischer all distinguish between the reception of Plenzdorf's *Die neuen Leiden des jungen W.* in East and West Germany.

[28] Ulrich Plenzdorf, "Diskussion" (1973), in Brenner, ed., *Plenzdorfs "Neue Leiden des jungen W.,"* 178.

[29] J. D. Salinger, *The Catcher in the Rye* (London: Penguin, 1958; first published in 1951), 194.

³⁰ See Thomaneck's chapter "Goethe, Salinger, and Defoe," in his *Ulrich Plenzdorf,* 44–51.

³¹ Daniel Defoe, *Robinson Crusoe* (1719). Cited in Thomaneck, *Ulrich Plenzdorf,* 50.

³² Volker Braun, *Unvollendete Geschichte* (Frankfurt am Main: Suhrkamp, 1989, first published in *Sinn und Form,* 1977), 43–44, Braun's emphasis.

³³ Goethe, *Dichtung und Wahrheit, HA,* 9:583.

³⁴ See Wapnewski, "Zweihundert Jahre Werthers Leiden oder": "Die Aufklärung als europäische Geistesbewegung hat die Voraussetzung für die Begründung des bürgerlichen Zeitalters geschaffen, also auch die ideologischen Voraussetzungen für die bürgerlichen Revolutionen des 18. und 19. Jahrhunderts. Diese mit großen Verzögerungen ausbrechenden Revolutionen sind vorbereitet durch eine lange Phase der Ungeduld, der *Frustration.* Werther ist ein symptomatisches Produkt dieser vorrevolutionären Unruhe, die das Gefühl für das Selbstgefühl des Individuums heftig gesteigert, dessen subjektives Selbstverständnis leidenschaftlich geschärft hat. Solch herrischem Ichgefühl aber entsprach der Kontext der Zeitgeschichte nicht. Es schlug mithin nach innen, sensibilisierte sich zu privaten Exzessen, wurde auch wohl tödlich" (339).

³⁵ See Wapnewski, "Zweihundert Jahre Werthers Leiden oder": "Die Jahre um 1970 werden schneller geschichtlich gesehen, als das gemeinhin mit Jahreszahlen geschieht. Ihr reformerischer Elan und die vielleicht allzu treuherzige Gläubigkeit an die Machbarkeit des sozial Wünschenswerten hat ihnen die Kennmarke *Neue Aufklärung* eingetragen. Der Elan ist dahin, und vieles ist steckengeblieben, als illusionär oder utopisch abgetan, vielleicht entlarvt — vieles, das doch beitragen sollte den *neuen Menschen* zu wecken. Ungeduld erst, dann Enttäuschung ist mächtig in vielen, vor allem in jenen, deren Wesen zu Ungeduld und Enttäuschbarkeit neigt: der jungen Generation" (340). Wapnewski's emphasis.

³⁶ Wilhelm Girnus, "Lachen über Wibeau . . . aber wie?" (1973), in Brenner, ed., *Plenzdorfs "Neue Leiden des jungen W.,"* 190. Girnus himself refers to a line from Goethe's *Faust:* "Was du ererbt von deinen Vätern hast, / erwirb es, um es zu besitzen." *Faust I,* 683–84.

Notes to Chapter 6

¹ John Banville, *The Newton Letter* (London: Warburg & Secker, 1982). Subsequent references to *The Newton Letter* are taken from the more readily available paperback edition (London: Minerva, 1992) and cited in the text using the abbreviation *NL* and page number.

² Goethe, *Die Wahlverwandtschaften* (1809), *HA,* 6. Subsequent references to *Die Wahlverwandtschaften* are cited in the text using the abbreviation *WV* and page number. See also Judith Ryan, "Views From the Summerhouse: Goethe's *Wahlverwandtschaften* and its Literary Successors," in W. J. Lillyman, ed., *Goethe's Narrative Fiction: The Irvine Symposium* (Berlin: Gruyter, 1983), 145–60. In her article, Ryan identifies a whole series of works in which motifs and the character constellation of Goethe's *Die Wahlverwandtschaften* are taken up to a greater or

lesser extent, but none of these uses the names and the shifting character constellation as strikingly as *The Newton Letter*.

[3] Hugo von Hofmannsthal, *Ein Brief*, in *Sämtliche Werke*, vol. 31: *Erfundene Gespräche und Briefe* (Frankfurt am Main: Fischer, 1991), 45–55. Also known as *Chandos-Brief* or *Chandos Letter*. Subsequent references to *Ein Brief* are cited in the text using the abbreviation *EB* and page number.

[4] A "tetralogy" is traditionally a series of four Greek dramas, including a satirical interlude after the second drama. *The Newton Letter* has "An Interlude" for subtitle.

[5] Kurt Gödel (1906–1978), *Über formal unentscheidbare Sätze der Principia Mathematica und verwandter Systeme*, 1931. "Gödel's results were a landmark in 20th-century mathematics, showing that mathematics is not a finished object, as had been believed. It also implies that a computer can never be programmed to answer all mathematical questions" (http://www-groups.dcs.st-and.ac.uk/~history/Mathematicians/Godel.htm).

[6] Niels Bohr, cited in Henri Bortoft, *Goethe's Scientific Consciousness* (Tunbridge Wells: Institute for Cultural Research, 1986), 27, my emphasis.

[7] See Rüdiger Imhof, "My Readers, That Small Band Deserve a Rest: An Interview with John Banville," *Irish University Review* 11 (1981): 5.

[8] John Banville, "Physics and Fiction: Order From Chaos," *The New York Times*, April 21, 1985, Book Review section.

[9] Rüdiger Imhof, *John Banville: A Critical Introduction* (Dublin: Wolfhound, 1989). "The novel consists in the reshaping of traditional material, from Hofmannsthal, from Newton, from Henry James, Andrew Marvell, Sartre, Yeats, Ford Maddox Ford and . . . Goethe" (145).

[10] Francis C. Molloy, "The Search for Truth: The Fiction of John Banville," *Irish University Review* 11 (1981): 41.

[11] Goethe, "Selbstanzeige," *HA*, 6:621. The emphases are mine, except for "*eine* Natur."

[12] Goethe to Cotta, October 1, 1809, *HA*, 6:622.

[13] The sycamore is also called the North American plane tree.

[14] Etymologically *Otto* comes from *ot* (OHG) meaning *possession*, a fitting attribute for the process of "finding one's own." Yet appearances are deceptive: the name *Charlotte* is not related to *Otto*. See, for example, Michael Niedermeier, *Das Ende der Idylle. Symbolik, Zeitbezug, 'Gartenrevolution' in Goethes Roman "Die Wahlverwandtschaften"* (Berlin: Peter Lang, 1992), 35–36.

[15] See Molloy, "The Search for Truth," 42.

[16] Goethe, *Vorwort zur Farbenlehre, HA*, 13:317.

[17] Werner Heisenberg, "Die Goethesche und die Newtonsche Farbenlehre im Lichte der modernen Physik" (1941), in Hans Mayer, *Goethe im XX. Jahrhundert* (Hamburg: Christian Wegner, 1967), 418–32. "Trennt man . . . die Wirklichkeit in verschiedene Gebiete, so löst sich der Widerspruch zwischen der Goetheschen und der Newtonschen Farbenlehre von selbst. Die beiden Theorien stehen an verschiedenen Stellen in jenem großen Gebäude der Wissenschaft. . . . Freilich wäre

die Hoffnung, daß wir von dieser Erkenntnis aus schon bald zu einer lebendigeren und einheitlicheren Stellung zur Natur zurückkehren könnten, noch verfrüht" (431–32).

[18] Cited in Molloy, "The Search for Truth," 45.

[19] See, for example, Harriet Murphy, *The Rhetoric of the Spoken Word in "Die Wahlverwandtschaften"* (Frankfurt am Main: Peter Lang, 1990). "The narrator's presence here [in the first two chapters] is not strategically important to the evaluation of the material presented. The narrator does not exercise any of his own analytical skills or express any personal preferences in the form of evaluative interpretation or commentary. In doing so, the narrator shows that there is no personal relationship between himself and the material presented" (18).

[20] Niedermeier, *Das Ende der Idylle:* "Die metaphorische Sprache . . . legt nahe, daß die Romanhandlung selbst das versprochene Experiment ersetzt und die Romanfiguren Versuchsobjekte sind, an denen das soziale Urphänomen der Wahlverwandtschaften in Raum und Zeit darstellbar wird" (111).

[21] Heinz Schlaffer, "Nachwort," in Goethe, *"Die Wahlverwandtschaften,"* 2nd ed. (Munich: Goldmann, 1988), 245–68. "Das 'chemische Kabinett,' so müssen wir daraus schließen, braucht gar nicht mehr eigens anzukommen, weil es im Roman, im Schicksal seiner Figuren Wirklichkeit wird. 'Die Wahlverwandtschaften,' der Roman selbst, ist eben das 'chemische Kabinett,' welches das Gesetz der Wahlverwandtschaften demonstriert. Was zunächst als blindes Motiv gelten mußte, hat sich als Grundriß von Goethes Konstruktion enthüllt" (250).

[22] Goethe, "Der Versuch als Vermittler zwischen Subjekt und Objekt" (1792), *HA*, 13:10–20. "Die Vermannigfaltigung eines jeden einzelnen Versuches ist also die eigentliche Pflicht eines Naturforschers" (18).

[23] The curious use of "das" referring to the two *human* protagonists occurs again later, describing the attraction between Eduard and Ottilie: "hätte man eins von beiden . . . festgehalten, das andere hätte sich nach und nach von selbst . . . zu ihm hinbewegt" (*WV*, 478).

[24] The paperback edition by Picador, 1999, of *The Newton Letter* has omitted the reference to *The Chandos Letter*.

[25] Hermann Broch, "Hugo von Hofmannsthals Prosaschriften" (1951), in Gotthart Wunberg, ed., *Hofmannsthal im Urteil seiner Kritiker* (Frankfurt am Main: Athenäum, 1972), 435–54. "Hier wird ein junger Mensch hingestellt, für den Ich und Non-Ich jeglichen Kontakt verloren haben, da ihm die Symbolketten schon vor der Schmiedung des ersten Gliedes abgerissen sind: nichts bleibt ihm mehr als die schiere Spaltung an sich, so daß alle Lebenswerte verlöschen; er befindet sich im Gegenzustand zur Ekstase, im Zustand der Panik, im tiefsten Absturz des Menschen" (441).

[26] This is equally the case in Volker Braun's *Unvollendete Geschichte,* a text closely modeled on Büchner's *Lenz*. See chapter 5.

[27] See, for example, Richard Westfall, *Never at Rest: A Biography of Isaac Newton* (Cambridge: Cambridge UP, 1980), 277.

[28] See, for example, H. W. Turnbull, ed., *The Correspondence of Isaak Newton, 1688–1694,* vol. 3 (Cambridge: Cambridge UP, 1961), letters 421, 425 and 426.

[29] There is a further parallel: in the same way that Newton renounced science after his breakdown in 1693, Hofmannsthal ceased to write poetry after 1902, the year of publication of *Ein Brief*. See, for example, Broch, "Hugo von Hofmannsthals Prosaschriften," 435.

[30] Goethe, *Materialien zur Geschichte der Farbenlehre*, HA, 14:81.

[31] Arthur Koestler, *The Sleepwalkers: A History of Man's Changing Vision of the Universe* (Harmondsworth: Penguin, 1968), 505.

[32] Michael Holquist, *Dialogism: Bakhtin and his World* (London: Routledge, 1990). "In Newton's universe, the sum of instants occurring simultaneously over all of space add up to a time that is absolute in the sense that it is a flux of simultaneous instants embracing the whole of the universe. It was, in other words, a dream of unity in *physics*, that could serve as the proper setting for a dream of unity in Newton's *theology*" (19–20).

[33] Mikhail Bakhtin, cited in Tzvetan Todorov, *Mikhail Bakhtin: The Dialogical Principle* (Manchester: Manchester UP, 1984), 14.

Notes to Conclusion

[1] Marcel Reich-Ranicki, "Der Fänger im DDR-Roggen. Ulrich Plenzdorfs jedenfalls wichtiger *Werther*-Roman" (1973), in Peter J. Brenner, ed., *Plenzdorfs "Neue Leiden des jungen W."* (Frankfurt am Main: Suhrkamp, 1982), 264.

[2] Götz Grossklaus, "West-östliches Unbehagen. Literarische Gesellschaftskritik in Ulrich Plenzdorfs *Die neuen Leiden des jungen W.* und Peter Schneiders *Lenz*," *Basis, Jahrbuch für deutsche Gegenwartsliteratur*, 5 (1975): 84–85.

[3] Walter Benjamin, "Goethes Wahlverwandtschaften," in *Gesammelte Schriften* (Frankfurt am Main: Suhrkamp, 1991), 126. See chapter 3.

[4] For example, Sigrid Damm, *Ich bin nicht Ottilie* and Christa Schmidt, *Die Wahlverwandten*, both published in 1992. Significantly, two works whose title refers to Fontane's *Effi Briest*, a novel concerned with form in the widest sense of the term, have both been published since 1996: Rolf Hochhuth, *Effis Nacht* (1996), and Dorothea Keuler, *Die wahre Geschichte der Effi B.* (1998).

Index

Aktualisierung, 8
allusion, 1, 4, 5, 13, 16, 34, 35, 44, 59, 71, 92, 95, 114, 118, 121, 177, 179
anti-work, 11, 36, 91, 124, 174
Apollo/Apollonian, 74, 87, 92, 93
Aristotle, 46, 47
Arthurian tradition, 2

Baader-Meinhof, 64
Bacon, Francis, 167, 169
Bakhtin, Mikhail, 173
Banville, John, 106, 151–74, 179, 180
Banville, John, works by: *Dr Copernicus,* 152; *Kepler,* 152; *Mefisto,* 152; *The Newton Letter,* 12, 15, 151–74, 178, 181, 183, 184, 207n.17
Baroque theater, 48
Bearbeitung, 4
Benjamin, Walter, 71, 72, 94, 181; truth content/*Wahrheitsgehalt,* 71–73, 94–95, 181; material content/*Sachgehalt,* 71–73, 94–95, 181
Berg, Jan, 51, 201nn.17, 18
Bible, 24, 50, 58, 171; Mary Magdalene, 54, 55, 58, 59, 68; prodigal son, 59; wedding at Cana, 58
Biermann, Wolf, 1
Bildungsroman, 120, 121, 122
blind obedience, 21, 22, 23, 24, 31, 36, 37, 38
Bobrowski, Johannes, works by: *Boehlendorf,* 206n.3
Bohr, Niels, 152

bourgeois tragedy/*bürgerliches Trauerspiel,* 46, 53, 202n.25
Braun, Volker, works by: *Iphigenie in Freiheit,* 2; *Unvollendete Geschichte,* 8, 124, 148, 196n.16, 206n.3, 212n.26
Brecht, Bertolt, 11, 13, 16–44, 45, 46, 47, 50, 51, 56, 65, 68, 121, 176, 177, 179, 184, 197n.8, 198n.21, 199n.27, 199n.33; Epic theater/Brecht's (revolutionary) theater, 25, 32, 47; *Verfremdung*/alienation device, 35, 47, 61
Brecht, Bertolt, works by: *Antigone,* 24; *Coriolan,* 24; *Daniel Drew,* 28; *Don Juan,* 25; *Die Dreigroschenoper,* 24; *Die Gesichte der Simone Marchard,* 19; *Die heilige Johanna der Schlachthöfe,* 11, 13, 16–44, 51, 65, 175, 176, 179, 183, 197n.8, 198n.19, 199n.33; *Der Hofmeister,* 24; *Joe Fleischhacker,* 28; *Das Leben Eduards II von England,* 24; *Die Mutter,* 24; *Mutter Courage und ihre Kinder,* 24; *Der Prozess der Jeanne d'Arc zu Rouen, 1431,* 19
Brigade, 130, 140, 142, 145, 209n.17
Broch, Hermann, 169, 212n.25
Büchner, Georg, 7, 8, 11, 96–122, 169, 179, 182; free indirect speech/*freie indirekte Rede,* 205n.2

Büchner, Georg, works by: *Der hessische Landbote*, 98, 99; *Lenz*, 14, 15, 96–122 (Kunstgespräch, 101, 104, 116), 146, 147, 167, 168, 177–78, 181–85, 205nn. 1, 2, 206n. 11, 212n. 27; *Woyzeck*, 42
Büchner Prize, 107
Bürger/Bürgertum, 39, 49, 57, 72, 81, 82, 86–88, 93, 139, 148, 201n. 16, 204nn. 22, 27, 210n. 34; *Bildungsbürger*, 25, 92; *Kleinbürger*, 14, 45, 66, 201n. 16
Burgess, Gordon J. A., 7, 9, 121, 195n. 6

canon, 7, 11, 25, 48, 69, 93
catharsis, 8, 47, 69
Celan, Paul, 107; Georg Büchner Prize, 107
censorship, 15, 143, 144, 178
character constellation, 1, 2, 3, 5, 6, 75, 125, 134, 151, 154, 176, 177
classical (Greek) tradition, 26, 36, 74, 92–93, 104, 127, 164, 177. *See also* Weimar Classicism
Cold War, 178
comedy/*Komödie*, 11, 14, 45, 48, 50, 51, 56, 57, 66, 67, 68, 69, 176
Copernicus, 172–73
corporate state/*Ständegesellschaft*, 46, 57
Cotta, Johann Friedrich, 156

Damm, Sigrid, works by: *Ich bin nicht Ottilie*, 196n. 23, 213n. 4
Defoe, Daniel, works by: *Robinson Crusoe*, 131, 146, 147
Dionysos/Dionysian, 74, 79, 83, 87, 92
Döblin, Alfred, works by: *Die Ermordung der Butterblume*, 206n. 4

Donnenberg, Joseph, 20, 197n. 8, 198n. 10
Dürrenmatt, Friedrich, works by: "Theaterprobleme," 10, 47, 48, 66, 67

Einstein, Albert, 152, 167, 173, 180
elective affinities, 156, 157, 163, 172, 178
Eliot, T. S., works by: *Tradition and the Individual Talent*, 121, 122
Engels, Friedrich, 99, 141
enlightenment/*Aufklärung*, 99, 149, 210n. 34; new enlightenment/*neue Aufklärung*, 149, 210n. 35
epistolary novel/*Briefroman*, 123, 125; (quasi-), 165
Erbaneignungsdiskussion, 134, 144, 209n. 21
Erlach, Dietrich, 83, 204n. 19
Erotikos, 92
Euripides, 2

Fascism/*Faschismus*, 82, 94, 205n. 33
Fleisser, Marieluise, 48, 51
fragmentation, 14, 71, 80, 82, 89, 90, 91, 95, 122
Franzos, Karl Emil, 98
Freiheit, 35, 40–44, 63, 88, 130, 141, 161, 208n. 11; freedom, 14, 18, 22, 37, 39, 40–44, 61, 140, 141, 145, 149, 161, 164, 183, 197n. 5, 199nn. 29, 30; liberty, 14, 20, 40, 149, 183
French Revolution, 150
Frenzel, Elisabeth, 16
Freud, Sigmund, 80, 112, 177
Frisch, Max, 1, 10, 185
Frye, Northrop, 7

Garland, Mary, 60, 61
Gay, John, *The Beggar's Opera*, 24
Girnus, Wilhelm, 150, 208n.13, 210n.36
Glenn, Jerry H., 202n.23
Gödel, Kurt, 152, 211n.5
Goethe, Johann Wolfgang von, 11, 18, 19, 26, 44, 123–50, 151–74, 175; and Newton, 162, 211n.17
Goethe, Johann Wolfgang von, works by: *Dichtung und Wahrheit*, 126, 128; *Erzählungen deutscher Ausgewanderter*, 196n.23; *Faust*, 3, 25, 28–30, 34, 37, 39, 44, 198n.17, 210n.36; *Iphigenie auf Tauris*, 2; *Italienische Reise*, 75, 120; *Die Leiden des jungen Werther*, 2, 8, 9, 12, 15, 123–50, 178, 180, 181, 182, 185, 208n.11, 210n.34; "Versuch als Vermittler" 162, 212n.22; *Vorwort zur Farbenlehre*, 161, 211n.17; *Die Wahlverwandtschaften*, 12, 13, 15, 71, 106, 151–74, 178, 180, 183, 184, 185, 212n.19, 21, 23
Gorki, Maxim, 24
Grass, Günter, 185
Grimm, Reinhold, 206n.4
Grimmelshausen, Johann Jakob Christoffel von, works by: *Die Landstörzerin Courasche*, 24, 198n.12
Grossklaus, Götz, 7, 181

Habermas, Jürgen, 96
Hacks, Peter, works by: *Jahrmarktsfest zu Plundersweilen*, 196n.23
Haffner, Herbert, 7
Handke, Peter, works by: *Die Angst des Tormanns beim Elfmeter*, 106

Hauptmann, Elisabeth, works by: *Happy End*, 28, 33, 198n.21
Hauptmann, Gerhard, works by: *Der Apostel*, 97; *Bahnwärter Thiel*, 206n.4; *Iphigenie in Aulis*, 2; *Iphigenie in Delphi*, 2
Hebbel, Friedrich, 8, 11, 14, 45–70, 176, 177; necessity, 52, 62, 69
Hebbel, Friedrich, works by: *Maria Magdalena*, 11, 37, 45–70, 73, 176, 200n.1, 202n.25
Hegel, Georg Friedrich, 9, 56
Hein, Christoph, works by: *Die Ritter der Tafelrunde*, 2
Heisenberg, Werner, 162, 211n.17
Herwig, Oliver, 74, 76, 85, 87, 203nn.7, 10, 204n.22, 205n.26
Heym, Georg, works by: *Der Irre*, 206n.4
Hildesheimer, Wolfgang, works by: *Mary Stuart*, 10, 196n.23
Hochhuth, Rolf, works by: *Effis Nacht*, 196n.23, 213n.4
Hoffmann, Michael, 71
Hofmannsthal, Hugo von, 106, 111, 151, 167–74, 180, 213n.29
Hofmannsthal, Hugo von, works by: *Ein Brief/Chandos Letter*, 12, 13, 106, 109, 111, 120, 122, 151, 167–74, 179, 181, 182, 212n.25; *Erlebnis des Marschalls von Bassompierre*, 8, 196n.23
Hölderlin, Friedrich, works by: "Hyperions Schicksalslied," 27
Hollis, Andy, 13
Holquist, Michael, 213n.32
Homer, 92, 127, 131
Honecker, Erich, 128, 208n.13
Horváth, Ödön von, 48, 51

humanism/humanist tradition, 2, 19, 25, 31, 33
Hurst, Matthias, 80, 204n. 14
Hutchinson, Peter, 13, 15

Imhof, Rüdiger, 153, 211n. 9
integration, 6, 14, 96, 129, 127, 128, 172, 177

Joan of Arc, 3, 11, 16–20, 23, 26, 44, 45, 176
Jauss, Hans Robert, 4, 7, 8, 10, 195n. 5, 196n. 15
Jentzsch, Kerstin, works by: *Iphigenie in Pankow,* 2
Jerusalem, Karl Wilhelm, 125, 128

Kafitz, Dieter, 91, 205n. 34
Kafka, Franz, 185
Kant, Immanuel, categorical imperative, 26, 31, 38; duty and inclination/*Pflicht und Neigung,* 18, 21, 22, 197n. 5; good will/*guter Wille,* 26, 28, 31, 33, 38, 199n. 32
Kaul, F. K., 208n. 13
Keitel, Eveline, 7, 196n. 12
Keller, Gottfried, works by: *Romeo und Julia auf dem Dorfe,* 1–2, 3, 175
Kestner, Christian, 128
Keuler, Dorothea, works by: *Die wahre Geschichte der Effi B.,* 9, 196n. 23, 213n. 4
Knapp, Mona, 195n. 2
Knopf, Jan, 36, 199n. 27
Koeppen, Wolfgang, 12, 71–95, 122, 177, 178, 185, 203n. 7, 203n. 10, 204n. 18, 205n. 34
Koeppen, Wolfgang, works by: *Die Mauer schwankt,* 204n. 16; *Der Tod in Rom,* 11, 14, 71–95, 98, 114, 177, 180, 183, 184, 203nn. 7, 9, 204nn. 17, 18, 205nn. 24, 27, 33, 35

Koestler, Arthur, works by: *The Sleepwalkers,* 173
Kraus, Karl, 8
Kroetz, Franz Xaver, 45–70, 95, 121, 169, 176, 177, 179, 180
Kroetz, Franz Xaver, works by: *Maria Magdalena,* 8, 11, 14, 45–70, 73, 151, 176, 179, 180, 184, 201nn. 16, 17, 18
Kurscheidt, Georg, 49, 57, 201n. 16, 202n. 25

Laemmle, Peter, 120
Lenz, J. M. R., 24, 97, 98, 100, 111, 121, 179
Lenz, J. M. R., works by: *Der Hofmeister,* 24, 98; *Die Soldaten,* 98
Lessing, Gotthold Ephraim, 40, 46, 49
Lessing, Gotthold Ephraim, works by: *Emilia Galotti,* 11, 37, 46, 128, 196n. 23, 208n. 11; *Miß Sara Sampson,* 46
Locke, John, 155, 167, 169, 171
Lustspiel, 48

Macpherson, James, works by: *The Poems of Ossian,* 127, 131, 133
Mann, Heinrich, Heinrich Mann Prize, 124
Mann, Heinrich, works by: *Professor Unrat,* 25
Mann, Thomas, 11, 12, 71–95, 177, 203n. 10; aestheticism/aesthetics, 12, 14, 72, 74, 81, 84, 92, 95
Mann, Thomas, works by: *Doktor Faustus,* 3, 204n. 23; *Der Tod in Venedig,* 11, 14, 71–95, 114, 118, 120, 177, 178, 179, 183, 184, 185, 203n. 8, 204n. 14, 205n. 24
Mao Tse Tung, 99, 116; "On the Relation Between Knowledge

and Practice, Between Knowing and Doing," 117
Marlowe, Christopher, works by: *Doctor Faustus*, 3; *Edward II*, 24
Marx, Karl, 9, 14, 26, 32, 40, 69, 99, 107, 115, 116, 177
Mayer, Hans, 3, 37, 40
McClelland, Denny, 197n.5
Menke, Timm Reiner, 97, 98, 102, 114, 115, 206nn.7, 13
Meyer, Herman, 7, 9
Miller, R. D., 37, 199nn.29, 30
Molière, works by: *Don Juan*, 25
Molloy, Francis C., 153, 155
Morris, Leslie, 121
Müller, Gerd, 49, 201n.11
Murphy, Harriet, 211n.19

National Socialism/*Nationalsozialismus*, 74, 81, 86, 92, 203n.7
Neuerzählung, 4, 98, 114
Neutsch, Erik, works by: *Forster in Paris*, 206n.3
Newton, Isaac, 152, 167–71, 172, 180, 211n.9; life, 154, 155, 213n.29; scientific concepts, 153, 154, 161, 162, 165, 173, 174, 211n.17, 213n.32
Niedermeier, Michael, 211n.14, 20
Norris, Frank, works by: *The Pit*, 32

Oberlin, 97, 100, 101, 111, 112, 119, 206n.10
Oedipus, 1, 2
Ossian, 127, 131, 133

Panzner, Evalouise, 69, 202n.32
Pascal, Roy, 96, 205n.2
pederasty, 74, 75, 83, 85, 90, 95, 204nn.19, 22
Phaidros, 74, 84, 93

Pisan, Christine de, works by: *Ditié de Jeanne d'Arc*, 16
Pizer, John, 82, 87, 204n.16
plagiarism/*Plagiat*, 8, 9, 25
Plato, 74, 84, 92
Plenzdorf, Ulrich, 8, 9, 15, 123–50, 169, 178, 180, 181, 182, 208nn.13, 16; Heinrich Mann Prize, 124
Plenzdorf, Ulrich, works by: *Die neuen Leiden*, 9, 12, 15, 123–50, 178, 180, 182, 208nn.13, 16, 209n.28
Plutarch, 92

quantum physics, 167, 172
quotation/*Zitat*, 7, 9, 13, 15, 25, 120, 123, 131, 132, 134, 135, 137, 138, 139, 143, 144, 150, 169, 179, 180, 196n.18, 209n.16

Raphael, 93, 104
Reddick, John, 100
Reed, T. J., 79, 203n.8
Reich-Ranicki, Marcel, 72, 94, 129, 180, 181, 205n.33
Reis, Ilse H., 9, 129, 196n.18, 209n.16
relativity, 165, 167, 172, 173
reproduction, 2, 4, 11, 45, 48, 49, 57, 70, 95, 179
reworking, characteristics of, 180–85; definition of, ix, 3–10, 195n.6; effect of, 3, 5, 12, 34–44, 61–70, 89–95, 114–22, 144–50, 172–74, 175–79; intention of, 4, 6, 97, 179–80
Richner, Thomas, 73, 82, 87, 88, 94, 204nn.17, 18, 205nn.24, 27, 35
Riordan, Colin, 206n.13
Rousseau, Jean Jacques, works by: *Nouvelle Héloïse*, 125
Rülicke-Weiler, Käthe, 32

Ryan, Judith, 210n. 2

Salinger, J. D., 131, 146–47, 169
Sartre, Jean-Paul, works by:
   La Nausée, 106
scientific paradigm, 12, 152, 161, 167, 178, 183
Schiller, Friedrich, 11, 16–44, 129, 176, 177, 197n. 5, 198n. 20, 199nn. 29, 30, 202n. 25; *das Ideale*, 35; *das Sinnliche*, 35; *Vergnügen und Unterricht*, 40, 41, 43
Schiller, Friedrich, works by:
   Die Jungfrau von Orleans, 11, 13, 16–44, 55, 56, 176, 183, 197n. 8, 202n. 25; *Maria Stuart*, 10, 30, 37, 198n. 20; "Die Schaubühne als moralische Anstalt betrachtet," 40–41; "Über den Gebrauch des Chors," 35; *Über die ästhetischen Erziehung des Menschengeschlechts*, 41, 200n. 38
Schlaffer, Heinz, 212n. 21
Schmidt, Christa, works by:
   Die Wahlverwandten, 196n. 23, 213n. 4
Schneider, Peter, 7, 12, 14, 15, 96–122, 169, 179, 181
Schneider, Peter, works by: *Lenz*, 7, 8, 12, 14, 96–122, 124, 147, 168, 177–84, 206n. 13
Schneider, Rolf, works by: *Reise nach Jarolsaw*, 124
Schreiner, Olive, 151
Schueler, H. J., 7
Schulz, Gudrun, 28, 30, 198n. 20
Seaman, A. T., 208n. 10
Shakespeare, William, 108
Shakespeare, William, works by:
   Coriolan, 24–25; *Henry VI*, 16; *Romeo and Juliet*, 1
Shaw, George Bernard, 16

Shaw, George Bernard, works by:
   Major Barbara, 33; *St Joan*, 18, 19
Sinclair, Upton, works by:
   The Jungle, 32
speechlessness/*Sprachlosigkeit*, 51, 178, 201nn. 17, 18
Socrates, 74, 93
Sophocles, works by: *Antigone*, 24
Spies, works by: *Faustbuch*, 2
Stich-Crelinger, Auguste, 55
student movement, 99, 105, 114, 179
Sturm und Drang, 98, 99
subjectivity, age of/*Subjektivität*, 123, 148; new subjectivity/ *neue Subjektivität*, 114, 122, 124, 185
Sudau, Ralf, 7

tableaux vivant, 158
Tate, Dennis, 96
Tauwetter, 128
tetralogy, 152, 211n. 4
third narrative, 5, 181, 185
Third Reich, 88
Thoma, Ludwig, *Magdalena — eine bayrische Emilia Galotti*, 196n. 23
Thomaneck, Jürgen, 137, 147
Thomas, N. L., 208n. 6
tragedy/*Tragödie*, 1, 9, 10, 11, 13, 14, 17, 18, 20, 23, 34, 35, 36, 37, 45–50, 55–57, 66–70, 201n. 16, 202n. 25; fear and compassion/*Furcht und Mitleid*, 16, 43, 46, 47, 66
tragi-comedy, 10, 49, 68
Trunz, Erich, 208n. 11, 209n. 25

Verständigungstext, 7
Volksstück, 48, 49
Voltaire, works by: *La Pucelle d'Orleans*, 16, 17
Vormärz, 98, 99

Wagner, Peter, 199n. 33
Wagner, Richard, works by: *Parsifal*, 2; *Tristan und Isolde*, 2
Waiblinger, Franz Peter, 123, 134, 209n. 21
Walser, Robert, works by: *Kleist in Thun*, 97
Walsøe-Engel, Ingrid, 45, 61
Wapnewski, Peter, 149, 150, 210nn. 34, 35
Weber, Max, 115, 116
Weimann, Robert, 129
Weimar Classicism/classical tradition, 2, 4, 8, 17, 19, 20, 25, 26, 28–31, 34, 35, 36, 39, 44, 45, 120, 134, 143, 174, 176. *See also* classical "Greek" tradition
Weltschmerz, 128
Wertheriaden, 124
White, Bouck, works by: *Das Buch des Daniel Drew, Leben und Meinungen eines Börsenmannes*, 32
Wieland, Christoph Martin, 17
Widdig, Bernd, 76, 81, 82, 94, 203n. 9
Wiederbearbeitung, 4
Wiedererzählung, 4
Williams, Rhys W., 106, 109, 112, 116, 120
Wolf, Christa, works by: *Kein Ort nirgends*, 206n. 3; *Lesen und Schreiben*, 97, 101; *Neue Lebensansichten eines Katers*, 196n. 23
Wolf, Gerhard, works by: *Der arme Hölderlin*, 206n. 3

Zmegac, Victor, 75

OHIO UNIVERSITY LIBRARY

Please return this book as soon as you have finished with it. In order to avoid a fine it must be returned by the latest date stamped below. All books are subject to recall after two weeks or immediately if needed for reserve.

CF